A Short Course of Economics

David Blake

Senior Lecturer in Financial Economics
Birkbeck College in the University of London
Chairman of Square Mile Consultants

McGRAW-HILL BOOK COMPANY

London · New York · St Louis · San Francisco · Auckland · Bogotá · Caracas
Lisbon · Madrid · Mexico · Milan · Montreal · New Delhi · Panama
Paris · San Juan · São Paulo · Singapore · Sydney · Tokyo · Toronto

Published by

McGRAW-HILL Book Company Europe

Shoppenhangers Road, Maidenhead, Berkshire, SL6 2QL, England
Telephone 0628 23432
Fax 0628 770224

British Library Cataloguing in Publication Data
Blake, David
  Short Course of Economics
  I. Title
  330

  ISBN 0–07–707726–1

Library of Congress Cataloging-in-Publication Data
Blake, David
    A short course of economics / David Blake.
      p. cm.
    Includes bibliographical references and index.
    ISBN 0–07–707726–1
    1. Economics. I. Title.
  HB171.5.B6526 1993
  330—dc20   93-12209 CIP

1234CL9543

Typeset by Keyword Publishing Services, London
and printed and bound in Great Britain by Clays Ltd, St Ives plc

Contents

Note

The 'Business Applications' were authored by Charlie Weir of Robert Gordon University.

Preface

The aim of this book is to give the reader a good understanding of the essential ingredients of economics in as concise a form as possible. While designed as a beginner's introduction to economics, the book is not supposed to be an 'idiot's guide': many sophisticated and up-to-date ideas in economics are examined in the end. This book has been planned to serve the needs of the busy and intelligent reader who wishes to acquire a good understanding of economics in as short a time as possible and in manageable chunks.

Economics is a very useful subject to have under one's belt. We are constantly bombarded with economic issues and economic arguments—in newspapers, on television, even in Parliament or the pub. It is one of the few subjects in which everyone can claim to be an 'expert'. Yet very often much nonsense is spoken or written. It is only after we understand the essentials of economics that we can start making a sensible contribution to the debate.

This book begins with the basics. How the markets for goods and services operate and how prices are determined in markets of various kinds are analysed. How a country's total output and income are determined and how inflation and unemployment arise are examined and how the economic actions of one country can affect those of another. Also analysed is the effect that governments can have on the economy. All this is done in the simplest possible terms, using diagrams wherever possible to help explain the arguments.

Having covered the basics, some of the latest issues in economics are analysed: privatization, contestable markets, interest rate volatility and exchange rate overshooting, monetary and exchange rate targeting, the European Monetary System and European Monetary Union. Again, this is done in a simple and concise manner.

By the end of the book, the reader will have covered over 80 per cent of the most important issues in economic analysis. He or she will then be able to begin to think like a professional economist. Professional economists tend to think in terms of economic 'models', which provide useful frameworks for analysing important economic issues. It might be a microeconomic model, such as a supply and demand model, or it might be a macroeconomic model, like the IS/LM model (all these models are fully explained in the text). So when a professional economist is asked a series of 'what if' questions, he or she will implicitly appeal to one of these models in order to answer the questions. The questioner may have no idea that an economic model is being used to answer the 'what if' questions. But all professional economists will have been trained to analyse the kinds of economic models covered in this book. So by the time the reader has finished the book, he or she should have a good idea of how professional economists think and the sorts of models or frameworks they have in the back of their minds. Initially, the reader might find the models somewhat artificial and unrealistic. Yes, they are indeed artificial and unrealistic. But they have to be just that in order to provide clear-cut predictions. With experience, the reader will realize just how useful they are in analysing an economic system which is virtually impossible to understand without the kind of simplified framework developed in this book.

If the reader would like some evidence that professional economists do use the models analysed in this book, he or she should read the stockbroker's report following this preface. After finishing the book, the reader should re-read the stockbroker's report in order to test how much their understanding has increased.

The book is written in a concise manner. This means that some readers might find that it takes some time to read each chapter. You should not be too concerned by this—after all, the book as a whole is not too long. It is recommended that you read each chapter completely, even if you find some passages difficult. You should then re-read the passages that you found difficult. You may well find that by covering the whole chapter, some particularly difficult parts may become easier to understand. Provided at the end of each chapter is a comprehensive summary. You should then do the exercises at the end of each chapter. You will find that this is an excellent way of testing your understanding of the text.

Not only do I hope that the book provides a useful introduction to individual readers, I hope that it will be used on courses in colleges and universities, and on professional training programmes. The book has been used successfully for teaching on both university courses for non-specialist economics students and on intensive (one-week) professional training programmes (in particular graduate induction and investment banking programmes in the City). As a teaching aid, I have prepared a comprehensive set of OHP slides, containing all the figures and tables in the book together with linking bullet point slides. In addition, I have prepared a solutions manual containing solutions to the exercises at the end of each section, plus some test exercises (again with solutions). I therefore hope that I have provided a turnkey training package for busy instructors. (The OHP slides and solutions manual are available from the publisher to those instructors who adopt the book for their courses.)

Finally, I would like to acknowledge other people who were involved in this exercise. Mahmood Pradhan, then of City University Business School, was commissioned to undertake some initial drafting; Ailsa Roell of the London School of Economics contributed the section on trade policy applications; Charlie Weir of Robert Gordon University contributed the nine business applications; and thanks are due to Sue Kirkbride for her superb, accurate and speedy typing of the manuscript, as usual. I would also like to thank David Owen of Kleinwort Benson Securities for permission to reprint the stockbroker's report at the end of this preface.

If I have whetted the appetites of my readers for economics, then I am of course delighted. If anyone would like to take their reading of economics further, then I can suggest the following additional reading (the first four items are UK economics texts and the last two are US texts).

Recommended reading

David Begg, Stanley Fischer and Rudiger Dornbusch (1990). *Economics*. McGraw-Hill, London.

Richard Lipsey (1989). *An introduction to positive economics*. Weidenfeld and Nicolson, London.

John Sloman (1991). *Economics*. Harvester Wheatsheaf, Hemel Hempstead.

Philip Hardwick, Bahadur Khan and John Langmead (1990). *An introduction to modern economics*. Longman, Harlow.

Paul Samuelson and William Nordhaus (1992). *Economics*. McGraw-Hill, New York.

William Baumol and Alan Blinder (1991). *Economics*. Harcourt Brace Jovanovich, New York.

D.B.

UK economic comment: Fiscal policy coming to the fore

30th August 1990
David Owen UK Economist

UK membership of the ERM would force investors to change the way they view the world. The Gilt-Edged market would have to take far more notice of what is happening in other European bond markets, particularly German Bunds and French OATS. The equity market might have to become accustomed to a prolonged squeeze on the corporate sector as the government grapples with a highly entrenched inflation problem and a long-term structural current account deficit.

Also interest rates will largely become subservient to keeping sterling within its agreed trading bands. As the OECD pointed out in its latest survey, fiscal policy will probably have to take a far more active role in fine tuning domestic demand. Reducing the real tax burden has been one of the central planks of Tory economic policy since 1979. Whoever is elected may have no choice but to do a U-turn on this government's tax cutting pledges, particularly if they find it difficult holding the line on public expenditure.

The impotence of monetary policy in a fixed exchange rate system is well founded in economic theory. The chart below depicts a model developed by the economists Mundell and Fleming almost thirty years ago. The IS curve describes all points of equilibrium within the goods market; a higher interest rate is associated with lower output, hence its downward slope. The LM curve describes all points of equilibrium within the money market; a rise in output puts upward pressure on interest rates, hence its upward slope. The point at which the IS and LM curves cross describes whole economy equilibrium and is associated with output Y_0.

Mundell and Fleming extended the IS/LM framework to include perfect capital mobility in a fixed exchange rate world. The UK is assumed to be a small economy, unable to influence the structure of world interest rates. Given the assumption of perfect capital mobility, UK rates have to equal the prevailing foreign interest rate r^*, for reasons explained below.

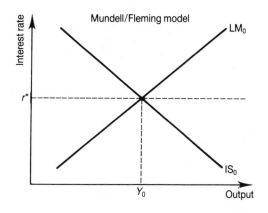

Case 1: Monetary tightening

Firstly assume the government tries to rein back domestic demand by tightening monetary policy, causing the LM curve to shift up to the left to LM_1—see first chart below. UK rates initially rise above the rates prevailing overseas, leading to a huge inflow of capital as investors take advantage of the interest rate gain. However, this interest rate gain does not last for long. The capital inflow expands the UK's money supply and puts downward pressure on UK rates, causing the LM curve to shift back to the right until equilibrium is restored—see second chart below. At the end of the day all that has happened is that the composition of the money supply has changed slightly. **Output is unaffected.**

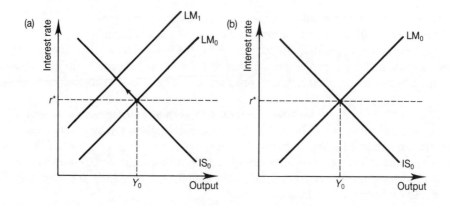

Case 2: Fiscal tightening

Contrast the above with what happens if the government tightens fiscal policy by raising taxes or cutting government expenditure. The IS curve shifts to the left to IS_1 as output is hit and interest rates fall—see first chart below. This initial fall in UK rates causes a huge outflow of capital and a contraction in the UK's money supply. The LM curve shifts to the left to LM_1 as interest rates are bid up, until equilibrium is restored—see second chart below. **Fiscal tightening proves highly effective. A contraction in the money supply compounds the initial fiscal tightening, leading to a significant fall in output.**

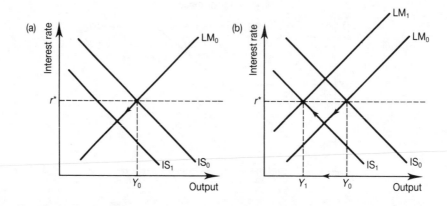

Of course the Mundell/Fleming model is by no means perfect. For a start the UK would be tied only to European currencies and the ERM is by no means as rigid as the model suggests. It will probably take several years for UK rates to come anywhere close to converging with those in Germany. In the interim investors will demand a risk premium, in the form of higher UK rates, to hold sterling. However, the model does give a flavour for the likely policy mix post-ERM. **Fixing sterling into the ERM will limit the government's scope to run an independent monetary policy. Fiscal policy could well have to come to the fore.**

[Reproduced with the permission of David Owen, Kleinwort Benson Securities Limited, London.]

I   MICROECONOMICS

If there were unlimited supplies of goods and services, there would be no need for economics or economists. Everyone could consume as much as they wanted of every good or service. *Economics exists as a discipline because resources are scarce and different people will bid to use them.* For example, a raw material such as iron ore could be used to make cars or washing machines or ships or knives and forks. Who decides how the iron ore should be allocated between these different uses? In a *centrally planned economy* (such as the Soviet Union between 1917 and 1991) this decision is made by the *state*. In a *competitive market economy*, on the other hand, the decision is made by *market forces*, with those believing that they can make the biggest profits from using the iron ore bidding the highest prices for it. In this way, some of the iron ore goes to car makers, some to washing machine makers, and so on, to the benefit of both consumers and producers. Similarly, almost all discussions of economic policy or economic performance employ an underlying framework which is based on the behaviour of individuals or companies, or the workings of markets for particular commodities.

It is for this reason that it is important to have an understanding of *microeconomics*, which is the area of economics specifically concerned with the explanation of the economic behaviour of individuals and companies and with the workings of markets. Consider, for example, the recent concern with the UK current account deficit and the particular concern about the exchange rate. The two are related, since the exchange rate affects the prices of domestically produced goods relative to those of foreign goods. If domestic residents continue to demand more foreign goods than they supply to the rest of the world, there will be downward pressure on domestic prices and foreign goods will become relatively more expensive. This, in turn, raises the question of how we finance the resulting current account deficit. Thus, even in the area of *macroeconomics*, which is concerned with the workings of the economy at the national and international levels, the underlying analysis frequently involves microeconomics.

We begin therefore with the analysis of individual markets for goods and services, where our primary concern is to examine what determines the prices and quantities transacted. For example, at a particular interest rate (price), what is the total amount (i.e. quantity) of lending that banks will be willing to advance? We examine how markets are brought into equilibium following changes in underlying supply and demand conditions. Clearly this is a relevant concern for all participants in the economy. The prices that consumers pay for goods and services affects their standard of living. Producers have a direct interest in predicting the volume of sales and therefore the revenue that they might receive. As for governments, the attainment of various policy goals depends crucially on underlying market conditions. We examine the effects of price controls and taxation with respect to their allocative impact (i.e. their effects on the distribution of income) and also from the narrower perspective of collecting tax revenue. We also apply our analytical tools to the interesting area of international trade policy. All of this is covered in Chapter 1.

In Chapter 2, we turn to the analysis of the responsiveness of demand to changes in prices, changes in consumer incomes and also to changes in the prices of related commodities. These are of interest to both producers and governments. If the changes in demand as a result of the above changes can be measured, then producers will be able to ascertain the effects on their revenue and thereby determine their pricing policies. Governments would like to know, for example, how much revenue a tax on a particular commodity will raise, or more generally, which types of goods should be taxed for revenue purposes. This will depend on the extent to which consumers change their consumption of a commodity as a result of higher prices induced by the higher taxes.

In Chapter 3, we consider how firms decide on how much to produce and offer for sale to the market. At each level of output, firms will be concerned about production costs (which depend on technology and the prices of factors of production, such as labour and capital) and how much revenue can be earned. Revenue earned will depend on the demand conditions facing firms. This in turn depends on the degree of competition from other suppliers, that is, on the market structure that they face. The two extreme cases of perfectly competititive markets and monopolistic markets are considered, as are the two intermediate cases of monopolistic competition and oligopoly. We also examine various types of non-price competition.

Finally, in Chapter 4, we examine what happens when markets fail to produce a socially efficient allocation of resources. This is known as market failure. This usually happens when there is monopoly power or when there are what economists call 'externalities', factors that the market does not take into account when determining prices. The government can do something about these problems through its taxation and competition policies. In the light of this, we consider the recent trend towards privatization of government enterprises. Of particular interest in the UK is the question of the changing form of privatization, i.e. the splitting-up of large nationalized industries into smaller private companies.

1 Demand, supply and the determination of prices in markets

1.1 Demand, supply, and market prices

A *market* for a good is a place which brings together buyers and sellers: a good is offered for sale by *producers* and purchased by *consumers*. Economists refer to *demand* in a market as the quantity of a good that consumers wish to purchase at each different price. At any given price, consumers will wish to buy a particular quantity. In general, if the price is higher, the quantity demanded will be lower. The intuitive reasoning behind this is that the greater the quantity of a good consumers have, the less they will value an additional unit. It follows that, if each additional unit is worth less to consumers, their willingness to pay is also lower for each additional unit. To induce consumers to purchase additional units, the price must be lower. When there is inflation (which is defined as an increase in the general level of prices), the price of a particular good might be constantly increasing. The inflationary increase in the price of a good (sometimes called the increase in the *absolute price* or *nominal price*) is not what is important here. What is important in microeconomics is the increase in the price of a good relative to the general level of prices (sometimes called the increase in the *relative price* or *real price*). If the increase in the absolute price of a good is less than the increase in the general level of prices, the relative price of the good has actually fallen. When economists talk about prices in microeconomics, they are talking about relative prices.

In Fig. 1.1, the negative relation between price and quantity demanded is illustrated. At the price P_0, consumers will purchase Q_0 units. If the price rises to P_1, consumers reduce their purchases to Q_1, and vice versa. In other words, the extra amount $(Q_0 - Q_1)$ is only purchased when prices are lower. The negative relation between price and quantity demanded is known as a *demand curve* (or *demand schedule*).

One may want to ask whether the price of the commodity in question is the only factor determining demand. Suppose, for example, that Q_1 is the number of books bought at a particular price P_1. The value of books to a consumer would, in general, depend on the availability of substitutes; for example, newspapers might contain similar material. If newspapers began including short stories, this might affect the demand for books of short stories. At price P_1, the demand for books might fall below Q_1. One could envisage a variety of factors that affect demand in this manner.

It is the availability of substitutes that leads to the very important idea in economics of *opportunity cost*. When someone considers buying a particular good, they implicitly compare the benefits that they will enjoy from consuming this good with the benefits that they could receive from consuming a range of alternative goods. Only if the benefits from consuming the good in question exceed the benefits from consuming the best of these alternatives will the individual buy the good in question. Economists equate the value of the benefits from consuming the good in question with the price of the good. They call the value of the benefits forgone from not consuming the best alternative the opportunity cost of consuming the good in question.

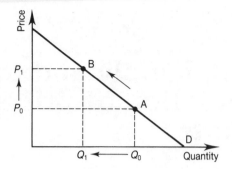

Figure 1.1   The demand curve

Individuals will therefore purchase a good only if its price exceeds the opportunity cost. The same argument applies to services as well as goods, since people tend to consume both goods and services.

For any given demand curve, the implicit assumption therefore is that all these other factors are held constant (this is the so-called *other things equal* or *ceteris paribus* assumption used by economists to make life easier). Instead of listing each possible factor, we simply identify three main categories that are held equal (or constant) along a given demand curve. These are:

1 The prices of related goods.
2 Consumers' incomes.
3 The tastes and preferences of consumers.

Note that any change in these will change the quantity demanded at any given price. This implies that the entire demand curve will shift (whether it shifts to the left or right is considered later).

Next we turn to the *supply* side of the market. No producer or supplier would wish to supply a good if the price were zero. At higher prices, supply would increase. A fairly simple rationalization of this is that there are costs involved in producing goods and services. The higher the price, the greater will be the quantity supplied as more revenue and profits can be earned from this activity. Alternatively, we could take the view that higher prices enable higher costs to be covered. Either way, this will yield an upward sloping *supply curve* (or *supply schedule*) with respect to prices. This is illustrated in Fig. 1.2.

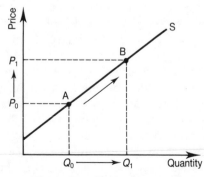

Figure 1.2   The supply curve

At price P_0, producers are willing to supply quantity Q_0. If the price rises to P_1, producers will be willing to increase supply to Q_1. As with our analysis of the demand curve, other factors are held constant along a given supply curve. Changing costs of inputs into the production process (e.g. labour, capital, land and premises, raw materials, energy) will shift the entire curve. For example, if oil prices rise, the cost of energy and transportation will rise and this will reduce the quantity of goods supplied at any given price (or in other words, any given quantity will only be supplied at a higher price). Similar considerations apply to the technology of production and government regulation (we return to these in more detail later).

1.2 Market equilibrium

Combining the demand and supply curves, we depict the *market clearing price* or the *market price* (P_0) and *quantity* (Q_0) in Fig. 1.3. The demand and supply curves tell us, respectively, the quantities that buyers wish to buy at any given price, and the quantities that suppliers wish to supply at any given price. At price P_0, and only at this price, these quantities are equal (point E), so that the supply offered to the market is just sufficient to meet the demand in full: in other words, the market clears. At all other prices, the quantities differ, implying that either buyers are willing to buy less than the quantity supplied (whenever $P > P_0$) or that suppliers are willing to supply less than the amount buyers wish to purchase (whenever $P < P_0$).

Equilibrium in a market occurs when, for given supply and demand conditions, there are no forces that will tend to alter the price. Everyone who wants to consume this good at the *equilibrium price* is able to do so. The equilibrium price is therefore an alternative name for the market clearing price.

When a market is not in equilibrium, there will be pressures (sometimes called *market forces*) that will tend to make the market adjust towards the market clearing price and quantity. These adjustment paths are often complex, and the type of analysis presented here can only tell us the direction of the change in prices to an equilibrium price. Figure 1.4 illustrates the two cases of *excess demand* and *excess supply*. In Fig. 1.4(a), at the current price P_1, quantity demanded is Q_1^D, whereas only Q_1^S is supplied. This shortfall in supply implies that some consumers will not have their demand satisfied: there is excess demand because the price is too low. There will be a tendency for prices to be bid up, as sellers of this good realize that they are having to turn some customers away. As the price rises, some consumers will reduce their demand. Only at the price P_0 will equilibrium be restored. The opposite case is depicted in Fig. 1.4(b), where suppliers will be left with unsold stock at price P_1: there is excess supply because the price is too high.

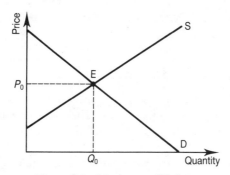

Figure 1.3 Market equilibrium

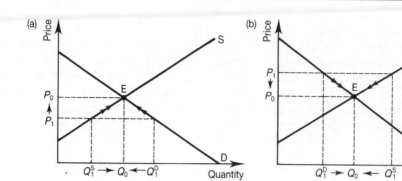

Figure 1.4   Price and quantity adjustments to maintain equilibrium: (a) excess demand; (b) excess supply

To reduce their inventories, suppliers will reduce prices, which will increase demand. This process will continue until the price is P_0.

Therefore, if a market experiences excess demand, the price will rise to choke off demand and to encourage additional supply; while if a market experiences excess supply, the price will fall to boost demand and curtail supply. Economists call these processes the operation of the *price mechanism* or the *market mechanism*. Prices provide *signals* to market participants. High prices for a good (relative to the prices of related goods) provide a signal to suppliers to increase the resources devoted to the production of this good (because higher profits can be made), but they provide a signal to consumers to switch their purchasing power to cheaper alternatives (because similar benefits can be enjoyed from consuming lower priced alternatives). In contrast, low prices for a good (relative to the prices of related goods) provide a signal to suppliers to transfer resources to the production of alternative goods (because higher profits can be made elsewhere), but they provide a signal to consumers to switch their purchasing power to this good (because they can now enjoy consuming this good more cheaply than was possible with alternatives). The *market clearing process* balances out these changes to supply and demand.

Note that we have made no mention of the speed of adjustment of prices. This depends on transactions costs and on how fast information becomes available to buyers and sellers regarding unsatisfied demands (Fig. 1.4(a)) and unsold stocks (Fig. 1.4(b)). In financial markets, security prices adjust almost instantaneously due to fairly low transactions costs (e.g. brokers' commissions and market makers' spreads—the difference between the buying price and selling price of securities—are fairly low) and the very rapid transmission of information, whereas in other markets they could take years to adjust. The labour market takes a particularly long time to adjust. For example, it takes a long time for workers made unemployed in one industry to be retrained and reskilled for work in another industry. Similarly, it takes a long time for workers made unemployed in one part of the country to move to find work in another part of the country.

1.3   The determinants of demand

Returning to the factors that we held constant along a given demand curve, we consider the effects of changes in these on price and quantity. The price of a particular good (sometimes called its *own price*) is only one of the determinants of its demand.

First, we have the *prices of related goods*. There are two cases to consider. Suppose the price of journeys on public transport services rises. More people would use their own cars for travel, raising the demand for petrol. So one of the determinants of petrol demand is the price of

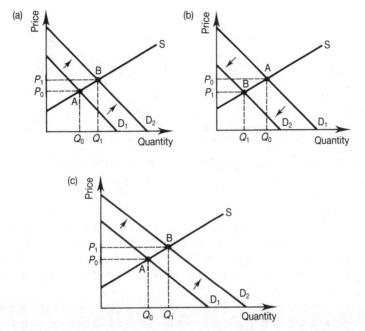

Figure 1.5   The determinants of demand: (a) an increase in the price of a substitute; (b) an increase in the price of a complement; (c) an increase in consumers' incomes (or a change in preferences in favour of a good)

substitutes for private car travel, namely public transport. In Fig. 1.5(a), beginning in equilibrium at point A, we show the demand curve shifting to the right (from D_1 to D_2) in the case where the price of a substitute good has increased. The effect is to raise the price to P_1 and the quantity demanded to Q_1. Demand is higher at all prices. The new equilibrium is at point B.

A second case is where two goods are *complements*. Suppose the price of cars increases. A lower demand for cars will also reduce the demand for petrol, in which case the price of petrol and the quantity of petrol sold both fall (Fig. 1.5(b)). Again the entire demand schedule will shift, this time to the left (from D_1 to D_2). The equilibrium moves from A to B.

In Fig. 1.5(c), the effect on demand of the two other factors held constant is analysed. A rise in *consumers' incomes* will raise demand at any given price, and therefore shift the entire demand schedule to the right (from D_1 to D_2). In some cases, higher income may well reduce demand: as consumers become richer they wish to consume more expensive, higher quality goods, and so reduce their demand for the lower quality goods that they have been consuming until now. As will be considered in Chapter 2, the classification of goods according to the effect on demand of changes in income can be useful for the purposes of forecasting demand. Finally, Fig. 1.5(c) can also be used to show the effect of a *change in preferences* in favour of a good away from other goods. This can happen, for example, when a new good is brought to the market and demand for it takes off. In both cases, prices rise and quantity sold rises as well.

1.4   The determinants of supply

Along the *supply curve*, the factors held constant were input prices, the technology of production and government regulation.

In Fig. 1.6(a), we consider the effect of a *rise in oil prices*, where oil is a major input in the

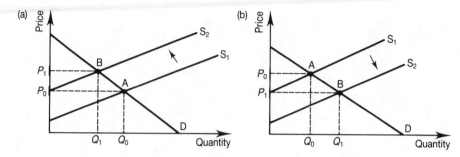

Figure 1.6   The determinants of supply: (a) a rise in input prices; (b) improvements in the technology of production

production process of a particular good. In this case, at the existing quantity being supplied to the market (Q_0), producers will be faced with higher costs and will only be willing to continue supplying this amount if they are able to charge higher prices. In effect, the supply schedule has shifted from S_1 to S_2. Since the demand schedule has remained constant, the equilibrium has moved from A to B. Note that there will necessarily be a contraction of the market, since costs of production are higher.

In Fig. 1.6(b), we show the effects of an improvement in the *technology of production*. The advent of computers and their use in the financial services industry has led to substantial reductions in the cost of providing banking services, for example. This is one of the reasons why banks are able to offer a variety of free banking services to bank customers. In this example, the fall in price can be interpreted as being equivalent to higher interest on bank accounts.

In the case of *government intervention*, the supply curve could shift either to the left or to the right. For example, if legislation is introduced to control pollution, firms' costs will increase because of the additional expense involved in complying with the legislation. This will lead to a decrease in supply at any given price, and hence to a leftward shift in the supply curve (as in Fig. 1.6(a)). An example of the opposite effect was the abolition of the restrictive monopoly held by opticians in the UK in the 1980s. This permitted new competitors to enter the industry and this expanded supply at each conceivable price, leading to a shift of the supply curve to the right (Fig. 1.6(b)). Similarly, the supply of banking services in the UK has also increased following the 1986 Building Societies Act, which removed all restrictions on building societies in the provision of banking services. Building societies now provide cheque accounts and also unsecured loans. As a result, the financial services industry has witnessed an unprecedented increase in competition among suppliers.

To summarize our discussion so far, we have considered the effects on demand and supply of both the own price changing and of changes in other factors which lead to shifts of entire curves. In terms of changes in demand, there can be movements along a given demand curve and shifts of the entire demand cuve. If the *quantity demanded* changes as a result of a change in the own *price*, then we *move along* a particular demand curve. If one of the *factors held constant* changes, then the demand curve *shifts*. Similarly, if *quantity supplied* changes as a result of a change in the own *price*, then we *move along* a particular supply curve. If one of the *factors held constant* changes, then the supply curve *shifts*.

1.5   The effect of price controls

The question we consider next is what happens to quantity supplied if some form of *price control* is introduced by the government.

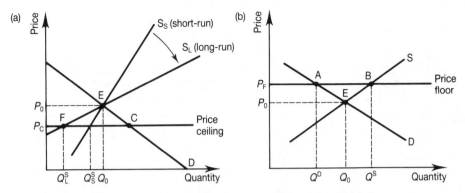

Figure 1.7 Price controls: (a) price ceiling; (b) price floor

1.5.1 Maximum price: price ceiling

One of the most common examples of a *price ceiling* is rent control on residential property. The government may be anxious that low-income groups in the economy are able to afford housing. In Fig. 1.7(a), we begin with the equilibrium point E, in the absence of any controls. The *short-run supply curve*, S_S, is fairly steep, implying that variations in price will not lead to large changes in quantity supplied. In the short run, there are limited alternative uses that can be made of residential property. The short-run supply curve shows the immediate response of suppliers to a change in the price of the good that they produce, before they have had a chance to transfer new resources into the production process for this good and away from the production of less profitable goods (in the case of a price rise), or to transfer resources to the production processes of other more profitable goods (in the case of a price fall). Suppose the government now imposes a ceiling on rents (P_C). Demand will increase to point C. However, the supply available for renting will be only Q_S^S. In the long run, supply will contract even further as landlords find alternative uses for their properties (for example, some landlords might just sell their properties rather than continue to let their properties for such low rents, and this will reduce the overall supply of rented property on the market). The *long-run supply curve* shows the final response of suppliers to a change in the price of the good that they produce, after they have had a chance to fully adjust their resources to the new price. The long-run supply curve is S_L, which is flatter than the short-run supply curve. The supply curve therefore tilts from S_S to S_L and the new long-run supply to the market will be Q_L^S. This is one of the disadvantages of such price controls: they may lower prices, but only by reducing the quantity available for sale. Also, while the price ceiling remains in force, excess demand ((C − F) in Fig. 1.7(a)) persists.

1.5.2 Minimum price: price floor

The Common Agricultural Policy of the European Community (EC) guarantees producers minimum prices for their output. They can supply as much as they wish at the minimum price or *price floor* (P_F in Fig. 1.7(b)). The result is that the EC has to be willing to buy any excess supply ((B − A) in Fig. 1.7(b)) and store it in 'butter mountains' and 'wine lakes' and so on. Note that in some cases the excess demands/excess supplies are eliminated via illegal *black markets*. This is usually the case with countries that impose foreign exchange controls: it is generally always possible to get black market dollars at a high price.

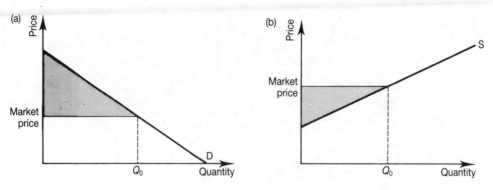

Figure 1.8   (a) Consumer surplus and (b) producer surplus

1.6   Consumer and producer surplus

1.6.1   Consumer surplus

The demand curve for a good indicates the amount that would be purchased at different prices. The downward sloping demand curve implies that consumers are willing to pay more for earlier units purchased than for later units. However, normally all units are purchased at a single price (the market price). Therefore for all units except the last one, consumers actually pay less than the amount they would be willing to pay. (Economists call the last unit purchased the *marginal unit*, and the earlier units purchased the *intramarginal units*.) The difference between what consumers are willing to pay and what they actually pay is called the *consumer surplus*. It measures the *social benefit* (or *social welfare*) accruing to consumers who buy this good. It is illustrated by the shaded area in Fig. 1.8(a). (Economists called it a *social benefit* because it is a benefit that arises to members of society as a result of the operation of the market mechanism: free markets allow consumers to acquire goods and services for a lower price than they would be prepared to pay for them.)

1.6.2   Producer surplus

Analogously, suppliers also receive a single price for all units (the market price). Earlier units are sold at a price greater than the minimum price at which they would have been willing to supply those units. This difference, shown by the shaded area in Fig. 1.8(b), is the *producer surplus*. It measures the social benefit accruing to producers who supply this good. (Free markets allow producers to sell goods and services at higher prices than they would be willing to supply them at.)

The market mechanism therefore provides social benefits for both consumers and producers.

1.7   The effect of taxation

The concepts of consumer and producer surplus are extremely useful in analysing the *efficiency* and *distribution* effects of tax policy.

Consider first the effect on the price and quantity of an indirect tax, such as a sales tax (e.g. value added tax (VAT) or customs and excise duties). Suppose that the government imposes a per unit tax of £x on the sale of a good. (A tax which imposes a constant money sum on each

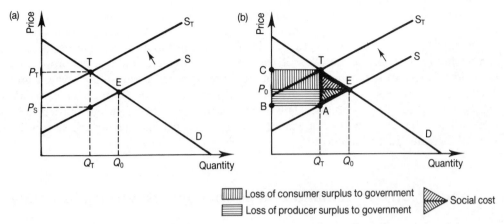

Figure 1.9   The effect of taxation: (a) indirect taxes; (b) redistribution effects and social cost

unit of a good that is sold is called an *ad valorem* tax.) The main effects are:

1 Consumers will now face a higher price and will demand less.
2 Suppliers will therefore sell less.
3 Suppliers thus receive less than the price paid by consumers (since £x per unit sold goes to the government).

These effects are shown in Fig. 1.9(a), where the equilibrium following the introduction of the tax moves from E to T. P_T is called the *market price* and P_S, the price received by the producer, is called the *cost price*. The amount $(P_T - P_S)$ is the tax per unit (i.e. £x) and total tax revenue is $(P_T - P_S)Q_T$, that is, the tax per unit *times* the quantity sold. The supply curve facing the consumer is different from the supply curve determining the behaviour of the producer. This is why the consumer is paying a higher price, despite the fact that the supplier is receiving a lower profit and therefore producing less.

The consumer is not bearing the whole *burden* (or *incidence*) of the tax, since the supplier has also suffered: the supplier is producing less and receiving a lower price. Figure 1.9(b) identifies the gains and losses for consumers, producers and the government. Two points to note are the *redistribution* of social benefit from consumers and producers to the government, and the net loss or cost to society. We can summarize them in the following way. The government's tax revenue consists of the rectangle CTAB, which is equal to the loss in consumer surplus *plus* the loss in producer surplus. In other words, part of the social benefit from consumers and producers is redistributed to the government. However, the consumer and producer have lost more than this. The triangle TEA is a further loss to them. This triangle represents a net loss to society as a whole, since it has been transferred to no one, not even the government. Economists call the triangle the *social cost* of (or *welfare loss* or *deadweight loss* from) indirect taxation.

Because of this social cost, economists argue that indirect taxation is a source of *inefficiency* in the market mechanism. The inefficiency is greater the flatter, or more *elastic* (see Chapter 2), the demand curve of the good being taxed. The government might well do something useful with the tax revenue that it receives (e.g. build more schools, hospitals or roads) so that the social benefit extracted by the government is eventually returned to consumers or producers. But the social cost of the indirect taxation cannot be recovered. It can, however, be minimized by taxing goods with steep (i.e. *inelastic*) demand curves.

The burden of the tax also depends on elasticities: both demand and supply elasticities (elasticities are discussed in more detail in Chapter 2). The greater the elasticity of demand (i.e. the flatter the demand curve), the less the burden falls on consumers and the more the burden falls on producers. That is, the more elastic the demand, the greater the relative proportion of the tax paid by producers, because consumers are more prepared to substitute away from this good towards other goods. On the other hand, the greater the elasticity of supply (i.e. the flatter the supply curve), the less the burden falls on producers and the more the burden falls on consumers. This is because producers are more able to reduce their production and so consumers must pay the greater part of the tax.

1.8   Applications of demand and supply analysis to trade policy

1.8.1   Opening up a closed economy

We will begin by considering a *small* economy which up till now has been closed to all trade with foreign countries (this situation is known as *autarky*). By 'small' we mean insignificant as far as the world market is concerned, so that any demand for imports or supply of exports from this country would not have any effect on world prices. We can distinguish two cases (see Fig. 1.10).

Case A

Case A shows a potential import: the equilibrium price under autarky exceeds the world market price of the product. Once free trade is introduced, the domestic price falls to the world market price: why would anyone pay more if they can buy the good for that price from foreign suppliers?

Who gains and who loses? Consumers benefit from the lower price and domestic producers lose. The net gain to consumers exceeds the loss to producers, suggesting the move to free trade is a good thing on balance, since there is a net benefit to society as a whole. However, if domestic producers have substantial political clout, they might be able to persuade the government to keep the economy closed to world trade. A recent example is Japan, which prohibits rice imports, a move supported by producers on the grounds that, since rice is a strategic commodity, it is important to have a strong source of domestic supply, even though the price of rice is much lower on the world market.

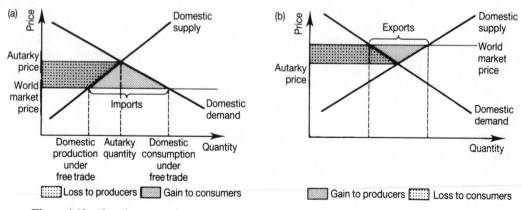

Figure 1.10   Opening up a closed economy: (a) an importable good; (b) an exportable good

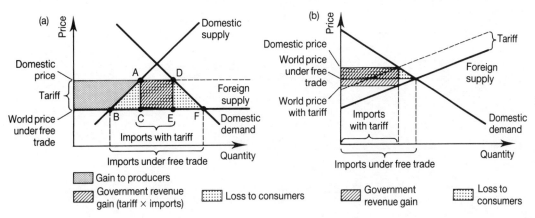

Figure 1.11   Import tariffs vs. free trade: (a) a small country; (b) a large country

Case B

Case B shows a potential export: the autarky price is lower than the world market price. This time the domestic price rises to the world level: why would producers ever sell the product for less than they can obtain abroad? Producers gain and consumers lose; but again gains exceed losses, favouring free trade over autarky.

1.8.2   Import tariffs vs. free trade

We can consider two cases, that for a small country and that for a large country (see Fig. 1.11).

Case A

Consider first a *small* country that is debating whether or not to impose an *import tariff* on a good that has up to now been freely traded. As shown in panel (a), the domestic price rises to the world price *plus* the tariff. The gainers are the domestic producers (who increase their producer surplus) and the government (which obtains revenue from the tariff). However, the losses to consumers exceed the gains to the other two groups: the net loss to society is the two triangles ABC and DEF.

This is the classic argument in favour of free trade, valid even if the world price is very low because of dumping by foreign exporters. Note, however, that the government may have other reasons for wishing the country to remain nearly self-sufficient in the production of this good (for example, a fear of future world price rises if foreign exporters succeeded in destroying domestic production through unfair competition).

Case B

A *large* country, in contrast, may derive a net benefit from an import tariff. By definition, import demand from such a country is significant enough to move the world price. We can represent this by showing the world supply curve with an upward slope in panel (b) (for simplicity we take the case where domestic supply is non-existent so that world supply equals foreign supply). As shown in the figure, the tariff restricts the country's import demand on the world market enough to lower the world price of the good. In that case the gain in tariff revenue may well exceed the loss of consumer surplus, as depicted.

The large country is exploiting its market power on the world market to move the *terms of*

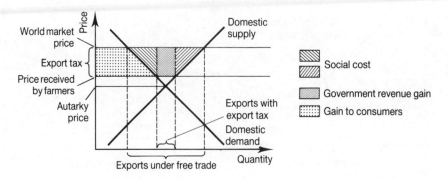

Figure 1.12   Raising revenue through an export tax

trade in its favour. Note that a small country cannot do this, so in the case of a small country, the loss in consumer surplus would exceed the tariff revenue. Note also that on a world scale, there is still a social cost from protectionism: foreign producers lose more than domestic consumers or the government gain. If foreign countries retaliate by setting up trade barriers of their own, every country can end up worse off (this is known as *beggar-my-neighbour*).

1.8.3   Raising revenue through an export tax

Many developing countries find it administratively infeasible to tax general economic activity. Instead, it may be easier for them to tax exports as they leave the country. For example, a government marketing board can buy up a cash crop from farmers and sell it abroad for the (higher) world market price, gaining revenue in the process. This is equivalent to the government imposing an *export tax*. A case in point is Senegal's main export crop, peanuts.

In Fig. 1.12, the farmers are paid a price that is below the world market price, but above the autarky price. It is assumed that farmers can easily circumvent the marketing board and sell directly to domestic consumers, who therefore pay the same price as the marketing board. As can be seen, this policy reduces exports to well below their free trade level. The farmers lose and domestic consumers gain, relative to free trade (this can be a political advantage, since cheap food for the urban masses is a prerequisite for retaining power). The social cost is measured by the two shaded triangles in Fig. 1.12.

1.8.4   Import tariffs, import quotas and voluntary export restrictions

In Fig. 1.13, an import tariff of T leads to imports of *M*. The domestic price and the quantities produced, consumed and imported are the same whether a tariff of T is imposed or a quota of *M* is imposed.

The only possible difference is in the beneficiary of the shaded rectangle. With a *tariff*, the tariff revenue is destined for the government's coffers. With a *quota*, it depends on how the *import licences* are awarded. If they are auctioned off by the government in a competitive bidding process, the government would receive the licence fee: importers would be prepared to bid up to T × *M* for the privilege of importing *M* units at the world market price and selling them at a price that is higher by T. If the auction is rigged, or if powerful business people can convince the government to award them import licences for free, then the benefit accrues at least in part to those individuals.

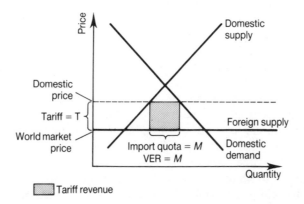

Figure 1.13   Tariffs, quotas and voluntary export restrictions

Recently, a number of Far Eastern countries, viewing European Community import restrictions on electronic goods as inevitable, have opted instead for *voluntary export restrictions* (or VERs). Essentially, these countries undertake to limit their exports to the EC to *M*. The advantage to them is that they retain the rectangle T × *M* for themselves. They might as well sell the *M* units at the domestic EC price (world price + T) and keep the excess over production costs for themselves.

1.9   Summary

1 A market is a place where buyers and sellers are brought together.
2 A demand curve shows a negative relationship between price and quantity demanded: the higher the price, the lower the quantity demanded.
3 The opportunity cost of consuming a good or service is the value of the benefit forgone from not consuming the best alternative good or service.
4 A supply curve shows a positive relationship between price and quantity supplied: the higher the price, the higher the quantity supplied.
5 The market clearing, or equilibrium, price is the price at which supply offered to the market is just sufficient to meet demand in full.
6 When there is excess demand in a market, prices will rise to choke off demand and encourage additional supply; when there is excess supply in a market, prices will fall to boost demand and curtail supply.
7 If the quantity demanded changes as a result of changes in the own price of the good, then there is a movement along a particular demand curve. If one of the factors held constant (e.g. the prices of related goods, consumers' incomes, or the tastes and preferences of consumers) changes, then the demand curve shifts.
8 If the quantity supplied changes as a result of changes in the own price of the good, then there is a movement along a particular supply curve. If one of the factors held constant (e.g. input prices, the technology of production, or government regulation) changes, then the supply curve shifts.
9 The short-run supply curve shows the immediate response of suppliers to a change in the price of a good that they produce, before they have had a chance either to transfer new resources into the production of this good and away from the production of less profitable

goods (in the case of a price rise), or to transfer resources to the production of other more profitable goods (in the case of a price fall).

10 The long-run supply curve shows the final response of suppliers to a change in the price of the good that they produce, after they have had a chance to fully adjust their resources to the new price.

11 Consumer surplus is the difference between the price that consumers would be willing to pay for a good and what they actually have to pay (the market price): it is positive for intramarginal units purchased and zero for the marginal unit purchased. It measures the social benefit that consumers enjoy from having a free market in this good.

12 Producer surplus is the difference between the price at which suppliers actually sell a good (the market price) and what they would be willing to sell it for: it is positive for the intramarginal units sold and zero for the marginal unit sold. It measures the social benefit that producers enjoy from having a free market in this good.

13 Indirect taxes, such as VAT, have the effect of raising the price paid by consumers, reducing the price received by producers, and reducing demand. There is a transfer of consumer surplus and producer surplus to the government, but also a net loss or social cost to society as a whole.

14 When a closed economy is opened up to world trade, goods will be imported if the world market price is below the autarky (closed economy) price, and goods will be exported if the world market price is above the autarky price.

15 In the case of a small country, an import tariff raises the domestic price above the world price by the amount of the tariff: producers and governments gain, but consumers lose more, so there is a net social cost. In the case of a large country, the world price with the tariff might actually be below the world price without the tariff: so although the domestic price is above the world price under free trade, the government gains more than consumers lose and there is a net social benefit (as long as other countries do not retaliate).

16 If the world market price is above the autarky price, a government can raise money from an export tax as long as the size of the export tax is less than the difference between the world price and the autarky price.

17 One alternative to an import tariff is an import quota, but as long as import licences are awarded through competitive bidding, the outcomes will be the same: the government gains some revenue. Another alternative is voluntary export restrictions: in this case the difference between the domestic price and the lower world market price is kept by the importer.

Exercises

1 Explain the idea of 'opportunity cost'.
2 Why do demand curves slope downwards?
3 What factors cause demand curves to shift?
4 Explain the significance of the 'ceteris paribus' assumption in economics.
5 Explain the difference between a movement along a demand curve and a shift in a demand curve.
6 Why do supply curves slope upwards?
7 What factors cause supply curves to shift?
8 How is the equilibrium market price determined? What happens out of equilibrium?
9 Why do some markets establish equilibrium more easily than others? Give examples.
10 Provide an example of two goods which are substitutes and examine the effect of a rise in the price of one good on the demand for the other good.

11 Provide an example of two goods which are complements and examine the effect of a rise in the price of one good on the demand for the other good.

12 What are the consequences of imposing (a) a price ceiling and (b) a price floor?

13 What is consumer surplus and why does it arise?

14 What is producer surplus and why does it arise?

15 Examine the possible consequences of imposing a sales tax. In what circumstances will the equilibrium price rise by the amount of the sales tax?

16 Examine the possible consequences for a small closed economy of opening up to world trade.

17 Examine the possible consequences for a small economy of imposing an import tariff.

18 The following data represent the demand and supply curves for a good:

Price (pence)	Quantity demanded per week	Quantity supplied per week
20	1	7
18	2	6
16	3	5
14	4	4
12	5	3
10	6	2
8	7	1
6	8	0

(a) Find the equilibrium price and quantity.

(b) Calculate the consumer surplus and producer surplus (in pence) at the equilibrium price.

(c) Calculate the excess demand or excess supply when the price is 18p.

(d) Calculate the excess demand or excess supply when the price is 8p.

(e) Suppose that, following an increase in consumers' incomes, the demand for the good increases by 2 units per week at each price level. Find the new equilibrium price and quantity.

(f) Suppose that (at the original level of consumers' incomes) the government imposes a sales tax of 4p per unit sold. Find the new equilibrium price and quantity and the tax revenue.

Business application: The commercial property market—boom to bust

During the period 1985–88 two factors played key roles in the boom in the overall property market: first, rapid economic growth, which averaged around 4.5 per cent over the three years, and second the fall in base interest rates from 14 per cent to 7.5 per cent. Confidence in the economy was high and this had a knock-on effect on the property market. The demand for commercial property—office space, warehousing and retailing—increased sharply and the market boomed.

Figure 1.14 shows the effects of these factors on prices within this market. The supply curve for commercial property is relatively inelastic given the time required to increase the stock of buildings. Reasons for this include the time involved in gaining planning permission as well as the actual construction time. We begin at point A on the original demand and supply curves, D_0 and S_0.

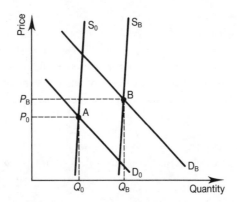

Figure 1.14   The property boom in the mid-1980s

S_0 = Original pre-boom supply of commercial property.
S_B = Boom supply of commercial property.
D_0 = Original pre-boom demand for commercial property.
D_B = Boom demand for commercial property.
P_0 = Original pre-boom price of commercial property.
Q_0 = Original pre-boom quantity.
P_B = Boom price of commercial property.
Q_B = Boom quantity.

In response to the favourable market conditions, the demand for commercial property increased to D_B and the supply rose to S_B, moving the commercial property market from A to B. The

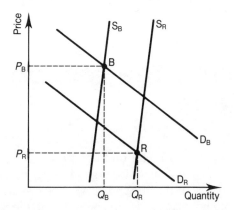

Figure 1.15   The post-1988 property slump

impact was a substantial increase in prices to P_B. Although much of the UK experienced such rises, they were most marked in London and the South East, where house prices also rose very sharply.

The attractiveness of the property market was further enhanced by the 1988 Budget which provided an additional stimulus to the economy by substantially cutting income tax. However, the economy was starting to overheat and, in response to rising inflation, the government increased base interest rates from 7.5 per cent to 15 per cent during 1988 and 1989.

The combination of high interest rates and an economy moving into recession had a devastating effect on the market. The demand for commercial property collapsed. Many property firms were highly geared, in that they had borrowed heavily to finance new developments. High interest rates therefore increased their repayment costs. However, a more serious problem was that they had borrowed against, not an appreciating asset (property) as they had expected, but a depreciating one. The inability to find tenants for their new developments further added to their cash flow problems. The consequences for companies such as Olympia and York, which was responsible for Canary Wharf in London's Docklands, clearly illustrated the problems faced in this sector. Figure 1.15 shows the post-1988 situation.

S_R = Recession supply of commercial property.
D_R = Recession demand for commercial property.
P_R = Recession price of commercial property.
Q_R = Recession quantity.

As the economy moved into recession and demand fell to D_R, there was an excess supply at the boom price of P_B. This was made worse by new property coming on to the market (with supply increasing to S_R). Consequently the market clearing price fell to P_R, which was too low for many companies to continue trading. As a result, many property-based firms went out of business as the commercial property market moved from B to R.

Although the recession has affected all parts of the UK, it has had most impact on London and the South East—therefore property companies most heavily involved there suffered the greatest difficulties. However, it is these same companies that are likely to benefit most when the upturn comes—assuming they survive.

2 Measuring the responsiveness of demand

In order to make demand analysis a useful tool for firms and also for governments, it is not sufficient just to know that a demand curve for a good slopes downwards. We need to be able to say something about the slope of the demand curve. For instance, if prices change by 10 per cent, by how much will demand change? The answers to questions of this type are important to firms in deciding what prices to charge. Firms are interested in the effect that any price change has on their total sales revenue. Governments are also interested in the same question for the purposes of tax policy. If, for example, demand is very responsive to price changes (so that the demand curve is fairly flat) a tax on that good will not yield much tax revenue because the quantity demanded will be much lower following the rise in price induced by the tax (we looked at this example in Chapter 1). Income and the prices of related goods are also important determinants of demand. We will therefore consider measures of the responsiveness of demand to these factors as well.

2.1 The price elasticity of demand

The *price elasticity of demand* is the measure of how demand responds to changes in the own price of the good (sometimes it is called the own-price elasticity of demand). In Fig. 2.1 we illustrate a hypothetical demand for bank loans at various rates of interest (interest measures the cost of borrowing and so is equivalent to the price of the loan). As the interest rate falls, the total amount of money that consumers wish to borrow rises.

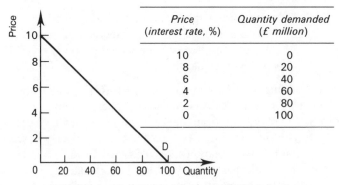

Price (interest rate, %)	Quantity demanded (£ million)
10	0
8	20
6	40
4	60
2	80
0	100

Figure 2.1 The demand for a good: bank loans

To measure how responsive demand is, two important points have to be taken into account:

1 We are more interested in the *percentage* change in quantity demanded than in the *absolute* change in quantity demanded. This is because we might wish to make a direct comparison

between the responsiveness of the demand for fish with that of the demand for meat to changes in their prices. Since one kilogram of fish is valued differently from one kilogram of meat, the absolute magnitude of the change in quantity consumed following a price change is not particularly useful. Furthermore, knowing the absolute change in quantity consumed of two goods is not particularly useful if consumers consume different initial amounts. For example, suppose that following price falls, a consumer buys 2 kilograms per month more fish and 4 kilograms per month more meat. But if initial monthly consumption was 2 kilograms of fish and 10 kilograms of meat, then the consumer's consumption of fish has increased by a much bigger percentage (100 per cent) than the consumption of meat (40 per cent).

2 Similarly, a given *absolute* change in price represents a different *percentage* change for goods with different initial prices. For example: a £1 fall in price from £11 to £10 is a smaller percentage change than a £1 fall in price from £2 to £1. Therefore, to make a comparison between the responsiveness of the demand for fish and meat to changes in their prices, it makes much more sense to use percentage changes in prices and quantities than absolute changes.

Formally, price elasticity is defined as follows:

$$\text{Price elasticity of demand } (e_p) = \frac{\text{percentage change in quantity demanded}}{\text{percentage change in price}} \quad (2.1)$$

i.e. the price elasticity of demand measures the percentage change in quantity demanded in response to a 1 per cent change in price. This measure of price responsiveness is independent of the units used to measure price or quantity.

In Table 2.1, we calculate the elasticity of demand for each successive price (i.e. interest rate) change of 2 percentage points for the bank loans given in Fig. 2.1. Note that as we move along the demand curve, the absolute value of the price elasticity falls. With this particular demand curve, each time the interest rate falls 2 percentage points, the quantity demanded rises by £20 million. However, each successive fall in price represents a larger percentage fall in prices, and the opposite is the case for quantity demanded. The price elasticity of demand is always negative

TABLE 2.1   **Price elasticity of demand: bank loans**

Price (interest rate; %)	Quantity demanded (£ million)	Price elasticity (e_p)
10	0	$-\infty$
8	20	-4
6	40	-1.5
4	60	-0.67
2	80	-0.25
0	100	0

Example: Price falls from 6 to 4 $= -33\%$
Quantity rises from 40 to 60 $= +50\%$

$$e_p = \frac{+50\%}{-33\%} = -1.5$$

Thus a 10 per cent fall in price increases quantity demanded by 15 per cent.

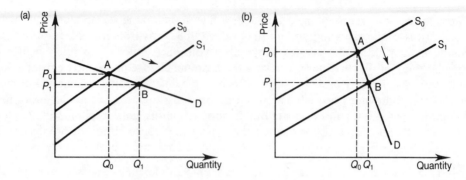

Figure 2.2 The implications of price elasticity for price and quantity variations: (a) elastic demand—small price changes, large quantity changes; (b) inelastic demand—large price changes, small quantity changes

since *either* the price change *or* the quantity change will be negative. In Table 2.1, the elasticity of demand at price 6 is -1.5. Since elasticity is a ratio of percentage changes, the implication in this case is that for any percentage change in price from 6 (either a 1 per cent rise to 6.1 or a 1 per cent fall to 5.9), the percentage quantity demanded will change in the opposite direction by one-and-a-half times the percentage change in price.

An equivalent definition is:

$$e_p = \frac{\Delta Q/Q}{\Delta P/P} = \frac{\Delta Q}{\Delta P} \times \frac{P}{Q} \tag{2.2}$$

where $\Delta Q/\Delta P$ (which is read 'delta Q by delta P') means the *change* in quantity demanded when the price *changes* by a particular amount, and P and Q are respectively the price and quantity demanded *before* the price change. From this we note that for straight line demand curves (as in Fig. 2.1), $\Delta Q/\Delta P$ will remain constant (since it measures the slope of the curve, which is constant throughout its length), whereas P/Q will fall as we move to the right. It therefore follows that the elasticity decreases as we move down a linear demand curve. For the above case, we have

$$e_p = \frac{\Delta Q}{\Delta P} \times \frac{P}{Q} = \frac{60 - 40}{4 - 6} \times \frac{6}{40} = -1.5 \tag{2.3}$$

Figure 2.2 shows how different demand elasticities affect equilibrium quantities and prices. In Fig. 2.2(a) an increase in supply results in a large rise in quantity demanded (Q_0 to Q_1), with a small change in price (P_0 to P_1). Demand in this case is said to be *elastic*. The opposite is the case in Fig. 2.2(b), where a similar increase in supply results in a large fall in prices, and only a small increase in quantity. Demand in this case is said to be *inelastic*. Technically, we have the following cases:

$$
\left.
\begin{aligned}
e_p &< -1 && \text{for elastic demand} \\
e_p &= -1 && \text{for unit-elastic demand} \\
e_p &> -1 && \text{for inelastic demand}
\end{aligned}
\right\} \tag{2.4}
$$

or using absolute values (since price elasticities are often reported without the minus sign in front):

$$|e_p| > 1 \quad \text{for elastic demand}$$
$$|e_p| = 1 \quad \text{for unit-elastic demand} \qquad (2.5)$$
$$|e_p| < 1 \quad \text{for inelastic demand}$$

Some typical price elasticities of demand in the UK are as follows:

Bread	−0.22
Fuel and light	−0.47
Alcohol	−0.83
Services	−1.02
Entertainment	−1.40

So bread, fuel and light, and alcohol have inelastic demands, services have a unit-elastic demand and entertainment has an elastic demand.

2.1.1   The implications of price elasticity for total revenue

Why is it important for a firm to know the price elasticity of demand that it faces? It is important because knowing the price elasticity helps it to predict changes in total revenue following changes in price. Consider the case of the privatized water companies, which now have to decide their own pricing policy. Pricing policy depends on the elasticity of demand, and water companies are in a powerful position because the demand for water is inelastic.

In Fig. 2.3, the pricing decision is illustrated in terms of the change in total revenue. In (a), a

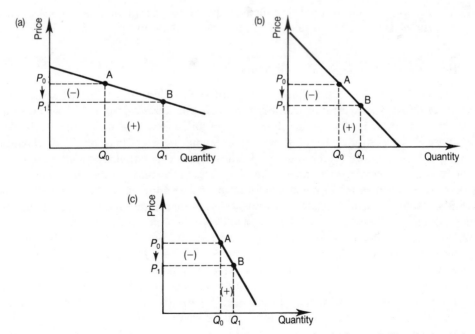

Figure 2.3   The implications of price elasticity for total revenue: (a) elastic demand; (b) unit-elastic demand; (c) inelastic demand

TABLE 2.2   Demand elasticities and changes in total revenue

Elasticity	Change in total revenue	Elasticity	Change in total revenue
For price rises: $\|e_p\| > 1$	<0	For price falls: $\|e_p\| > 1$	>0
$\|e_p\| = 1$	$=0$	$\|e_p\| = 1$	$=0$
$\|e_p\| < 1$	>0	$\|e_p\| < 1$	<0

decrease in price from P_0 to P_1 changes *total revenue* (where total revenue is defined as price × quantity) from $P_0 \times Q_0$ to $P_1 \times Q_1$. Considering gains and losses, the ($-$) area indicates the loss of revenue from lower prices and the ($+$) area indicates the gain in revenue from higher sales. In this case, the change in total revenue is positive. This means that the demand curve is elastic at this point. This is because the percentage change in quantity is greater than the percentage change in price, so that total revenue is higher after a price fall. In other words, the absolute value of the price elasticity of demand is greater than unity. It would pay the water companies to cut prices where demand is elastic.

In Fig. 2.3(b), a similar price change results in no change in total revenue. That is, the loss ($-$) is equal to the gain ($+$). The elasticity here is equal to unity. The demand curve is unit-elastic at this point. In this case, the water companies would gain nothing by changing prices.

In part (c), a similar price fall leads to only a small increase in demand. The gain ($+$) in total revenue is much smaller than the loss ($-$) in total revenue, resulting in a net loss. The elasticity of demand for this demand curve is less than unity in absolute value. Demand is inelastic at this point. Here it would not pay the water companies to reduce prices. Note that exactly the same analysis is applicable to other pricing decisions, e.g. football clubs setting entrance fees for their grounds, the pricing of cinema tickets etc.

Table 2.2 shows the change in total revenue in response to price changes as a consequence of different demand elasticities. The results for price rises are the opposite of those for price falls.

2.1.2   Short-run and long-run price elasticities

When the price of a good rises, the change in quantity demanded can be derived easily from its price elasticity of demand. Consumers will reduce their purchases and possibly switch some of their consumption towards other goods. The extent of this switch depends on the availability of goods that are close substitutes. In the short run it may not be possible to find close substitutes, or more importantly, there may be significant adjustment costs entailed in switching between goods. Suppose, for example, wage rates in the UK rise. Firms may not be able to adjust their production processes in order to manage with fewer workers for quite some time. Over time, however, high labour costs may encourage firms to use more capital (and various labour-saving technologies) instead of labour. Thus the *long-run elasticity of demand* (after full adjustment to a change in price has taken place) will be greater than the *short-run elasticity of demand*. In Fig. 2.4 this difference between short- and long-run elasticities is illustrated with the use of two demand curves. D_S is the *short-run demand curve*, which implies that a rise in price from P_0 to P_1 reduces quantity demanded to Q_S^D. As more substitutes become available, the demand curve shifts to D_L, causing the quantity demanded to fall even further to Q_L^D. D_L is the *long-run demand curve* for this commodity: D_L is always flatter or more elastic than D_S.

In terms of the arguments presented earlier about the use of elasticities for pricing policy, we can now add an important qualification. For the supplier of a commodity, it is important to

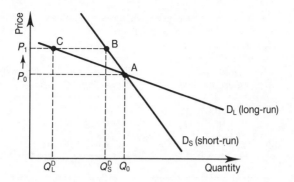

Figure 2.4 Short-run and long-run elasticities

bear in mind the long-run response of consumers and not just what will happen in the market immediately. This qualification has often been emphasized with respect to wage demands. In the long run, workers can price themselves out of their jobs if they receive substantial wage increases, even if they keep their jobs immediately after a wage increase.

So, the long-run elasticity depends on the extent to which consumers can find substitutes, and the definition of long run is the time it takes to switch to other goods. The 'long run' for some commodities might take longer to reach than the 'long run' for other commodities. The implication is that when the price of one good rises, the demand for other (related) goods is also affected. For producers, the effect on the demand for their commodities, as a result of changes in the prices of other goods, will be an important consideration when forecasting demand.

2.2 The cross-price elasticity of demand

Up till now, we have held the prices of related goods constant. In order to measure the responsiveness of the demand for a good to changes in the prices of related goods, we hold the own price constant and ask what happens when the price of a related good changes. This measure is termed the *cross-price elasticity of demand*. It is defined as the percentage change in quantity demanded of one good (say good i) *divided by* the percentage change in the price of a related good (say good j). Formally:

$$e_{ij} = \frac{\text{percentage change in quantity demanded of good } i}{\text{percentage change in price of good } j}$$

$$= \frac{\Delta Q_i/Q_i}{\Delta P_j/P_j} = \frac{\Delta Q_i}{\Delta P_j} \times \frac{P_j}{Q_i} \tag{2.6}$$

Whether e_{ij} is positive or negative depends on the relation between the two goods. If two goods are *substitutes*, this cross-price elasticity will be *positive*. A price increase for one good results in demand falling for that good and increasing for the substitute good. Conversely, when two goods are *complements* to each other, the cross-price elasticity will be *negative*. In this case, a positive price change for one good will reduce the quantity demanded of the complementary good.

Two hypothetical cases of substitutes and complements are shown in Table 2.3.

TABLE 2.3   Cross-price elasticity of demand

(a) Substitutes		(b) Complements	
Price of bank finance	Quantity of equity finance	Price of underwriting	Quantity of equity finance
11.5	100	10	70
12.0	120	20	63
$e_{ij} = \dfrac{120 - 100}{12.0 - 11.5} \times \dfrac{11.5}{100} = 4.6 > 0$		$e_{ij} = \dfrac{63 - 70}{20 - 10} \times \dfrac{10}{70} = -0.1 < 0$	

Case A: Substitutes (equity finance and bank finance)

In this case, an increase in the price of bank finance from 11.5 to 12.0 ($\Delta P_j = 0.5$), leads to an increase in the quantity of equity finance demanded from 100 to 120 ($\Delta Q_i = 20$). The cross-price elasticity is positive, since

$$e_{ij} = \frac{\Delta Q_i}{\Delta P_j} \times \frac{P_j}{Q_i} = \frac{120 - 100}{12 - 11.5} \times \frac{11.5}{100} = 4.6 \tag{2.7}$$

Case B: Complements (equity finance and underwriting)

If the price of underwriting rises from 10 to 20 ($\Delta P_j = 10$), the quantity of equity finance demanded falls from 70 to 63 ($\Delta Q_i = -7$). (Underwriting is a service provided by a bank whereby the bank agrees to buy any equity issued by a firm that is not purchased by investors in the market place; the bank gets a fee and the firm gets a guaranteed equity issue.) In this case, the cross-price elasticity is negative, since

$$e_{ij} = \frac{\Delta Q_i}{\Delta P_j} \times \frac{P_j}{Q_i} = \frac{63 - 70}{20 - 10} \times \frac{10}{70} = -0.1 \tag{2.8}$$

An example of substitutes in the UK is cider and beer, with a cross-price elasticity of 0.50 (a 1 per cent increase in the price of beer increases the demand for cider by 0.50 per cent). An example of complements in the UK is food and travel, with a cross-price elasticity of -0.12 (a 1 per cent increase in the price of travel reduces the demand for food by 0.12 per cent).

In terms of the demand curve, the changes that we have been considering lead to shifts of the entire curve. This follows from the fact that we hold all other prices constant when drawing a demand curve. When any of the other prices change, the demand curve will shift. In Case A, the demand curve for equity finance shifts to the right, and in Case B, the demand curve for equity finance shifts to the left (see Fig. 2.5).

The importance of cross-price elasticities of demand lies in their use for forecasting the demand for goods. In our example above, companies will be interested in the prices of all forms of financing instruments and in the price of bank services such as underwriting, when forecasting the demand for their own product.

2.3   The income elasticity of demand

The second factor that is held constant along a given demand curve is consumers' incomes. A rise in incomes implies that, at any given price, consumers can afford to buy a larger quantity

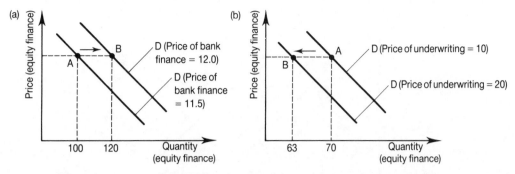

Figure 2.5 Cross-price elasticity and demand shifts: (a) substitutes; (b) complements

of the good. However, not all goods are affected in the same way. There are some goods for which the demand may fall when incomes rise. These goods are termed *inferior goods*, because they are purchased only when consumers have low incomes. As incomes rise, consumers are able to afford better substitutes. Goods which have a positive change in demand as a result of income increases are termed *normal goods*.

The sensitivity of demand to changes in income (Y) is called the *income elasticity of demand* (e_y), and is formally defined as:

$$e_y = \frac{\text{percentage change in quantity demanded}}{\text{percentage change in income}} = \frac{\Delta Q/Q}{\Delta Y/Y} = \frac{\Delta Q}{\Delta Y} \times \frac{Y}{Q} \tag{2.9}$$

Depending on the nature of the good and the need that it satisfies, the income elasticity can be positive or negative. In Table 2.4, a worked example is shown where this elasticity is positive.

The higher the income elasticity, the greater will be the shift of the demand curve. In Fig. 2.6 (see p. 28), beginning with demand curve D_0 (and point A), a given increase in income (holding own price constant at P_0) could shift the demand curve to D_1, D_2 or D_3. The income elasticity is positive but less than unity when the shift is from A to B_1. It is positive and greater than unity when the shift is from A to B_2. The income elasticity is negative when the move is from A to B_3.

TABLE 2.4 Income elasticity of demand

Income	Quantity demanded
100	60
110	65

$$e_y = \frac{65 - 60}{110 - 100} \times \frac{100}{60}$$

$$= \frac{5}{10} \times \frac{100}{60} = 0.83$$

Thus a 10 per cent rise in income increases quantity demanded by 8.3 per cent.

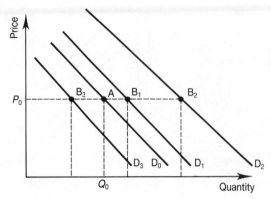

Figure 2.6   Income elasticity and demand shifts

Goods can be classified according to their income elasticities:

$$e_y > 0 \text{ for a } normal \ good.$$
$$e_y < 0 \text{ for an } inferior \ good.$$
$$e_y > 1 \text{ for a } luxury \ good.$$
$$e_y < 1 \text{ for a } necessity.$$

A good is known as a *normal necessity* if its income elasticity lies betweeen 0 and 1. We can consider some examples of income elasticities for the UK:

Bread	−0.50
Fuel and light	0.30
Alcohol	1.14
Services	1.75
Entertainment	1.99

So bread is an inferior good, consumed mainly by the poor: if someone's income fell by 10 per cent, their consumption of bread would increase by 5 per cent. Fuel and light are normal necessities: if someone's income increases by 10 per cent, their consumption of fuel and light would increase by 3 per cent. In contrast, alcohol, services and entertainment are luxury goods.

It is also possible for income elasticities to change over time. For example, if the income elasticity for a good increases over time, we would expect to see a movement from A to B_1 to B_2 in Fig. 2.6. For most applications of income elasticities, one-off changes in income elasticities might not be very useful: it would be more useful to have data over a sufficiently long period in which there have been continuous increases in income (i.e. economic growth).

There are a variety of uses of income elasticities. For example, consider the decision facing producers of where to target their marketing (advertising) efforts. Knowledge of income elasticities both over time and also across different income groups is extremely useful in reducing unnecessary marketing expenditure. Certain types of banking services, such as 'gold' credit cards, are marketed to higher income groups only, for instance.

Income elasticities of demand are also extremely useful in judging how particular firms or industries will perform over the course of the business cycle. As incomes grow, high income elasticity markets will expand most rapidly (but also contract fastest in a recession). Low income elasticity markets tend to be safe but unexciting in terms of future profits growth. For example, the demand for entertainment changes at twice the rate that consumers' incomes change: entertainment is a good industry to be in during an economic boom, but a bad one to be in during a slump!

2.4 Demand elasticities and taxation

We saw earlier the importance of the price elasticity of demand for determining total sales revenues of producers. Exactly the same underlying features of demand curves are also relevant for determining government tax revenue (as we saw in Chapter 1). The amount of tax revenue collected from sales and excise taxes depends on the effect the tax has on consumer demand. If, as a result of the increase in price induced by the imposition of a tax, the demand for the good falls considerably, then the total tax revenue that the government collects will be small. The reason for this is that the total quantity sold (which determines the tax base) will be small. We know that this is the case when demand is highly elastic. Conversely, if there is a very small change in demand when the price changes, tax revenue will be larger. This occurs when demand is inelastic.

In Fig. 2.7 we consider two goods which are characterized by identical supply conditions, but differ in terms of the elasticities of demand, i.e. the slope of the demand curves. D_E is the demand curve for a good with elastic demand, and D_I is the demand curve for a good with inelastic demand. The initial equilibrium quantity is Q_0. The imposition of a tax has the effect of shifting the supply schedule to the left. In Fig. 2.7, this is shown as the movement from S to S_T. For both goods, demands falls (a movement along the demand curve). The new equilibrium quantities are Q_E and Q_I respectively. For the good with elastic demand, the tax revenue is shown by the lower shaded rectangle, which is the market price (P_E) *minus* the price the supplier receives (P_{ES}), all *times* the quantity sold (Q_E), i.e. $(P_E - P_{ES})Q_E$. For the good with inelastic demand, the corresponding area (the upper shaded rectangle) is shown as $(P_I - P_{IS})Q_I$. The tax take when demand is inelastic is clearly larger. This explains why products with inelastic demands (such as tobacco and alcohol) have higher excise duties imposed on them than products with elastic demands.

In practice, maximizing tax revenue may be just one consideration for government tax policy, albeit an important one. The government may also have the objective of reducing aggregate consumption in order to control inflation, in which case taxing goods which have elastic demands

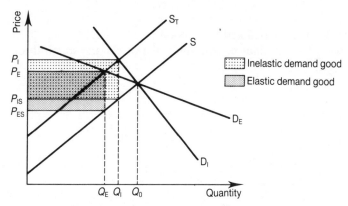

Figure 2.7 Demand elasticities and taxation

will help to do this. In either case, whether the objective is to maximize revenue, reduce consumption or both (as may be the case with tobacco and alcohol taxation), price elasticities of demand are crucial in setting tax rates.

2.5 Summary

1 The price elasticity of demand measures the percentage change in quantity demanded when the own price changes by 1 per cent. The demand for a good is said to be elastic when the absolute value of the price elasticity exceeds unity: in this case, a 1 per cent increase in price reduces demand by more than 1 per cent. The demand for a good is said to be inelastic when the absolute value of the price elasticity is less than unity: in this case, a 1 per cent increase in price reduces demand by less than 1 per cent.

2 When demand is elastic, a fall in price increases total revenue, while an increase in price reduces total revenue. When demand is unit-elastic, total revenue is unchanged whether price rises or falls. When demand is inelastic, a fall in price reduces total revenue, while an increase in price increases total revenue.

3 Demand tends to become more elastic in the long run: a rise in price will reduce demand in the short run, but lead to an even bigger reduction in demand in the long run as consumers switch to less expensive substitutes.

4 The cross-price elasticity of demand measures the percentage change in quantity demanded when the price of a related good changes by 1 per cent. The cross-price elasticity is positive for substitutes: the demand for a good increases when the price of a substitute good rises. The cross-price elasticity is negative for complements: the demand for a good falls when the price of a complementary good rises, since less of both goods will be consumed.

5 The income elasticity of demand measures the percentage change in quantity demanded when income changes by 1 per cent. The income elasticity is positive for normal goods: the demand for normal goods increases when income increases. The income elasticity is negative for inferior goods: the demand for inferior goods falls when income increases. The income elasticity is greater than unity for luxury goods and less than unity for necessities.

6 The government will raise greater tax revenue if it taxes goods with inelastic demands than if it taxes goods with elastic demands.

Exercises

1 Define the price elasticity of demand for a good.

2 You are given the following information about the prices and quantities demanded of two goods:

	Price	Quantity demanded
Good A	100	10
	110	9
Good B	15	30
	20	25

Calculate the price elasticities of demand for both goods. Which good is more price elastic?

3 Is the following statement true or false? 'When demand is price inelastic, lower prices mean both higher sales and higher revenues for sellers.'

4 Is the following statement true or false? 'When the price elasticity of demand is unity, a firm's revenue is independent of the price that it sets.'

5 Why is the long-run price elasticity of demand greater than the short-run price elasticity of demand?

6 Define the cross-price elasticity of demand.

7 'When two goods are substitutes, the cross-price elasticity is negative.' True or false?

8 You are given the following information about the prices of good A and the quantities demanded of good B:

Price of A	Quantity demanded of B
100	10
110	11

Calculate the cross-price elasticity of the demand for good B with respect to the price of good A. Are A and B complements or substitutes?

9 You are given the following own price and cross-price elasticities of demand:

Good	Percentage change in quantity demanded in response to a 1% change in price of		
	Petrol	Cars	Public transport
Petrol	−1.1	−0.6	0.2
Cars	−0.4	−1.3	0.1
Public transport	0.3	0.7	−0.7

(a) For which goods and services is demand elastic?

(b) Which goods and services are substitutes and which are complements?

(c) Suppose that the price of petrol rises by 20 per cent. What happens to the demand for cars and public transport?

(d) Draw a diagram of the market for cars before and after the change in the price of petrol.

10 The following table shows the number of personal computers sold, the price of personal computers and the incomes of buyers in each of four years:

Year	Number sold	Price (× £100)	Income (× £1000)
1	100	5	10
2	120	4	10
3	130	4	11
4	110	5	11

(a) You want to examine the effect of price on quantity sold, holding everything else constant. Draw a diagram plotting the relevant points. What is your conclusion?

(b) Is price the only determinant of quantity sold?

(c) What is the effect of income on the sales of personal computers?

(d) Holding income constant at £10,000, calculate the price elasticity of demand.

(e) Holding the price constant at £500, calculate the income elasticity of demand.

11 The following table shows an individual's income and expenditure on four goods in each of two years (assuming prices were constant between the two years):

Good	Year 1 Income = 1000	Year 2 Income = 2000
A	150	600
B	250	200
C	300	700
D	300	500

(a) Calculate the expenditure (or budget) shares in each year for each good.

(b) Calculate the income elasticity of demand for each good.

(c) Determine whether the goods are normal or inferior.

(d) Determine whether the goods are luxuries or necessities.

12 Why do governments prefer to tax goods that are price inelastic?

13 If the price of a good falls by 15 per cent, calculate the percentage change in expenditure on the good if the elasticity of demand for the good is:

(a) −0.8.

(b) −1.0.

(c) −1.4.

3 Output supply and market structure

In Chapter 1, the analysis of market equilibrium prices and quantities was conducted under the assumption that the supply curve for output was upward sloping. We provided some plausible reasons for this. In this chapter, we explore the underlying determinants of output supply in more detail.

What determines the *level of output* that firms supply? We will find that the level of output depends first on the *costs* incurred in the production of goods and second on the *revenues* that firms receive by selling their output (see Fig. 3.1).

We first look at the determinants of the cost of production and how these costs vary with different levels of output. Other things being equal, it is reasonable to assume that firms are interested in minimizing their costs of production (which is equivalent to maximizing their profits). These costs in turn will depend on the choice of *production technology* made by the firm and also the prices and quantities of the *factors of production* used to produce each level of output. Over time, technological innovations occur which tend to reduce costs of production. In this chapter, however, we are concerned with a much shorter time horizon in order to focus on firms' decisions about output when the production technology that they face is fixed.

The revenue that a firm receives from sales will in general depend on the *degree of competition* it faces in its particular market; in other words on the *market structure* that firms face. A competitive market structure implies negligible market power for individual firms, which in turn implies that the price that they can charge is determined to a large extent by factors outside their control. This is known as *price-taking behaviour*. Firms that have considerable market power will be able to determine, to some extent, the prices that they charge. This is known as *price-setting behaviour*. These differences in the degree of competition are important in determining the level of output, total revenue and ultimately profitability. First we consider the

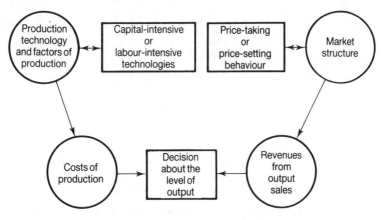

Figure 3.1 The theory of supply

two polar cases: *perfect competition* and *monopoly*. Then we consider two cases lying between these extremes: *monopolistic competition* and *oligopoly*.

3.1   Output levels and costs of production

Most production processes require a variety of inputs or *factors of production* (e.g. labour, capital, land and premises, raw materials, and energy). Some production processes, for example, are *labour-intensive*, using many workers but little capital equipment or machinery; other production processes are *capital-intensive*, using large amounts of capital equipment or machines operated by only a small number of workers.

The *total costs* of production will clearly increase as output is increased. However, the important question is whether or not costs increase proportionately with the increase in inputs. In other words, we would like to know whether the *average cost* of producing each unit of output rises as production increases, falls or just stays the same (average cost is defined formally below). The answer depends on whether there are *economies of scale* present in the production process. In Fig. 3.2 we depict three possible cases. Where there are *increasing economies of scale* or *increasing returns to scale* in the production process, the average cost of producing goods falls as the scale of operations increases (Fig. 3.2(a)). Where there are *constant economies of scale* or *constant returns to scale*, the average cost of producing goods remains unchanged as the scale of operations increases (Fig. 3.2(b)). Where there are *decreasing economies of scale* or *decreasing returns to scale*, the average cost of producing goods rises as the scale of operations increases (Fig. 3.2(c)).

In general, it is likely that at fairly low levels of production all factor inputs are not being utilized fully. Overhead costs (such as the salaries of administrative staff or the rent on factories) or the number of machines, for example, may not have to be increased every time more workers are hired. This is the stage in the production process of economies of scale: additional output can be supplied with a less than proportionate increase in costs. After some level of output, however, diseconomies of scale are likely to occur. That is the stage in the production process

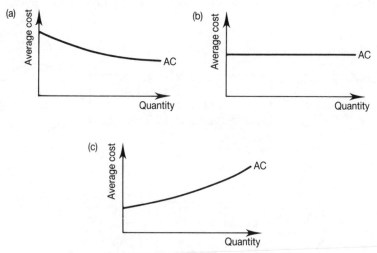

Figure 3.2   Returns to scale and costs of production: (a) increasing returns to scale; (b) constant returns to scale; (c) decreasing returns to scale

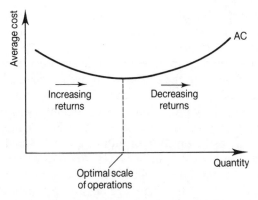

Figure 3.3 The optimal scale of operations

where most factors have to be increased (for example, a new factory may have to be built) to raise output by just a small amount. In Fig. 3.3, the production process is such that the U-shaped average cost curve exhibits all three types of returns to scale. Initially, we have increasing returns to scale. Then there is a turning point after which decreasing returns set in. The minimum point of the average cost curve can only be attained again by replicating the entire production process in another factory. In other words, there is an *optimal scale of operations* (or *minimum efficient size* for the production process chosen) determined at the output level at which average costs are minimized.

Whether average costs fall, rise or remain unchanged as output is increased depends on the behaviour of the total costs and the marginal costs of production as output increases.

3.1.1 Total costs and marginal costs

Figure 3.4 shows the typical shape of a firm's total cost curve as a function of quantity produced. *Total fixed costs* are fixed overhead costs that must be met whatever the level of output, even when output is zero in a particular period. For example, a shirt-making company will need to rent a factory or workshop. The rent will have to be paid whatever the level of production. Such

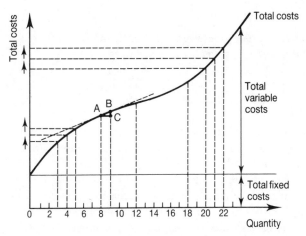

Figure 3.4 Total costs and marginal costs

costs can only be avoided if a firm decides to stop production altogether. *Total variable costs are costs that increase with (i.e. vary with) the level of output*: more workers, raw materials and other inputs must be used to produce more output. For example, in order to produce more shirts, the firm will have to employ more sewing machine operators, buy more cloth and use more electric power. *Total costs are the sum of total fixed costs and total variable costs*. Total costs will always be increasing as output increases, initially less than proportionately with increases in output, but eventually more than proportionately with increases in output.

When there are increasing returns to scale, total costs will be rising less than proportionately with output. In Fig. 3.4 this is the position at output levels 3, 4 and 5, for example. The slope of the total cost curve decreases as output increases. After 18 units are produced, however, the slope of the total cost curve stops falling and instead begins to increase. Decreasing returns to scale have set in and total costs begin rising more than proportionately with output. In Fig. 3.4 this is the position at output levels 20, 21 and 22, for example.

The changing returns to scale feature of the production process also implies that the cost of producing each additional unit of output differs, depending on the scale of production. The cost of producing an additional unit of output is called the *marginal cost*. Formally, *marginal cost (MC)* is defined as the *increase in total cost (ΔTC) as output increases by one unit (ΔQ)*:

$$MC = \frac{\Delta TC}{\Delta Q} \tag{3.1}$$

This is equal to the slope of the total cost curve at a particular level of output. The slope of the total cost curve at any level of output is equal to the slope of the line tangent to the total cost curve at that level of output. For example, the marginal cost of producing the ninth unit is given by BC/AC in Fig. 3.4.

In Fig. 3.4 the slope of the total cost curve is decreasing between 0 and 12 units of output. This is because the total cost curve is concave to the origin between 0 and 12 units. For example, the increase in output from 4 to 5 units adds less to total cost than the increase from 3 to 4 units. At 12 units of output, the slope of the total cost curve is at its flattest and marginal cost is minimized. After 12 units, the slope of the total cost curve begins to increase. This is because the total cost curve is convex to the origin after 12 units. For example, the increase in output from 21 to 22 units adds more to total cost than the increase from 20 to 21 units.

3.1.2   Total costs and average costs

Figure 3.5 shows the relationship between total cost and *average cost*. Formally, *average cost (AC)* is defined as *total cost (TC) divided by total output (Q)*:

$$AC = \frac{TC}{Q} \tag{3.2}$$

By simple geometry, the average cost of producing any level of output is equal to the slope of the line segment from the origin to the point on the total cost curve corresponding with the total cost of producing that level of output. For example, the average cost of producing 9 units is given by BD/OD in Fig. 3.5, while the average cost of producing 18 units is given by B′D′/OD′.

In Fig. 3.5 the slope of the line segment is decreasing between 0 and 18 units of output, indicating that average costs are decreasing over this range. At 18 units of output, the slope of the line segment is at its flattest and average cost is minimized. After 18 units, the slope of the line segment begins to increase and average costs also begin to increase.

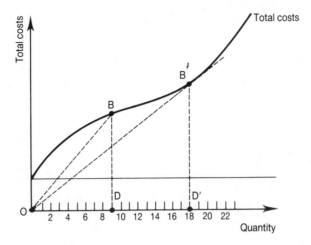

Figure 3.5 Total costs and average costs

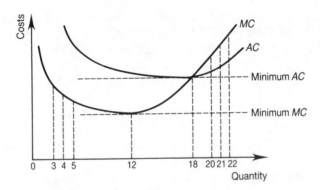

Figure 3.6 Marginal costs and average costs

3.1.3 Marginal costs and average costs

Figure 3.6 shows the relationship between marginal and average costs. Marginal costs fall initially, reach a minimum at 12 units and thereafter rise. Average costs also fall initially, reach a minimum at 18 units and thereafter rise. Below 18 units, average costs are higher than marginal costs; above 18 units, average costs are lower than marginal costs. What explains this relationship between marginal and average costs?

When marginal costs are falling, the addition to total costs is smaller for each additional unit produced. This means two things. First, it means that the marginal cost of the next unit produced is lower than the average cost of all preceding units, and therefore the average cost at this level of output must be greater than the marginal cost. Second, it means that average costs must be falling, because each successive unit being produced is being produced at lower marginal cost and this brings down the average cost.

After 12 units of output, marginal costs start rising and the addition to total costs increases for each additional unit produced. The decline in average costs begins to slow down. At 18 units of output, marginal cost equals average cost: the addition to total cost equals the average cost

TABLE 3.1 Relationship between marginal and average costs: bank loans and interest rates

Amount of additional loan (m)	Interest rate charged (%)	Average interest rate (%)	Marginal interest rate (%)
£100	12	12	12
£50	13	12.33	13
£40	15	12.89	15

Average interest rate, e.g.:

$$12.89 = \left(\frac{100}{190} \times 12\right) + \left(\frac{50}{190} \times 13\right) + \left(\frac{40}{190} \times 15\right)$$

of all previous units produced, so the average cost will not change. Not only does marginal cost equal average cost at 18 units, but average cost reaches a minimum at this level of output.

After 18 units of output, the effect of the rising marginal costs is to add more to total costs than the average cost of all preceding units. This means that marginal cost will be higher than average cost after 18 units and this will have the effect of causing average costs to rise.

An alternative way of seeing this is to re-examine the total cost curve in Figs 3.4 and 3.5. Recall that the slope of the line tangent to the total cost curve at any level of output measures the marginal cost at that level of output, while the slope of the line segment from the origin to the same point on the total cost curve measures the average cost at that level of output. It is clear from the figures that the slope of the tangent is less than the slope of the line segment for all levels of output below 18. At an output level of 18, the slopes are the same (see point B' in Fig. 3.5). At output levels above 18, the slope of the line tangent exceeds that of the line segment. This precisely confirms the relationship between marginal and average costs shown in Fig. 3.6.

The relation between marginal and average cost is summarized as follows:

$$MC < AC \Rightarrow AC \text{ is falling}$$

$$MC = AC \Rightarrow AC \text{ is at its minimum}$$

$$MC > AC \Rightarrow AC \text{ is rising}$$

As an example, Table 3.1 shows the relationship between marginal and average interest rates on bank loans.

Further, it is clear from the analysis that when marginal cost is below average cost the production process exhibits increasing returns to scale; when marginal cost equals average cost it exhibits constant returns to scale; and when marginal cost exceeds average cost it exhibits increasing returns to scale. This can be expressed in a slightly different way. We can define the *cost elasticity of production* as follows:

$$e_C = \frac{\text{percentage change in quantity produced}}{\text{percentage change in total cost}}$$

$$= \frac{\Delta Q / Q}{\Delta TC / TC} \tag{3.3}$$

$$= \frac{TC/Q}{\Delta TC/\Delta Q}$$

$$= \frac{AC}{MC} \qquad\qquad (3.3 \; Continued\,)$$

in other words, as the ratio of average costs to marginal costs. It is clear that

$$e_C > 1 \Rightarrow \text{increasing returns to scale}$$

$$e_C = 1 \Rightarrow \text{constant returns to scale}$$

$$e_C < 1 \Rightarrow \text{decreasing returns to scale}$$

The costs of production are one important determinant of the level of output. To determine what the actual level of output will be, we need to specify the demand or market conditions facing the firm. This in turn is given by the *market structure*, which varies considerably between industries. The extreme cases outlined in the next two sections will uncover the essential principles involved.

3.2 Market structure: perfect competition

3.2.1 Necessary conditions for perfect competition

The first case we analyse is that of *perfect competition*, which is the most competitive environment possible that any firm can face. There are a number of conditions necessary for markets to be perfectly competitive:

1 *A large number of buyers and sellers.* This is a minimum requirement for any one supplier or consumer not to be able to exercise *market power*. Each supplier is small enough in relation to the size of the market that it cannot influence market prices by variations in its output; each consumer is small enough in relation to the size of the market that it cannot influence market prices by variations in its demand.
2 *Free entry and exit.* An additional condition preventing suppliers from being able to exercise market power is for there to be a number of potential entrants who could enter the market and supply output at or near existing prices. In equilibrium, there may not actually be any new entrants coming into the industry, since current demand may already be satisfied, but the possibility must always be there.
3 *Absence of restrictive government regulations.* This ensures that *barriers to entry* do not exist. There should be no requirement, for example, to have licences to engage in production, or for there to be formal qualifications to engage in production. Note that in some industries, government regulations exist to prevent existing firms erecting barriers to entry (e.g. telecommunications in the UK or car manufacturing within the European Community).
4 *Homogeneous products.* All firms in the industry produce identical products, i.e. perfect substitutes indistinguishable from each other. Without this, there will be some product differences that will give firms some degree of market power. In this case, it would be possible for firms to increase prices without losing all their market share, something which is not possible under perfect competition.
5 *Buyers and sellers have full information.* Buyers need to be aware of all suppliers' prices, so

that firms are not in a position to charge different prices as a result of imperfect knowledge on the part of consumers.

Together, these five conditions define perfect competition, where firms are said to be *price takers*. Price takers face horizontal demand curves for their products. At the existing market price, each firm is able to sell as much as it likes without affecting the price. Any rise in its price above the market price will result in zero sales; consumers will immediately switch their demand to suppliers offering the identical product at the market price. Any lowering of price will result in the firm attracting all the demand in the market, which, because it is such a small supplier, it would not be able to meet. For example, if there are 10 000 firms in a perfectly competitive industry with equal market shares, and one firm cut its prices, it could not possibly satisfy market demand. Similarly, even if it doubled or tripled its output, this would have a negligible effect on changing market supply (and hence market price) and the firm will be able to sell all its output at the same price. Thus the demand curve that it faces is horizontal. Two examples of perfectly competitive activities are wheat farmers and newspaper vendors: both produce homogeneous products (one farmer's wheat is indistinguishable from the next farmer's wheat; the newspapers from one vendor are identical to those of any other) which have to be sold at the same market price.

3.2.2   Total revenue, marginal revenue and average revenue

In Fig. 3.7 we illustrate the horizontal demand curve facing a firm in perfect competition: it is a horizontal line at P_0, the equilibrium price established from the intersection of industry supply with industry demand.

Since every unit produced by a perfectly competitive firm is sold at the same price, and each additional unit produced can also be sold at the same price, the additional revenue the firm receives as a result of supplying one more unit is equal to the price. In other words, the *marginal revenue* from an additional unit sold is equal to the price. Furthermore, the *average revenue* from each unit sold is also equal to the price, since all units are sold at the same price. Formally, *marginal revenue (MR)* is defined as the *increase in total revenue* (ΔTR) *as sales increase by one unit* (ΔQ). *Total revenue (TR)* is *price (P)* times *quantity (Q)*:

$$TR = P \times Q \tag{3.4}$$

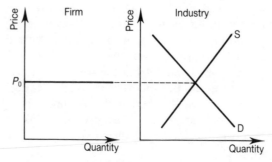

Figure 3.7   A competitive firm's demand curve

When all units produced can be sold at the same price:

$$MR = \frac{\Delta TR}{\Delta Q} = P \tag{3.5}$$

Further, *average revenue (AR)* is defined as *total revenue (TR) divided by total sales (Q)*:

$$AR = \frac{TR}{Q} = P \tag{3.6}$$

So, under perfect competition, marginal revenue and average revenue are both equal to price.

3.2.3 Profit-maximizing output for a competitive firm

Given these demand conditions (i.e. $MR = AR = P$) and the structure of costs facing the firm, we can determine the *profit-maximizing level of output*.

First, for any profit-maximizing firm, the decision as to whether to supply an additional unit of output will depend on whether the addition to total revenue from selling this additional unit (i.e. the marginal revenue) is greater than the cost of producing the additional unit (i.e. the marginal cost). *The firm will find it profitable to expand production up to the level of output at which marginal cost is equal to marginal revenue.* Any level of output below this level implies that profits are not being maximized, since additional units could be sold and the marginal revenue from the sales would exceed the marginal cost of producing them. Profits could therefore be increased by increasing output. Any level of output above this level will imply a reduction in profits (possibly absolute losses) since the marginal revenue from the additional sales will be less than the marginal cost of producing the sales. Profits could therefore be increased by reducing output.

In Fig. 3.8(a), point E depicts the *short-run equilibrium* for the firm where profit-maximizing output is Q_0. Since marginal revenue is equal to the price, it follows that marginal cost is also equal to the price. *The profit-maximizing level of output for a competitive firm in short-run equilibrium is therefore equal to the level of output at which marginal cost is equal to the market price,* i.e. $P = MR = MC$.

To determine the level of profits for the firm, we note that for each unit of output, profits are equal to the price *minus* the average cost: that is $(P_0 - C_0)$. Total profits are then given by the per unit profit *times* the quantity produced, i.e. $(P_0 - C_0)Q_0$. This measure of profits is a measure of *excess profits*. Excess profits are any profits earned above *normal profits*, which are the required return on capital. Normal profits are a cost of production (as are wages to workers, rent to factory and land owners, interest on bank loans etc.) and this cost has already been incorporated in the average and marginal cost curves in Fig. 3.8. Suppliers of capital will expect to make

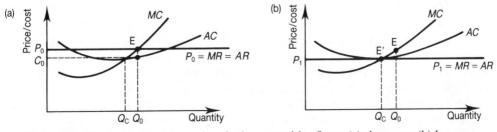

Figure 3.8 The output decisions of perfectly competitive firms: (a) short-run; (b) long-run

normal profits on any activity in which they invest, otherwise they will transfer their capital to more profitable uses.

The scenario in Fig. 3.8(a) is only a short-run equilibrium, because the existence of excess profits encourages new entrants. As more and more firms enter the industry, the total supply of output will increase, leading to a reduction in market price. Lower prices (and hence lower marginal revenues) lead to each firm reducing its production along its marginal cost curve. The excess profits will be eliminated at the point where prices are equal to the minimum point on the average cost curve. Figure 3.8(b) depicts this new equilibium at E' with market price P_1. Each firm is now just covering costs, which include the required return on capital (i.e. normal profits), but no excess profits are being made. Therefore *the profit-maximizing level of output for a competitive firm in long-run equilibrium is equal to the level of output at which marginal cost and minimum average cost are both equal to market price and marginal revenue, i.e. $P = MR = MC = minimum AC$.*

The supply curve for each firm is its marginal cost curve above the minimum point of the average cost curve. Below this point, all firms (assuming all firms are equally efficient and use the same production process and therefore have the same cost curves) will be making losses, and if prices remained below P_1 for a sustained period there would be no firms left in the industry. Above minimum average cost, firms will be willing to supply additional output along their marginal cost curves, i.e. as long as they are paid the marginal cost of the additional output.

3.3   Market structure: monopoly

At the other extreme to perfect competition is *monopoly. A monopolist is the sole supplier in the industry.* Examples are the letters service of the Royal Mail, and water, gas and electricity suppliers to domestic residents. These are examples of *regulated monopolies*, over which the government has established regulatory authorities (such as Ofwat, Ofgas and Offer) to prevent them exploiting their monopoly position. There are very few examples of pure *unregulated monopolies*, mainly because the high profits generated by them sooner or later encourage other firms to enter the industry and compete against them; for example, Rank Xerox was a monopoly supplier of photocopiers until the 1970s. For an unregulated monopoly to maintain its monopoly position it will generally need to be protected by legal barriers to entry, such as patent or copyright laws.

For producers to have some *monopoly power* they must face a downward-sloping rather than a horizontal demand curve for their product. Indeed, the slope of a firm's demand curve (i.e. the price elasticity of demand e_p) can be used to measure a firm's degree of monopoly power:

$$\text{Degree of monopoly power} = \frac{1}{|e_p|} \tag{3.7}$$

If $|e_p| = \infty$ (so that the firm's demand curve is horizontal), the firm's monopoly power is zero. The steeper the demand curve, the lower is $|e_p|$ and the higher the monopoly power. If $|e_p| = 0$ (so that the firm's demand curve is vertical), the monopoly power is infinite. Note that monopoly power is given to monopolists by consumers: if consumers did not have such an inelastic demand for the output of the monopolist, the monopolist would not have such a high degree of monopoly power. (The market structure in which there is a single buyer in the industry is called *monopsony*; e.g. where the state buys all the output of oil produced on its territory.)

3.3.1 The demand for a monopolist's output

When a monopolist changes the level of output he or she will necessarily be faced with a different price. Since a monopolist is the sole supplier, the demand curve he or she faces is the entire industry's demand curve, which is downward-sloping. (A *firm* can face a horizontal demand curve as in the case of perfect competition, but the *industry* demand curve is always downward sloping.) An important implication of this is that for the monopolist marginal revenue is not equal to average revenue or price. If output is raised by one unit, the price will fall not only for the marginal unit, but for all units supplied (including intramarginal units). Therefore the change in total revenue (i.e. marginal revenue) is the price of the last unit sold *minus* the reduction in revenue resulting from the reduced sale price on all intramarginal units. For example, if 10 units can be sold for £2.00, but the 11th unit can only be sold at £1.90, then all 11 units have to be sold at £1.90: why should anyone pay £2.00 for something that they can get for £1.90? So the marginal revenue from selling the 11th unit is not £1.90, but the difference between the total revenue from selling 11 units and the total revenue from selling 10 units:

$$\text{Marginal revenue} = (£1.90 \times 11 \text{ units}) - (£2.00 \times 10 \text{ units})$$

$$= £20.90 - £20.00 \tag{3.8}$$

$$= £0.90$$

or

$$\text{Marginal revenue} = \text{Price of 11th unit} - \text{Reduction in revenue from the reduced}$$
$$\text{sale price on the preceding 10 units}$$

$$\tag{3.9}$$

$$= £1.90 - (£2.00 - £1.90) \times 10$$

$$= £0.90$$

in other words, £0.90 rather than £1.90. Figure 3.9(a) shows that the marginal revenue curve is downward-sloping and to the left of the demand (or average revenue) curve.

The total revenue for a monopolist is the price (average revenue) *times* the quantity sold. By definition, total revenue must be at a maximum when marginal revenue is zero. This can be seen in Fig. 3.9(b), which plots total revenue as the revenue (price × quantity) rectangles under the demand curve in Fig. 3.9(a). Note, however, that until we specify the costs of production, we cannot determine the level of output that will actually be supplied by the monopolist. The objective of the monopolist is profit maximization and not revenue maximization. (However, if a firm was interested in maximizing its revenue it would produce at Q_1 in Fig. 3.9.)

All this implies that a monopolist is a *price setter*, in the sense that he or she has some control over the price at which the output is sold.

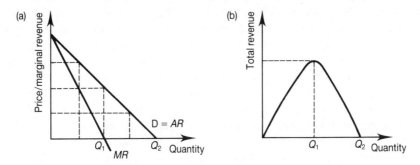

Figure 3.9 Demand for a monopolist's output

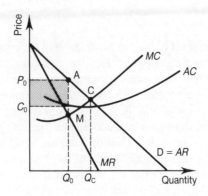

Figure 3.10   Profit-maximizing output for a monopolist

3.3.2   Profit maximizing output for a monopolist

To maximize profits, the monopolist will choose to produce the level of output at which marginal revenue equals marginal cost. This is a similar condition to firms in perfect competition, and indeed is the general rule for any firm seeking to maximize profits. The essential difference is that with monopoly, marginal revenue is *not* equal to the price, since marginal revenue is always less than the price with a downward-sloping market demand curve.

In Fig. 3.10, the profit-maximizing output level is Q_0, at which point $MR = MC$ (i.e. point M). At that output level, the price for each unit of output will be P_0, given by the demand curve D. Excess profits will equal price *minus* the average cost for each unit, i.e. $(P_0 - C_0)$, and the maximum profits will therefore be given by the shaded area $(P_0 - C_0)Q_0$.

The crucial difference from the case with perfectly competitive firms is that the price charged is *greater than* the marginal cost. An additional unit of output between Q_0 and Q_C would cost less to produce than the price at which it could be sold, i.e. consumers would be willing to pay a higher price than the marginal cost of production. However, total profits would fall, since marginal revenue is lower than marginal cost at output levels above Q_0. The reason for this is that the marginal revenue curve is downward sloping and to the left of the demand or average revenue curve. In other words, because the monopolist would have to reduce the price for all previous units, he or she stops at Q_0. The competitive level of output would be Q_C at C in Fig. 3.10, where $P = MC$.

3.3.3   Price discrimination

Suppose that a monopolist did not have to reduce the price for intramarginal units when he or she sold an additional unit of the good. This would be the case when a different price could be charged for each and every unit. The first unit would be sold to the consumer willing to pay the highest price (where the demand curve meets the vertical axis), the next unit would be sold at the next highest price, and so on. Figure 3.11 depicts this situation of *perfect price discrimination*. The marginal revenue curve would now coincide with the demand curve, since the change in total revenue would be equal to the price of the last unit sold. Profit maximization would be at point C with output level Q_C, where $P = MC$ for the last unit sold, and the resulting output level is exactly the same as under perfect competition.

The major difference however is that the monopolist has extracted the entire consumer surplus for himself or herself. Every consumer has had to pay the maximum price that he or she would be prepared to pay for every unit purchased and not just for the last unit purchased. This implies

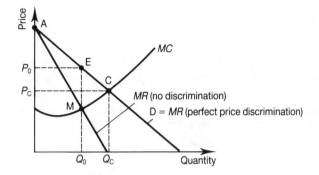

Figure 3.11 Perfect price discrimination

that the consumer surplus is zero for all units purchased and not just the last unit: all the consumer surplus (the triangle ACP_C) has been transferred to the monopolist. (Note that a monopolist who is not able to engage in perfect price discrimination sells all Q_0 units at P_0 in Fig. 3.11, and this leaves some consumer surplus (the triangle AEP_0) in the hands of consumers.)

Perfect price discrimination can only occur if the monopolist can successfully isolate all consumers and prevent them from trading with each other. In practice, this is extremely unlikely to be the case. It is, however, quite common to see different prices being charged for the same good or service to different groups of consumers. For example, passenger fares on British Rail are different at different times of the day. Similarly, British Gas and British Telecom charge different prices to domestic and business users. The reason why they are able to do this is that it is not possible for domestic and business users to trade with each other, i.e. it is not possible for the user being charged the lowest price to buy all the monopolist's output and resell it to users being charged higher prices, sharing some of the cost savings with them. The ability to engage in differential pricing comes from the fact that the monopolist is faced with different demand curves for each segment of market demand, and different buyers of the monopolist's output are unable to trade with each other.

Figure 3.12 illustrates the profit-maximizing behaviour of a *discriminating monopolist* who is faced with two types of customer in two segmented markets, but with constant marginal costs in each market. To maximize profits, the monopolist will equate marginal revenue in both markets. Suppose initially the same price is charged in both markets. Because of different demand

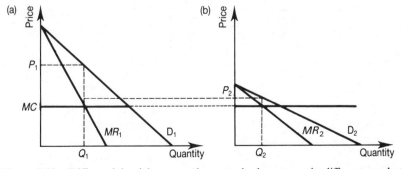

Figure 3.12 Differential pricing: equating marginal revenues in different markets

elasticities in each market, marginal revenues would differ. The monopolist could then switch some output from the market where marginal revenue is lower to the market where marginal revenue is higher and increase total revenue without any change in total output or total cost. This process continues until the marginal revenues are both equal to each other and equal to marginal cost. (Note that this process, whereby marginal revenues are being equalized, is exactly analogous to the process of *arbitrage* in financial markets, where asset prices are equalized across markets. For example, the shares of leading UK companies are traded in both New York and London, and arbitrage ensures that both markets trade at the same price.)

3.4 Market structure: monopolistic competition

Between the extreme cases of perfect competition and monopoly lie a range of *imperfectly competitive* market structures. The two most distinctive ones are monopolistic competition and oligopoly.

Monopolistic competition (sometimes called *imperfect competition*) shares some of the features of perfect competition in that there exist a large number of small suppliers and that there is freedom of entry to and exit from the industry. However, it shares some of the features of monopoly, in that each firm has some degree of monopoly power. Each firm faces a downward sloping demand curve for its product and so has some control over the price that it charges, at least in the short run. This is because there is some degree of *product differentiation* operating in the industry, with each firm supplying a slightly differentiated product to the market.

The classic example of a monopolistically competitive firm is the corner shop. Corner shops might sell similar or even identical goods, but the source of product differentiation lies in their location, i.e. in their proximity to where customers live. A corner shop has some monopoly power, since consumers tend to prefer to use the nearest shop to where they live. A corner shop with no nearby competitors can therefore charge higher prices. But if it makes excess profits, this will encourage competitors to establish a corner shop across the road. The new shop will charge marginally lower prices and will take away some of the market share of the original shop. The demand curve facing the original shop will shift to the left and the final equilibrium will involve lower prices, lower sales and the elimination of excess profits.

Figure 3.13 shows the profit-maximizing position of a monopolistically competitive firm in the short run and the long run. In the short run (Fig. 3.13(a)), the demand curve is D_S. Profit-maximizing output is determined at the point where short-run marginal revenue equals marginal cost. The firm will sell Q_0 at price P_0 and make excess profits of $(P_0 - C_0)Q_0$. The

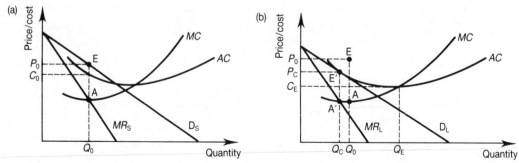

Figure 3.13 The output decisions of monopolistically competitive firms: (a) short-run; (b) long-run

excess profits will attract new entrants to the industry. Existing firms will lose market share and their demand curves will shift to the left. The long-run equilibrium position is shown in Fig. 3.13(b), with the long-run demand curve given by D_L. Profit-maximizing output is determined at the point where long-run marginal revenue equals marginal cost *and* also where price is equal to average cost, so that excess profits are zero. In long-run equilibrium, the firm will sell Q_C at P_C. However, the long-run equilibrium, while not characterized by excess profits, is characterized by *excess capacity*. The firm's output is not being produced at minimum average cost (C_E) and so there is excess capacity of ($Q_E - Q_C$).

3.5 Market structure: oligopoly

Oligopoly refers to an industry in which only a few firms compete against each other. The firms are *interdependent*, so that the actions of each firm can affect the behaviour of every other firm, as with rival players in a dynamic game. (The market structure in which there are only a few buyers is known as *oligopsony*. Typically oligopsonists will operate a *price ring*, as in the case of an auction where artificially low prices are bid by members of the price ring.)

3.5.1 Cartels

The best strategy for interdependent firms to pursue is to collude and form a *cartel*. A cartel is a group of firms that agrees to cooperate and act like a single monopolist. The firms agree to limit total output to the level that the monopolist would produce. The cartel then agrees how much of total output is supplied by each firm (i.e. the production quota set for each firm) and also how total profits are divided up between firms.

To illustrate, we can consider a cartel formed by two firms with identical constant returns to scale cost structures. This is shown in Fig. 3.14. Average and marginal costs are constant and equal for both firms. The combined demand curve is D. The optimal strategy for the cartel is to restrict output to Q_0, which is sold at P_0. If the production quota for each firm is 50 per cent, and profits are also shared equally, then each firm produces $Q_0/2$ and makes profits of $(P_0 - C_0)Q_0/2$.

However, each firm has an *incentive to cheat*. Because price exceeds average cost, each firm has an incentive to sell more than its quota. In Fig. 3.14, each firm has an incentive to produce twice its production quota; that is, each firm has an incentive to produce Q_0. But if both firms

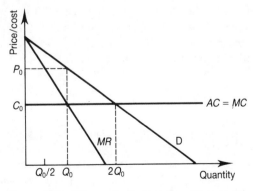

Figure 3.14 The optimal strategy with a cartel

attempt to do this and total output increases to $2Q_0$, the market price will fall to C_0 and total profits will be zero.

The success of a cartel in being able to act like a monopolist depends on a number of factors. The smaller the number of firms in the cartel, the easier it is to monitor every firm's activities and hence detect cheating if it occurs. The greater the degree of product differentiation, the more difficult it is to monitor the activities of different firms, to determine cost structures and to set monopoly prices. On the other hand, if all firms in the industry produce identical products, it is impossible to identify the member firm which is cheating by selling above its quota. The effectiveness of the cartel is enhanced if the trading prices of all members are published, and correspondingly weakened if prices are kept confidential.

Even if the members of the cartel keep to their quotas, there might be problems in sustaining the cartel in the long run. First, there is the threat of new entrants coming into the industry, attracted by the excess profits being made by cartel members. Even if the new entrants are invited to join the cartel, this will only reduce the share of profits going to existing members. Second, the high prices charged by the cartel will encourage consumers to search for substitutes and for new producers to design and make such substitutes. If this is successful, the demand for the cartel's product will both be reduced and become more price-elastic, thereby reducing the cartel's ability to maintain monopoly prices and excess profits.

Cartels are illegal in the UK and in certain other countries, such as the USA. However, every now and again, informal cartels are discovered and prosecuted—a recent example in the UK being an informal cartel in the cement industry. The world's most famous cartel is OPEC (the Organization of Petroleum Exporting Countries), which was established in 1973. Initially, OPEC was effective in sustaining a high price for oil, but widespread cheating by OPEC members, new sources of supply from formerly uneconomic sources (such as the North Sea and Alaska) by non-OPEC members and the use of substitutes (such as gas or coal in power stations, and petrol extracted from coal) have reduced the effectiveness of OPEC in recent years.

3.5.2   Price leadership

A cartel is an agreement to control the quantities that each member of the cartel produces. It is an explicit form of collusion, and, as we have said, it is illegal in many countries. There are alternative forms of collusion which are tacit rather than explicit and so do not involve a deliberate conspiracy. The most important of these is *price leadership*.

Under price leadership, one firm acts as a price leader. The role of the *price leader* is to set the price of the product. The other firms in the industry merely follow the price set by the leader; the other firms are known as *price followers*. The price leader will typically be the largest firm in the industry or the one with the lowest costs. It must be in a position to punish any firm which does not follow its price lead. This is usually achieved by the price leader pushing prices down and driving the offending firm out of business. The price leader therefore needs sufficient excess capacity for this punishment to be a *credible threat*.

3.5.3   Price wars

Cartels and price leadership are the two main forms of cooperative solution with oligopoly. However, in many cases, the rivalry between oligopolistic firms is so great that a cooperative solution is not possible. In such cases, the solution will be non-cooperative, and the most important non-cooperative solution is the *price war*. A price war leads to firms cutting prices aggressively in order to maintain market share. Sometimes, firms are forced temporarily to sell

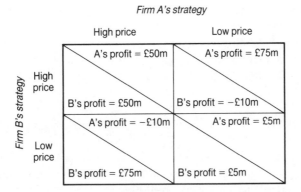

Firm A's strategy

Figure 3.15   The pay-off matrix in a price war

their products at a loss. Examples of oligopolistic firms that have engaged in price wars in the past are car manufacturers and petrol stations.

We can examine why price wars break out between interdependent oligopolistic rivals using a technique known as *game theory*. The objective of each *player* or *rival* in a *game* is to choose a *strategy* that maximizes the *pay-off* from the game, taking into account the likely strategies pursued by the other players in the game. The non-cooperative solution that emerges from this is known as the *Nash solution.*

To illustrate, we can consider two oligopolistic firms (A and B) whose strategies and pay-offs are shown in the *pay-off matrix* given in Fig. 3.15. We will suppose that each firm knows the possible strategies and pay-offs of itself and its rival. If both firms set high prices, the profit for both firms is £50m, while if both firms set low prices their profits are only £5m each. But if firm A sets a high price and firm B sets a low price, B will make profits of £75m and A will lose £10m. The opposite pay-offs hold if B sets a high price and A undercuts B's price.

So each firm's pay-off depends not only on its strategy, but also on the strategy pursued by the rival. The best strategy for both firms is to collude and set high prices. This is the cooperative solution and leads to maximum combined profits of £100m divided evenly between the two firms. But each firm has an incentive to cut its price and increase market share, as long as the other firm does not retaliate. For example, if B held its prices high and A cut its prices, then A's market share would increase, A's profits would rise to £75m and B would make a loss of £10m. But B could recover its market share and turn its £10m loss into a £5m profit by engaging in a price war with A and cutting its prices to match those of A. The non-cooperative Nash or price war solution involves minimum combined profits of £10m divided evenly between the two firms.

In the absence of cooperation between firms, the optimal behaviour of each firm is to choose the strategy that minimizes the maximum potential loss that can be inflicted on it by the rival firm. This is known as a *minimax* decision criterion. Since both firms recognize this, both firms choose a low price, profits are minimized and a price war breaks out.

3.6   Non-price competition

So far in this chapter we have concentrated on the way in which firms compete against each other on the basis of price. If some firms are generating excess profits, other firms will enter the industry, produce and sell products at lower prices, and, in long-run equilibrium, the market price is such that only normal profits are made by the remaining firms in the industry. Price competition is clearly important, but it is only one aspect of the way in which firms compete against each other. Firms also engage in forms of *non-price competition*. The type and degree of both price and non-price competition chosen by firms is called the *marketing mix*.

3.6.1   The marketing mix

The marketing mix has four elements, the first based on price decisions and the rest on non-price decisions:

1 Price—covers policy on price setting, discounts, payment and credit terms.
2 Advertising—covers publicity and sales promotion.
3 Product—covers all aspects of the goods and services provided, including product range, product characteristics and technological developments.
4 Location—covers all aspects of the firm's production, sales and administration facilities in relation to the location of the firm's inputs and the location of the firm's markets.

Each of these elements affects either the firm's revenues or its costs or both. The marketing mix therefore affects the firm's profits and the optimal marketing mix is clearly the one that maximizes the firm's profits. We can demonstrate this by examining the effect of increased advertising on the firm's profits, for example.

Advertising
Advertising expenditure will affect a firm's profits in the following manner. If the advertising is successful, it will increase the demand for the firm's product and hence its revenues, but it will also increase the firm's costs, both directly, as a result of the cost of advertising, and indirectly, since the firm will have to increase its production to meet the increase in demand for its product.

The firm will maximize profits from advertising expenditure by increasing expenditure on advertising until the sales revenue generated from the last £1 spent on advertising just equals the cost of the advertising *plus* the additional costs of producing the extra output sold:

$$\frac{\Delta TR}{\Delta A} = 1 + \frac{\Delta TC}{\Delta A} \tag{3.10}$$

where $\Delta TR/\Delta A$ is the addition to total revenue generated by an additional £1 spent on advertising and $\Delta TC/\Delta A$ is the additional production cost resulting from the extra advertising.

An alternative expression for determining the optimal expenditure on advertising is known as the *Dorfman–Steiner condition*:

$$\frac{A}{TR} = \frac{e_a}{|e_p|} \tag{3.11}$$

which states that the ratio of advertising expenditure (A) to total sales revenue (TR) should equal the ratio of the advertising elasticity of demand ($e_a = (\Delta Q/\Delta A)(A/Q)$) to the price elasticity of demand ($|e_p| = (\Delta Q/\Delta P)(P/Q)$). The Dorfman–Steiner condition says that advertising expenditure as a proportion of total revenue should be greater the greater the advertising elasticity of demand and the lower the price elasticity of demand. Perfectly competitive firms with horizontal demand curves (so that $|e_p| = \infty$) do not need to advertise at all; neither do firms such as monopolists, who, because they already supply the whole market, would not be able to use advertising to increase their market share (i.e. $e_a = 0$).

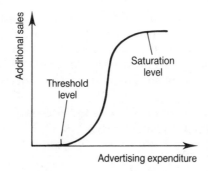

Figure 3.16 The effectiveness of advertising

The advertising elasticity of demand e_a measures the effectiveness of advertisng. There are several factors that determine e_a. The first is total advertising expenditure. Figure 3.16 shows the relationship between advertising expenditure and the additional sales generated. There is a *threshold level* of advertising before any additonal sales arise. Thereafter, sales increase first slowly and then rapidly. Eventually, sales begin to tail off and at some point the *saturation level* is reached. The second factor is the type of product. The advertising elasticity will be greater for new products and luxuries than it will be for existing products and necessities, for example. The third factor is market structure. For example, the advertising elasticity will be low if a firm's market share is high or if rivals respond with similar advertising campaigns; in the latter case, advertising may be necessary to maintain market share, rather than to increase the overall level of demand. The fourth factor is the general state of the economy: in a recession, when unemployment is high and confidence is low, advertising is likely to be less effective than when the economy is booming and consumers have money to spend.

Product
Firms have to make three main decisions about the products that they make. The first is the product range decision, the second is the product characteristics decision and the third is the speed with which technological developments are incorporated into product design.

Most firms do not produce just a single product; rather, they produce a variety of products. Firms will develop an extended *product range* if there is a competitive advantage from doing so either on the supply side or on the demand side or both.

On the supply side, there may be *cost synergies*, whereby the production of one product in the range helps to reduce the cost of manufacturing another product in the range. This is sometimes called *economies of scope*: the costs of producing two products X and Y jointly ($TC(X, Y)$) is less than the costs of producing them separately:

$$TC(X, Y) < TC(X) + TC(Y) \qquad (3.12)$$

One of the most important sources of economies of scope is *complementarity of supply*, whereby the production and marketing of the whole product range benefits from the same resources. The existence of economies of scope therefore provides an incentive for the development of multi-product firms.

On the demand side, there might be *demand synergies*, whereby the demand for one of the firm's products is increased because the firm is making related products. There are also benefits from *product diversification*. If some products sell well in an economic boom, while others sell well in an economic slump, so that poor performance from one product line is compensated for by good performance from another line, then selling both lines can help reduce the overall variability of the firm's revenues and hence the variability of its profits. When demand is high and there are capacity limitations, it may be necessary to cut back on the full product range in order to concentrate resources on the most profitable lines. When demand is low and there is excess capacity, the range can be expanded to cover all the products that can make a contribution to profit.

The *product characteristics* decision deals with the attributes that each product will possess. There are five main sets of product characteristics:

1 Features.
2 Quality.
3 Style.
4 Brand name/mark.
5 Packaging.

To illustrate, consider the manufacturer of a video cassette recorder (VCR). The manufacturer might decide to produce a variety of VCRs, ranging from a basic model, through models of increasing sophistication, to a model offering every imaginable recording feature. For each model in the range, the manufacturer must decide on whether to use low quality or high quality components and how much effort and resources to devote to the manufacturing process. The manufacturer has to decide on the style of the VCR. Should it make a purely functional VCR, or should it aim to produce a stylish piece of room furniture? Branding a product, through the use of brand names or brand marks, is more expensive than offering a generic product, but adds to the distinctiveness of the product. Packaging can also be important. In the case of a VCR, the packaging is designed purely for the purpose of taking the VCR home safely and is then discarded. But for many goods, such as perfumes and chocolates, the packaging is a very important part of the product and can constitute a significant proportion of the total cost of the product. These product characteristics are important for product differentiation, i.e. to help a firm to differentiate its product from that of rivals and to help reduce the elasticity of demand that it faces, thereby helping to reduce the degree of substitutability for the firm's products.

The final aspect of the product that will concern the firm deals with technological developments and the speed with which the firm incorporates them. The firm has to decide whether to be a *technological leader* (or *first-mover*) or a *technological follower*. A technological leader has to engage in expensive *research and development* (R&D) activities which may lead nowhere, or which may lead to new inventions which have to be protected through *patents* if they are successful. However, the advantages of being the first into the market with a new product may well outweigh the costs, and the first-mover may gain a position of market dominance that is unassailable. The technological follower, on the other hand, will have to decide how it gains access to the technology developed by the leader. It may be able to develop a clone version without having to incur the full R&D costs. Alternatively, it may have to license the new technology from the leader.

Location
Location is the final component in the marketing mix, and covers the geographical placing of a firm's production, sales and administration facilities. The optimal location for each of these facilities depends on

1 The effect of location on costs.
2 The proximity to the market.
3 Government policy.

The most important location-sensitive costs are those of labour, energy and raw materials. Capital mobility means that capital costs are becoming increasingly equalized on a global basis, but labour mobility is not as widespread on a global or even on a national basis. Also, energy and raw material costs are lower in some locations than others, especially when distribution and transportation costs are taken into account. Accordingly, firms have incentives to locate in low-cost sites in respect of their labour, energy or raw material requirements. For example, many companies making electronic equipment or computers have located in the Far East, where labour costs are lower than in Europe or the USA. Similarly, steel mills tend to be located close to coal supplies.

The firm also has to decide how close to its final market it wants to be located. This will depend partly on how much it costs to transport the finished product in comparison with the cost of transporting the raw materials. However, there may be advantages to locating production facilities close to the market in terms of superior market intelligence or more flexible responses to changing customer demands. In addition, there may be cost savings if after-sales and maintenance facilities are located near production facilities.

Finally, government policy may influence location decisions in a number of ways. For example, a government might have a regional policy that aims to reduce unemployment in areas of the country where unemployment is high. Government subsidies can therefore help to reduce the cost of locating in locations that are otherwise undesirable from the firm's point of view. As another example, import tariffs or quotas might force an overseas company to establish production plants in a particular country when it would not otherwise wish to do so.

3.7 Summary

1 The level of output chosen by a firm depends on the costs involved in producing the output and the revenue received from selling it.
2 The production process requires a range of factors of production (e.g. labour, capital, land and premises, raw materials and energy) and a production technology which may be capital-intensive or labour-intensive.
3 The production process exhibits increasing, constant or decreasing returns to scale when average costs respectively fall, remain unchanged or rise as output increases. The minimum efficient size for the production process occurs at the output level at which average costs are minimized.
4 Total costs are the sum of total fixed costs which do not change with the level of output and total variable costs which increase with the level of output.
5 The marginal cost of producing an additional unit of output is the addition to total costs from producing that unit.
6 The average cost of producing a given number of units is equal to the total cost of producing that number of units divided by the number of units produced.
7 When marginal costs are falling as output increases, average costs will also be falling, but will be higher than marginal costs. At the output level at which average costs are minimized, marginal costs will equal average costs. As output increases above this level, marginal costs are rising; average costs will also be rising, but will be lower than marginal costs.
8 The revenues received from selling its output depend on the demand conditions facing the firm. These in turn depend on the market structure in which the firm operates. There are four main types of market structure: perfect competition, monopoly, monopolistic competition and oligopoly. The type of market structure determines the level of output and price, and hence the profit that a firm can achieve.

9 Perfect competition is characterized by a large number of buyers and sellers, free entry to and exit from the industry, absence of restrictive government regulation, homogeneous products, and full information on buyers and sellers. Firms are price takers and face horizontal demand curves. The profit-maximizing level of output for a competitive firm is the level of output at which marginal cost is equal to market price. In the long run, the profit-maximizing level of output is the level of output at which average cost is minimized. In the long run, price also equals average cost, so that firms make normal profits, but not excess profits.

10 Monopoly is characterized by having a single supplier in the industry. The monopolist faces the downward-sloping industry demand curve and so has some role in setting prices. The degree of monopoly power is greater the steeper or more inelastic the demand curve. The profit-maximizing level of output is the level of output at which marginal cost is equal to marginal revenue. The monopolist is able to make excess profits in the long run.

11 A price-discriminating monopolist is able to segment the market effectively and hence can charge a higher price in the sub-market with the more inelastic demand.

12 Monopolistic competition is characterized by having a large number of small suppliers and free entry to and exit from the industry, but each supplier has some degree of market power. This means that each firm has some degree of local monopoly power and has some control over price in the short run. This is because there is some degree of product differentiation operating in the industry. In the short run, the profit-maximizing level of output is the level of output at which marginal revenue is equal to marginal cost. In the long run, the profit maximizing level of output is the level of output at which average cost equals price. A monopolistically competitive firm can make excess profits in the short run, but only normal profits in the long run. Entry into the industry will ensure this.

13 With oligopoly, there are only a few competing firms, whose actions are interdependent.

14 The best strategy for oligopolists is to collude and form a cartel: joint profits are maximized by limiting output to the level that a monopolist would produce. The problem is that each member of the cartel has an incentive to cheat and expand output above its quota. Also, the high prices charged by the cartel will both attract new entrants into the industry and encourage a search for substitute products. This may make a cartel unsustainable in the long run.

15 Price leadership is a tacit form of collusion. One firm acts as a price leader and other firms raise prices when the price leader raises prices.

16 When explicit or implicit cooperation between oligopolistic firms breaks down, price wars often break out. Firms cut prices aggressively in order to maintain market share. The non-cooperative Nash equilibrium results in lower joint profits than the cooperative joint profit-maximizing equilibrium.

17 Oligopolistic firms also engage in non-price competition. The type and degree of both price and non-price competition is called the marketing mix. There are four elements to the marketing mix: price, advertising, product and location. The firm will maximize profits from advertising expenditure by selecting the level of advertising expenditure at which the marginal revenue from the additional sales generated by the advertising equals the cost of the advertising plus the additional costs of producing the extra output sold. The product mix chosen by the firm will depend on the presence of cost synergies, such as economies of scope, and demand synergies resulting from product diversification, i.e. producing a range of different products or a range of similar products with different characteristics. The optimal location of a firm's production, sales and administration facilities depends on the costs of resources in different locations, the proximity to the market and government policy.

Exercises

1 What factors determine the level of output supplied by a firm to the market?
2 What are economies of scale?
3 'With increasing returns to scale, average costs rise as output increases.' True or false?
4 How would a firm determine its optimal scale of operations?
5 Define marginal cost.
6 The following table shows total cost at each level of output.

Output	0	1	2	3	4	5	6	7	8	9
Total cost	1	13	24	33	40	50	66	84	104	126

(a) Calculate the average cost and marginal cost at each output level.
(b) How are average and marginal cost related?
7 What is meant by market structure? Give examples of different types.
8 What are the main conditions necessary for markets to be perfectly competitive?
9 Explain what it means for a firm to be a price taker. What implications does price-taking behaviour have for the demand curve that a firm faces?
10 Explain how average revenue is equal to price.
11 Define marginal revenue.
12 How does a competitive firm determine its profit-maximizing level of output?
13 Suppose that a competitive firm can sell all that it likes at a price of 18.
(a) What is the firm's marginal revenue?
(b) If the firm has the same cost structure as given in Exercise 6, what is the profit-maximizing level of output?
(c) What are the profits at this level of output?
(d) Is this profit sustainable in the long run? If not, what is the long-run price, profit-maximizing level of output and level of profits?
14 Why is marginal revenue less than price when the demand curve is downward sloping?
15 Prove the following statement: 'Total revenue reaches a maximum when marginal revenue is zero'.
16 How does a monopolist determine the profit-maximizing level of output?
17 Suppose that a monopolist faces the following relationship between sales and marginal revenue:

Sales	1	2	3	4	5	6	7	8	9
Marginal revenue	27	26	25	24	23	22	21	20	19

(a) Calculate total revenue for each level of sales.
(b) Calculate the demand curve that the monopolist faces.
(c) If the monopolist has the same cost structure as given in Exercise 6, what is the profit-maximizing level of output?
(d) What are the monopolist's profits?
18 What is perfect price discrimination?
19 Suppose that a discriminating monopolist faces the following two sets of markets for its output:

Sales	Marginal revenue	
	Market 1	Market 2
1	18	16
2	17	15
3	16	14
4	15	13
5	14	12
6	13	11
7	12	10
8	11	9
9	10	8

(a) Calculate total revenue for each level of sales in each market.

(b) Calculate the demand curve that the monopolist faces in each market.

(c) If the monopolist produces its output at constant marginal cost of 15, calculate the profit-maximizing output in each market.

(d) Calculate the prices and price elasticities of demand at the profit-maximizing output levels in each market. Comment on your results.

20 Under what circumstances will marginal revenue equal price even though the demand curve is downward sloping?

21 'A monopolistically competititve firm will produce a level of output at which price is above minimum average cost; it will therefore make excess profits in the long run.' True or false?

22 What are the main similarities and differences between perfect competition and monopolistic competition?

23 What is the main distinguishing feature of oligopoly?

24 What is the main difficulty with sustaining a cartel over time?

25 Suppose that two oligopolists form a cartel. They have constant marginal costs of 9. Find the optimal price and output strategy for the cartel and the profits to each member if they are divided equally when the market demand curve is as follows:

Sales	1	2	3	4	5	6	7	8	9
Price	15	14	13	12	11	10	9	8	7

26 Examine the following pay-off matrix for two firms A and B and find the cooperative solution and the Nash solution:

		Firm A's strategy	
		High price	Low price
Firm B's strategy	High price	A's profit = 10 B's profit = 20	A's profit = 14 B's profit = 10
	Low price	A's profit = 6 B's profit = 18	A's profit = 12 B's profit = 8

27 Why do price wars break out?

28 What kind of firms do not need to advertise?

29 Calculate the optimal expenditure on advertising for a firm with the following characteristics:

Price elasticity of demand $= -0.75$

Advertising elasticity of demand $= 0.12$

Total revenue $= £250m$

30 Explain what is meant by a firm's 'marketing mix'.

31 What are the main sets of product characteristics that a firm must consider when designing a new product?

Business application: Company borrowing costs—fixed versus variable interest rates

There are numerous sources of finance available to companies. These include shares, bonds and bank loans. Since loans incur interest payments, and these are an outgoing, the payments represent a cost to the company. If firms can minimize their interest payments, costs will fall and the profits available to shareholders, and to the business, will rise.

The interest rate charged on bank loans is linked to the base interest rate. The extent to which the rate charged exceeds the base rate depends on three main factors: the size of the loan, the length of the repayment period and the perceived riskiness of the company. The lowest rates will be available to companies with the highest credit rating. These include the UK's top 100 companies, for example, Marks and Spencer, Glaxo, BT and BP. Such companies are sometimes called 'blue chip' companies. As the riskiness of companies increases (loans to medium-sized firms, small firms and new businesses are riskier than loans to blue chips, for example), the rate charged by the banks will increase.

In addition, the type of loan negotiated will have a direct effect on a firm's interest payments and hence its costs. There are two main types of loan:

1 *Fixed interest loan*—the interest rate charged does not vary over the life of the loan. A fixed interest loan would be advantageous to a company if it was felt that interest rates were going to rise, because the bank could not increase its charges. This type of loan is usually only available to blue chip and other large companies.
2 *Variable interest loan*—the interest rate charged alters with changes in the base rate. Thus increases in base rates will increase the rate charged to companies, while lower base rates will reduce the amount payable.

    Companies will benefit from this type of loan if base rates are expected to fall, since this will mean lower repayments and hence lower costs. The largest companies will be able to negotiate the lowest premiums above base, whereas new and small businesses will probably have to pay a higher premium.

If interest rates have been static for some time, and are expected to remain so, companies will be indifferent to the type of loan they undertake, assuming that both types carry the same initial interest rate.

To illustrate the potential repayment differences from fixed and variable interest loans, assume two blue chip companies wanted to borrow £1 million for two years, over the period 1 January 1990 to 31 December 1991. For the purposes of the example, assume that the interest is charged daily and is calculated on a simple basis rather than compounded. The interest *plus* the principal are payable at the end of the period in one lump sum. One company negotiates a fixed interest loan at base rate *plus* 1 per cent, the other a variable interest loan also at base rate *plus* 1 per cent.

The economic situation around late 1989 could have justified either type of loan. Government policy had been concentrating on defeating inflation by means of high, and rising, interest rates.

Given the upward trend in inflation at the time, with the possibility of further increases in interest rates, a fixed interest loan would have appeared to be a sensible option. On the other hand, there were fears being expressed about a possible recession, in which case cuts in interest rates could have been expected. In the event, we know that the base rate was cut on eight occasions during this period, falling from 15 per cent to 10.5 per cent.

1 *Fixed interest loan*
   Fixed interest rate: 16 per cent (base rate + 1 per cent)

$$\text{Loan} = £1m \text{ at 16 per cent for 2 years}$$

$$\therefore \quad \text{Interest payment} = £320,000$$

2 *Variable interest loan*
   Interest charged:
   (a)

$$1 \text{ Jan–7 Oct} = 16 \text{ per cent (base rate + 1 per cent)}$$

$$= 280 \text{ days at 16 per cent}$$

$$= 160,000 \times \frac{280}{365}$$

$$\text{Interest repayment} = £122,739.73$$

   (b)

$$8 \text{ Oct–12 Feb} = 15 \text{ per cent (base rate + 1 per cent)}$$

$$= 128 \text{ days at 15 per cent}$$

$$= 150,000 \times \frac{128}{365}$$

$$\text{Interest repayment} = £52,602.74$$

   (c)

$$13 \text{ Feb–26 Feb} = 14.5 \text{ per cent}$$

$$= 14 \text{ days at 14.5 per cent}$$

$$= 145,000 \times \frac{14}{365}$$

$$\text{Interest repayment} = £5,561.64$$

   (d)

$$27 \text{ Feb–21 Mar} = 14 \text{ per cent}$$

$$= 23 \text{ days at 14 per cent}$$

$$= 140,000 \times \frac{23}{365}$$

$$\text{Interest repayment} = £8,821.91$$

   (e)

$$21 \text{ Mar–11 Apr} = 13.5 \text{ per cent}$$

$$= 21 \text{ days at 13.5 per cent}$$

$$= 135,000 \times \frac{21}{365}$$

$$\text{Interest repayment} = £7,767.12$$

(f)
$$\text{12 Apr–23 May} = 13 \text{ per cent}$$
$$= 42 \text{ days at 13 per cent}$$
$$= 130,000 \times \frac{42}{365}$$

$$\text{Interest repayment} = £14,958.90$$

(g)
$$\text{24 May–10 July} = 12.5 \text{ per cent}$$
$$= 48 \text{ days at 12.5 per cent}$$
$$= 125,000 \times \frac{48}{365}$$

$$\text{Interest repayment} = £16,438.35$$

(h)
$$\text{11 Jul–3 Sept} = 12 \text{ per cent}$$
$$= 55 \text{ days at 12 per cent}$$
$$= 120,000 \times \frac{55}{365}$$

$$\text{Interest repayment} = £18,082.19$$

(i)
$$\text{4 Sept–31 Dec} = 11.5 \text{ per cent}$$
$$= 119 \text{ days at 11.5 per cent}$$
$$= 115,000 \times \frac{119}{365}$$

$$\text{Interest repayment} = £37,493.15$$

$$\therefore \quad \text{Total interest repayment} = £284,465.73$$

$$\text{Total saving with variable interest loan} = £35,534.27$$

Clearly substantial cost savings are gained by choosing the more favourable option, and so great care needs to be taken when deciding the most cost-effective method of borrowing money. If a fixed rate loan is not available to a company, it should endeavour to obtain the lowest interest rate penalty possible. For example, if a medium-sized firm was being charged base rate + 4 per cent on a variable interest loan as outlined above, its repayments would be £59,999.98 higher than a blue chip company which was charged base rate +1 per cent. This clearly illustrates the financial cost advantages of being able to obtain favourable interest rates.

4 Market failure and government policy

In this chapter, we investigate *market failure*, which arises when the equilibrium generated by a free unregulated market fails to produce a socially efficient allocation of resources. We examine the principal distortions that lead to market failure, such as the existence of externalities and monopoly, or the absence of a complete set of insurance markets and forward markets. We also examine what role, if any, there is for government intervention in the market mechanism. In particular, we examine the *taxation policy* and the *competition policy* that a government might adopt to help to reduce the effects of market failure, especially in the light of recent experience in the UK concerning the privatization of state-owned industries. We begin by examining what is meant by an efficient allocation of resources.

4.1 The efficient allocation of resources

The market has an important role in allocating scarce resources between competing alternative uses. We would like to know whether the market performs this role efficiently or inefficiently. We can distinguish between a privately efficient allocation of resources and a socially efficient allocation of resources. We can show that when there is perfect competition there will be at least a privately efficient allocation of resources.

4.1.1 The benefits of perfect competition

There are three main benefits from perfect competition. First, the price paid by consumers is equal to the marginal cost of the resources used up in producing the good. This implies what economists call a *privately efficient allocation of resources*. This is because consumers value the benefits from the goods that they consume in relation to the price that they have to pay and will increase their consumption of a particular good until the point where the *marginal private benefit* from the last unit consumed equals the price that must be paid. Another way of looking at this is that consumers will increase their consumption of a particular good until the consumer surplus from the last unit consumed is equal to zero. Producers also value the goods that they produce in relation to the price that they receive and will be willing to supply additional units of that good until the point where the *marginal private cost* of the last unit produced equals the price that they receive. Another way of looking at this is that producers will increase their production of a particular good until the producer surplus from the last unit produced is equal to zero. Therefore, when price equals marginal cost neither consumer nor producer can be made better off in the sense of achieving greater consumer surplus or producer surplus; i.e. the joint welfare of both consumers and producers is maximized when price equals marginal cost. This is sometimes called a state of *pareto optimality* (after the Italian economist Pareto). When price differs from marginal cost, a reallocation of resources can improve welfare (i.e. be *pareto improving*). For example, if the market price of cars exceeds their marginal cost of production, car makers can improve their welfare by buying more raw materials, such as iron ore, and making more cars. This will help to lower the market price of cars, and car makers will stop supplying more cars when car prices equal their marginal costs of production. On the other hand, if the market price of washing machines is lower than their marginal cost of production, washing machine makers can improve their welfare by buying fewer raw materials, such as iron ore, and making fewer washing machines. This will help to raise the market price of washing machines, and washing machine makers will stop supplying fewer washing machines when washing machine prices equal their marginal costs of production. In this way, a competitive market reallocates resources between competing alternative uses until neither consumers nor producers can improve their welfare. In short, the efficient allocation of scarce resources requires *marginal cost pricing* (sometimes called *efficient pricing*).

The second benefit is that the long-run perfectly competitive equilibrium implies that firms are producing on the minimum point of their average cost curves. This implies that economies of scale are being fully exploited and the output is being produced at the lowest unit cost.

The third benefit is that there is full capacity utilization in the long run. Free entry and exit imply that any resources not being used will not be employed in the industry, so under perfect competition there is no wasteful use of scarce resources.

4.1.2   Market failure

Market failure is said to occur when an equilibrium in a free unregulated market fails to achieve a *socially efficient allocation of resources*. A socially efficient allocation of resources is achieved when marginal private and social costs and benefits are equated to prices:

$$MPC = MSC = P = MSB = MPB \qquad (4.1)$$

where

$$MPC = \text{marginal private cost}$$
$$MSC = \text{marginal social cost}$$
$$MSB = \text{marginal social benefit}$$
$$MPB = \text{marginal private benefit}$$
$$P = \text{price}$$

A socially efficient allocation occurs when private costs and benefits are respectively equal to the costs incurred and the benefits enjoyed by society as a whole. In this case *marginal social costs* and *marginal social benefits* are also equal to price. This is because the costs and benefits to society are identical to the costs and benefits to the individual producer or consumer respectively.

Market failure occurs when there are *distortions* that prevent a socially efficient allocation occurring. We can consider some examples of such distortions.

4.2   Externalities and taxation policy

Externalities arise when one individual's production or consumption decisions affect either the production or consumption decisions or the welfare of other individuals other than through

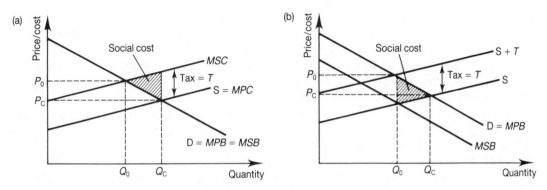

Figure 4.1   (a) Production externalities and (b) consumption externalities

market prices. When one firm increases its production and this causes the market price to fall, which in turn forces other producers to transfer resources to other industries, this is an example of the market working. On the other hand, if one firm increases its production and this causes an increase in pollution and noise in the vicinity and these additional 'costs' are not taken into account in the market mechanism, then this is an example of the market failing, in this case, failing to take into account the social costs of production. An externality is any factor not taken into account by (i.e. external to) the market mechanism. We will examine the two main types of externalities, production externalities and consumption externalities, and how the government can use the tax system to remove the distortions caused by externalities.

Production externalities lead to the social costs of production exceeding the private costs of production, as in the case of a smoky factory polluting the neighbourhood with soot. This is demonstrated in Fig. 4.1(a) which shows that the marginal social cost (*MSC*) of production exceeds the marginal private cost (*MPC*) of production as a result of the pollution. The *MPC* curve is the supply curve of the product to the market. The demand curve for the product produced by the factory is given by D, which also measures both the marginal private benefit (*MPB*) and the marginal social benefit (*MSB*) from consuming the good. The private competitive equilibrium is given at output level Q_C and price P_C, where *MPC* intersects *MPB*. But the socially efficient equilibrium is given at output level Q_0 and price P_0, at which *MSC* intersects *MSB*. The private competitive equilibrium produces 'too much' output ($Q_C - Q_0$) and the *social cost* of this excess production is given by the shaded triangle in the diagram. The appropriate solution is for the government to impose a *pollution tax* of T on the output of the firm, thereby increasing the *MPC* of production to equal the *MSC* of production. This would reduce the firm's output to the optimal level Q_0. Note that the optimal level of output implies an optimal level of pollution. The only way to eliminate the pollution would be to stop producing the good altogether, but the lost social benefits (consumer surplus) from doing this would exceed the social cost savings.

Consumption externalities lead to the social benefits from consumption being lower than the private benefits from consumption, as in the case of someone smoking a cigarette in a restaurant or on public transport. This is demonstrated in Fig. 4.1(b), which shows that the marginal social benefit (*MSB*) from consuming cigarettes is lower than the marginal private benefit (*MPB*), given by the demand curve D. Given the industry supply curve for cigarettes, the private competitive equilibrium is at output level Q_C and price P_C where supply intersects with demand or *MPB*. But the socially efficient equilibrium is given at output level Q_0, where supply intersects with *MSB*. The private competitive equilibrium again produces 'too much' consumption ($Q_C - Q_0$) and the social cost of this excess consumption is given by the shaded triangle in the diagram. To achieve the socially efficient allocation, the government should impose a *health tax T* on the production of cigarettes. This would have the effect of shifting the supply curve from S to $S + T$. By raising the price of cigarettes to P_0, demand would be reduced along the demand curve to the socially optimal level Q_0.

These examples provide a case for government intervention in production and consumption decisions by using the tax system to help to remove the distortions caused by market failure. In the past, there have been only a few examples of government taxation being used in this way, e.g. excise duties on tobacco and alcohol acting as implicit health taxes. However, in the future, as environmental issues such as 'global warming' cause increasing concern, we may find that the tax system is being increasingly used to influence the production decisions of firms and the consumption decisions of consumers. Currently, for example, there is talk of introducing a *carbon tax* to help reduce the carbon emissions that lead to global warming.

It is, of course, possible for powerful pressure groups to press for government intervention in production and consumption decisions other than through the tax system. For example, the government now prohibits smoking on most forms of public transport rather than simply using the tax system to reduce it to a 'socially optimal level'.

4.3   Incomplete insurance and forward markets

A socially efficient allocation of resources requires that *MSC* and *MSB* are equated to prices for all goods produced and consumed today under all *contingencies* or *states-of-the-world*. During the course of the next year, for example, someone might move from being employed to being unemployed, from being healthy to ill, from having a house to having their house burned down, or from owning a car to having their car stolen. Each of these moves takes an individual from a desirable state-of-the-world to an undesirable state-of-the-world. People who dislike risk would like to be able to insure against the consequences of becoming unemployed, becoming ill, having their house burned down or having their car stolen. In short, what is needed is a complete set of *contingent insurance markets* that allow risk to be transferred from those who are averse to risk to insurance companies which are prepared to take on risk for a price. The equilibrium price or insurance premium would equate the *MSC* and *MSB* of risk-bearing for every contingency or state-of-the-world, i.e. a socially efficient allocation must also be *contingent-state-efficient*.

But the reality is that a complete set of contingent insurance markets does not exist, i.e. there is an incomplete market in *risk transference*. This is because of the problems of adverse selection and moral hazard. Insurance works because a large number of people make low premium payments which are used to make much larger payouts to a small number of people who might unfortunately have to make claims. The amount collected in premiums must be sufficient to meet valid claims and to give normal profits to insurance companies. Insurance only works if the claims are generated randomly as a result of genuine accidents and insurance companies are able to determine the probabilities of accidents occurring so that they can fix premiums.

Adverse selection is the problem of insurance being taken out mainly by people who are likely to make subsequent claims. The classic examples are medical insurance being taken out by people who know that they are ill and likely to make a claim, rather than by healthy people who are not likely to make a claim, and fire insurance being taken out by people who know that they are innately careless and likely to make a claim, rather than by careful people who are not likely to make a claim. The problem is really one of what is known as *asymmetric information*: the insurance applicant knows more about his or her condition or character than the insurance company. Sometimes the insurance company can avoid adverse selection through effective *screening* as, for example, in the health screening of applicants before offering medical insurance. Where effective screening is not possible, the problem of adverse selection remains and it makes some risks uninsurable at any price. This is because if the insurance premium is raised to cover the additional risk of adverse selection, good risks will be driven away and it will not be profitable for the insurance company to provide the insurance at all.

Moral hazard is the problem of people becoming less careful (either consciously or unconsciously) after insurance has been taken out. For example, some people might become less careful about locking up or making sure that the gas and electricity are turned off when they leave their homes. Similarly, some people might deliberately leave their old battered car unlocked in the hope that it is stolen and they can claim on the insurance. Again, insurance companies can do something about moral hazard by requiring evidence that a claim is valid, such as evidence of forced entry into a home in the case of a burglary claim. If the front door had been left unlocked, so that entry into the home was unforced, then it is likely that the insurance company would not meet the claim on the grounds that there had been *contributory negligence*. But in many cases moral hazard is difficult to prove (such as in the case of a stolen car), and again it makes some risks uninsurable at any price.

There is very little that the government can do about adverse selection or moral hazard, since it has no better means than insurance companies of determining the true risks of individuals. However, the government might decide as a matter of public policy to insure certain risks that private insurance companies would be unwilling to take on. This is the principle underlying the National Health Service in the UK, whereby treatment is provided 'free at the point of need', regardless of the National Insurance contribution record of the user.

A socially efficient allocation of resources also requires that *MSC* and *MSB* are equated to prices for all goods produced and consumed today. However, if the allocation of resources is also going to be *intertemporally efficient* as well (i.e. continuously efficient over time), then the *MSC* and *MSB* of goods consumed in the future must be equated to the future prices of those goods. To do this, we would need to have a complete set of *forward markets* into the future. In these forward markets, producers and consumers would make agreements today for goods to be produced and consumed at future dates at prices agreed today; and the prices agreed today would be such that expected future marginal social costs and benefits would be equalized for every good produced in the future.

But the problem is that a complete set of forward markets does not exist in reality. There are a number of reasons for this. First, we do not have any reliable information today about new types of goods that might be available in the future as a result of technological progress. A quarter of a century ago, cars and washing machines existed, but personal computers and fax machines did not. It would therefore not have been possible to have arranged forward contracts in PCs and fax machines a quarter of a century ago. Second, we do not have any information today about the tastes and preferences of generations as yet unborn. It is therefore not possible to incorporate their future demands for goods and services in the current determination of forward prices for these future goods and services.

As a consequence of these factors, the market mechanism is much more effective at establishing an efficient allocation of goods between consumers today than it is at establishing an efficient allocation of goods between consumers today and consumers in the future. This is a problem of *incomplete information* about the future. There is also very little that a government can do about this, since it has no better information about future technological developments or about the future tastes and preferences of consumers than the rest of us.

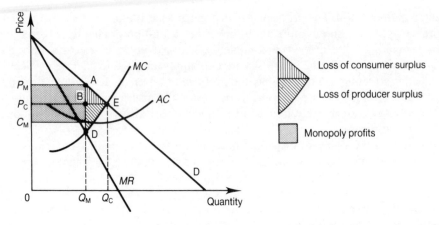

Figure 4.2   The social cost of monopoly

4.4   Monopoly and competition policy in the UK

Another distortion is caused by the existence of *monopoly*. In this section, we consider exactly what is wrong with monopolies and what may be the appropriate form of control over them. In particular, we investigate the competition policy that the UK government has towards industry. Then we examine natural monopolies: those that do not result from any regulatory barriers preventing competitive entry into the industry.

4.4.1   The social cost of monopoly

Figure 4.2 illustrates the profit-maximizing level of output for a monopolist. Q_M is the level of output at which marginal revenue is equal to marginal cost. The *inefficiency* of monopoly results from the fact that at this level of output marginal cost is less than the price (A is at a higher point than D). At output levels greater than Q_M, the consumer is willing to pay a price greater than the marginal cost of production. This is true until output level Q_C. Therefore the triangle ABE in Fig. 4.2 represents the loss of consumer surplus. Similarly, if we compared monopoly with a competitive industry, the latter's output level would be Q_C and price would be P_C. So for the producers the existence of monopoly implies a loss in producer surplus shown by the triangle BDE in Fig. 4.2. (The producer surplus is the difference between the price of a unit sold and the marginal cost of producing that unit of output.) The combined area ABDE measures the social cost of monopoly. This cost arises from having a lower level of output (smaller market) than would be the case with a competitive industry. Therefore, for efficiency considerations, the existence of monopoly is undesirable.

Monopoly also leads to a transfer of resources or income from consumers to the monopolist, compared with the position under competition. The area $(P_M - P_C)Q_M$ measures the consumer surplus that is transferred to the monopolist from the consumer. It represents a *redistribution of income* rather than a net loss or cost to society. However, the government might be concerned about the distribution of income between members of society, and it may be argued that the excess profit accruing to monopolists is socially undesirable. It is possible to deal with this by imposing a *lump sum tax* on monopoly profits. The advantage of lump sum taxes is that they do not alter the profit-maximizing output level of the monopolist. Profits will be lower than before by the amount of the tax, but Q_M will still be the output level at which profits are maximized. Lump sum taxes are therefore *non-distortionary*. (This contrasts with *ad valorem taxes* which are *distortionary*: they involve a social cost because they change the profit-maximizing level of output to one that is socially inefficient.)

In the UK, during the early 1980s, a period of high interest rates (engineered by the government to reduce inflation) generated considerable profits (often termed *windfall profits*) for commercial banks, whose liabilities tended to be fixed rate deposits whereas their assets were earning variable rates. The government imposed a special one-off *profits tax* which was simply a fixed sum of money. It was only imposed in a single tax year. The government justified its imposition on the grounds that the banks had benefited from government policy (i.e. high interest rates). These extra profits were not a result of increased efficiency.

4.4.2 Competition policy

The UK's legislative framework dealing with monopoly or a firm with a *dominant position* in a market is as follows:

1 *Fair Trading Act 1973*. The Director General of Fair Trading can make a monopoly reference to the Monopolies and Mergers Commission (MMC). The criterion for a reference is evidence that 25 per cent or more of a particular good or service is supplied in the UK by a single firm, or by two or more firms acting in a way that appears to restrict competition between them. If the MMC finds evidence of monopoly behaviour, the Director General of Fair Trading can recommend the Secretary of State for Trade and Industry (also known as the President of the Board of Trade) to make an order prohibiting the anti-competitive behaviour.
2 *Competition Act 1980*. A reference to the MMC results in an investigation of the whole market which can be time-consuming. The Competition Act allows the Director General to investigate a single firm if it is believed it is engaged in anti-competitive practices in the UK.
3 *Article 86 of the Treaty of Rome 1957*. This article prohibits the abuse of a dominant position, which is defined as the power to prevent effective competition in an important part of the European market. The European Court of Justice has ruled that abuse of a dominant position includes discriminatory pricing and refusal to supply. If the European Court finds evidence of an abuse, the European Commission can order an end to the abuse or impose fines.

For monopolies which have cost advantages, the policy issues are far more complex. The extreme case of this arises when the size of the market is such that the average cost of the firm is still decreasing when market demand is fully satisfied. These are called decreasing cost industries or *natural monopolies*.

4.4.3 Natural monopolies

Figure 4.3 illustrates the problems involved in generating efficient outcomes when an industry is characterized by increasing returns to scale at all levels of output. Such industries will have room for only one firm, since that is when maximum benefits can be gained from the economies of scale.

In Fig. 4.3, given the size of the market, marginal cost is below average cost at all levels of output. If this industry is run by a private firm, output produced would be Q_M, where $MR = MC$ (point A). However, this is inefficient since there are significant economies of scale still present. At higher levels of output the average cost will be lower and consumers are willing to pay more than the marginal cost of production. The efficiency criterion requires *marginal cost*

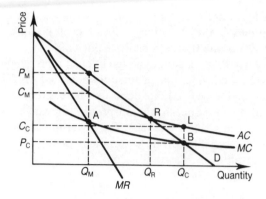

Figure 4.3   Natural monopolies

pricing. However, at $MC = P$ (point B), average cost is above marginal cost, implying that at price P_C losses will be incurred equal to $(C_C - P_C)Q_C$. There are a number of solutions to this problem.

One solution is *average cost pricing* at point R and output level Q_R, where there are no excess profits, but no losses either.

Another solution is *two-part tariffs.* This is where the payment for the good (or service) comes in two parts. The first is a *fixed charge*, which is levied for the right to be able to consume at all, and then a *variable charge* per unit of the good consumed. In the UK, almost all *utilities* are priced in this way. Gas, electricity and telephones are a good example of this form of pricing. The result is that, in principle, marginal cost pricing may still be possible. At $MC = P$, the losses that are made can be recovered by extracting some of the consumer surplus in the form of the fixed charge. To avoid losses, the total value of the fixed charge levied on all consumers must be at least $(C_C - P_C)Q_C$.

A final solution is to take such industries into *public ownership.* This strategy was quite common in the past (especially during the period 1945–79), although the recent trend in the UK is the reverse. The argument for *nationalization* relates to the ability of the government to exercise a direct form of control over pricing and output decisions. Also, in some industries, marginal cost pricing with fixed charges may still not generate positive profits. In this case, losses may have to be *subsidized* through general taxation.

In practice, all of these pricing formulae require considerable monitoring to ensure that regulated industries keep some control over costs and that the *regulators* themselves are not working perversely in the interests of the industry rather than those of the consumer (this is known as *regulatory capture*).

4.5   Privatization in the UK

In this final section we examine what in the UK has been a major plank of competition policy since the beginning of the 1980s. The trend in government policy in the UK since the beginning of the 1980s has been to take industry out of public ownership by selling it to the private sector. This strategy is known as *de-nationalization* or *privatization.* The aims and objectives of the government's privatization programme have never been comprehensively defined. The objectives have probably differed between industries, between government departments, and also over time.

The principal aims appear to be:

1 To increase efficiency and competition.
2 To reduce the public sector borrowing requirement (PSBR).
3 To reduce government interference in commercial decision-making.
4 To widen share ownership.
5 To encourage employee share ownership.

In this section we will concentrate on the aspects which deal with the promotion of efficiency and increased competition.

4.5.1 Management

It has often been argued that private sector management has greater ability and is generally better trained than public sector management. Public sector managers are more likely to be administrators than entrepreneurs and are also more likely to have political constraints imposed on them by government departments. Private sector managers' performance is monitored by actual and potential shareholders. Furthermore, ineffective management may result in a lower share price and hence in the firm becoming a target for a takeover bid, which, if successful, would force the existing management out of office. Together these threats are supposed to discipline managers and ensure that they work in the interests of shareholders. In practice, however, individual shareholders may face considerable *free-rider* problems. Each shareholder may rely on other shareholders to monitor management performance (which is costly), and effectively no one is monitoring performance adequately. To avoid this, shareholders sometimes offer managers performance-related salaries or insist on having non-executive directors on the boards of companies to represent shareholder interests.

4.5.2 Ownership

In the UK, the question of the ownership of an enterprise has received considerable attention. Public ownership of enterprises is often seen as enabling social objectives to be met. However, such objectives have never been clearly defined, and it is therefore difficult to compare the performance of these industries with private sector performance. Moreover, public enterprises are frequently used to further the political objectives of the political party in power.

One of the major problems with public ownership is the method of finance. The borrowings of nationalized industries in the UK are counted as part of the public sector borrowing requirement. However, once a firm has been privatized, its borrowings are no longer counted as part of the PSBR. Furthermore, because of a curious public sector accounting convention, the proceeds from the sale of public assets directly reduce the PSBR, because they are treated as 'negative public expenditure'. The privatization policy therefore accorded well with the government's aim of reducing the PSBR, in order to meet fiscal and monetary policy targets. However, much of this reduction in the PSBR is transient and therefore largely illusory.

4.5.3 Competition or regulatory framework

Privatization enhances efficiency if it increases corporate incentives to cut costs and set prices more in line with costs. The achievement of efficiency, however, is not a function of ownership. Primarily, efficiency is dependent on the degree of competition faced by the privatized firm and also on the appropriate regulatory framework in cases where competition is not possible as a result of the underlying returns to scale characteristics of the industry. There is no essential difference between private sector natural monopolies and publicly owned natural monopolies.

The question then is whether a privatized industry operates in a competitive environment. This does not simply depend on the number of firms operating in the industry, but more importantly on the existence of potential entrants. This in turn depends on whether the privatized firm is operating in a contestable market.

4.5.4   Contestable markets

A *contestable market* is one in which existing firms are vulnerable to *hit-and-run entry*. We can assume that all firms—actual and potential—have access to the same production methods, and hence their cost functions are identical. Moreover, entry involves no sunk costs: a firm can enter the market without incurring irrecoverable expenditures and there are no barriers to exit.

Sunk costs are the fixed costs that cannot be recovered when a firm leaves an industry. Not all fixed costs are sunk costs. For example, entry into the oil industry may require investing in oil rigs for off-shore extraction. Exit from the industry would involve sunk costs, since oil rigs have almost no second-hand value. This is because they have no alternative use. In contrast, entry into the banking industry may involve high fixed costs (e.g. leasing a building, installing a computer system, etc.), but many of these costs are recoverable if a firm leaves banking (since leases and computer systems can be sold). Therefore the presence of high fixed costs is not necessarily an indication that a market is not contestable. In the above example, the oil industry is not contestable, whereas the banking industry is contestable. In addition, the degree of contestability increases with technological progress. What may not be contestable in one technological age becomes contestable in another. An example of this is telecommunications.

Examples: British Telecom, British Airways and Electricity Supply
British Telecom (BT) was a natural monopoly owned by the state until 1984. There were no competing firms. Following privatization, the degree of competition BT faces depends on whether there are potential entrants into different parts of its services and also on the terms and conditions of the privatization. Suppose that the government had simply sold off BT to the private sector unconditionally. The investment required to enter the industry is both high and irrecoverable. Installing telephone lines throughout a country and building exchange networks is costly and the investment, once made, has little alternative use. Any new firm entering the industry and having to construct its own networks would be extremely vulnerable to the pricing policies of British Telecom. BT could reduce prices so that the new firm always made losses. Since there is no second-hand value for most of the capital investment, sunk costs would be very high. These factors would be sufficient to deter entry, and therefore the telecommunications industry without additional regulatory protection for new entrants is not contestable in most of its services. However, the government did provide some protection for new entrants by requiring BT to give access to its network in exchange for a fee. This was the only way in which Mercury Communications could enter the industry and compete for the business of commercial customers. As a result, the prices charged by BT to commercial customers tend to rise by less than those charged to residential customers. BT has also protested that the fee that Mercury must pay to BT to use its network is too low, prompting the comment is that 'British Telecom is the only monopoly ever to complain about unfair competition'. Supplying the actual telephones is, on the other hand, quite different. As soon as that market was de-regulated many new firms entered. That part of the market is contestable.

The privatization of British Airways in 1986 did not involve the same issues. There already existed many other airlines. The only important question concerned the extent to which British Airways should be allowed to retain its monopoly over certain routes. These are subject to constant review. The point here is that, since there is a market for second-hand aeroplanes, sunk costs are not very high. So this market is contestable.

Another important consideration is the way in which the company (or industry) is privatized. Competition can be encouraged at different levels: the supply of telephones is one example. More importantly, the way the electricity supply industry was privatized in 1990 and 1991 (with a national grid, two electricity producers/generators (PowerGen and National Power), and many regional electricity companies (such as London Electricity plc) as distributors) will encourage competition in those areas where competition will benefit the consumer. Being able to break up a nationalized industry into separate economically viable companies can increase competition, but clearly is only possible in some cases. At the time of the BT privatization, the authorities did not consider breaking up BT as feasible.

4.5.5 Regulation of privatized industries

The question of whether newly privatized industries should be regulated is directly related to the degree of competition. In the case of British Airways, regulations cover only safety standards to which all airlines are subject. There is no control over its pricing policies from the national government, except through reciprocal agreements with other state airlines. The market can ensure competitive pricing. For British Telecom, however, there are few competitors, other than Mercury. It was recognized that BT was primarily a natural monopoly, and as such would not have sufficient incentives to hold costs down to promote efficiency. Profits could always be maintained by raising prices. Therefore in order to provide incentives, BT is subject to what is called the *RPI − X pricing formula*. BT can only raise prices annually by the rate of inflation (measured by the increase in the Retail Price Index) *minus* X, which for the first five years after privatization was 3 per cent and after 1992 was set at 7 per cent. Therefore if retail price inflation is running at 5 per cent per annum, BT has to cut prices by 2 per cent. This is a mechanism which forces BT to cut costs (principally overmanning costs) to maintain profitability.

There are considerable problems with such crude regulations. BT will have an incentive to reduce some of its services, particularly those that are not profit-making, such as public telephones. This has been the subject of much criticism from the telecommunications regulator Oftel, which has the responsibility for monitoring the quality of service provided by BT. Moreover the RPI − X rule only covers around 45 per cent of BT's sales. Therefore there is still a very large proportion of BT's activities over which it has complete independence in setting prices. Furthermore, technological advances in the telecommunications industry imply that there are some markets (e.g. facsimile transmission) which are still in their infancy, and for which at the time of privatization it would have been very difficult to design the appropriate regulation.

In the privatization of the water industry in 1991, the pricing rule applied by the government was actually an *RPI + X formula*. The industry's prices will therefore rise by more than the rate of retail price inflation. This is because the water companies had to spend large sums to raise the quality of the water supplied to customers. This requirement stems from a Directive from the European Commission in Brussels.

In both cases, it is extremely difficult for regulators to ascertain what the value of X should be. Even if this difficulty is overcome, the regulatory authority still has to determine whether the water companies have made sufficient improvement to water quality. The authorities will have to rely totally on the water companies for this information. The same is true of British Telecom, which is responsible for supplying all cost information to Oftel.

4.5.6   The form of privatization

The concern about promoting efficiency and the recognition that efficiency depends critically on competition has led many people to question the form of privatization that has been introduced. The main issue is whether state-owned monopolies should be sold as single firms, or whether they should be divided into independent units and sold off separately.

Returning to our example of British Airways, suppose that British Airways and BAA (the former British Airports Authority), which owns and operates the main airports in the UK, had been sold off as one company. In that case, other airlines would have to pay this firm for landing rights: that is, to rent services from a competing airline. The aviation market would then not be contestable, since potential entrants would have to build their own airports, which clearly is not feasible. A similar point can be made about BT. In principle, it would have been possible for the exchange networks and the telephone lines to be sold as one company which would then rent these to competing operating companies which would supply the instruments to the users, thereby making telecommunications more competitive from the start.

Some lessons had been learnt by the time it came to privatize the water and electricity industries. These two state-run monopolies were split up into regional units (in the case of water) and by function (in the case of electricity). For example, in the case of electricity, power generating activity was separated from electricity distribution and the marketing of electrical appliances. Some competition was introduced within each function: e.g. National Power and PowerGen are separate companies generating electricity. Exactly the same thing could have been done with British Gas and British Telecom.

4.6   Summary

1 Perfect competition results in a privately efficient allocation of resources because marginal cost pricing is used (where marginal private costs and benefits are both equated to prices), economies of scale are being fully exploited, and there is full capacity utilization.
2 Market failure occurs when an equilibrium in a free unregulated market fails to achieve a socially efficient allocation of resources. A socially efficient allocation of resources is achieved when marginal private and social costs and benefits are equated to prices. Market failure arises when there are distortions that prevent a socially efficient allocation occurring.
3 One example of a distortion is externalities. These arise when one individual's production or consumption decisions affect either the production or consumption decisions or the welfare of other individuals other than through market prices. Production externalities, such as factory pollution, result in the marginal social costs of production exceeding the marginal private costs of production and too much output. The solution is a pollution tax to bring marginal private costs into line with marginal social costs. Consumption externalities, such as someone smoking in a restaurant, result in the marginal social benefits of consumption being less than the marginal private benefits and too much consumption. The solution is health tax to bring marginal private benefits into line with marginal social benefits. These examples provide a case for government intervention in production and consumption decisions by using the tax system to help remove the distortions caused by market failure.
4 Another distortion is caused by incomplete forward markets. A socially efficient allocation of resources has to hold continuously over time. This requires the marginal social costs and benefits of goods consumed in the future to be equated to the future prices of those goods. Forward markets would allow a socially efficient allocation of resources at all future dates to be determined today. However, a complete set of forward markets does not exist. This is

because it is impossible to know what new products might be invented in the future or to know the demands for products from future generations yet unborn. There is little that governments can do about this problem.

5 Yet another distortion is caused by incomplete insurance markets. A socially efficient allocation has to hold under all states-of-the-world. This implies that individuals would like to insure against the consequences of bad states-of-the-world occurring, such as unemployment or ill health. This in turn requires the existence of insurance companies that are prepared to insure against all risks for a price. However, it is not possible to insure against all contingencies because of the problems of adverse selection and moral hazard. Adverse selection is the problem of insurance being taken out mainly by people who are likely to make a subsequent claim. Moral hazard is the problem of people becoming less careful after insurance has been taken out. Insurance companies can do something to screen applicants, but again there is little the government can do about the problem.

6 Monopoly or dominant position in a market involves social costs since efficient marginal cost pricing is not used. This leads to lost consumer surplus and producer surplus. One solution to this problem is to impose a lump-sum tax on monopoly profits, as for example the government did on UK bank profits in the 1980s. More generally, the UK government has a competition policy to deal with monopoly or dominant position: the Fair Trading Act 1973, the Competition Act 1980 and Article 86 of the Treaty of Rome 1957.

7 However, natural monopolies (which exhibit increasing returns to scale at all output levels) will make losses if marginal cost pricing is used. Possible solutions to this problem include average cost pricing, two-part tariffs and public ownership to subsidize losses.

8 The government's policy of privatizing state-owned industries in the 1980s and 1990s has had the following aims: to increase efficiency and competition, to reduce the public sector borrowing requirement, to reduce government interference in decision making, to widen share ownership and to encourage employee share ownership. Whether a firm operates more efficiently in the private sector compared with the public sector depends on whether it faces effective competition or whether there is an appropriate regulatory framework in the case where the privatized firm is a natural monopoly. Effective competition depends on whether the firm operates in a contestable market. This is a market that is vulnerable to hit-and-run entry since it does not have irrecoverable sunk costs of entry. For example, British Airways operates in a contestable market, but most of the activities of British Telecom are not contestable. British Telecom therefore needed a regulator and an RPI − X pricing formula to ensure that it operated efficiently, whereas British Airways did not.

Exercises

1 What are the social benefits of perfect competition?
2 Explain the notions of (a) an efficient allocation of resources and (b) marginal cost pricing.
3 What are externalities? Explain how the government's taxation policy can be used to deal with them.
4 What is intertemporal efficiency?
5 What is contingent-state efficiency?
6 What is the social cost of monopoly?
7 What is a natural monopoly? Discuss some possible solutions to the problems posed by a natural monopoly.
8 What are the aims of the government's privatization programme?

 9 What is a contestable market?
10 Give two examples of a market that is contestable and two examples of a market that is not contestable.
11 How would you go about the privatization of a nationalized monopoly? Use an example to illustrate your answer.
12 Does it really matter whether a natural monopoly is in the private sector or the public sector?

Business application: Competition policy—the control of mergers

United Kingdom regulation

The government minister in overall charge of competition policy is the Secretary of State for Trade and Industry, also known as the President of the Board of Trade. Policy operation, which involves monitoring monopolies, mergers, restrictive practices and anti-competitive practices, is undertaken by the Office of Fair Trading, which is overseen by the Director General of Fair Trading. Investigation into referred merger bids is one of the tasks of the Monopolies and Mergers Commission (MMC).

The conditions under which a merger bid, or an existing merger situation, may be referred to the MMC are laid down in the 1973 Fair Trading Act. A bid is eligible for reference if it fulfils either or both of the following criteria: that the value of acquired assets exceeds £30m or that the combined market share is at least 25 per cent. In all, around 3 per cent of eligible bids are finally referred to the MMC.

Each reference is treated separately from previous ones; that is, a case-by-case approach is adopted, with no presumptions as to the advantages or disadvantages of the individual bids under investigation. After assessing the evidence presented to it, the MMC must decide how a merger is likely to affect the public interest. If it decides that it is expected to operate against the public interest, it will recommend that the bid should not be allowed to proceed. However, if a proposed merger is expected either to operate in the public interest or to have no effect on it, the recommendation will be that it should be allowed to go ahead. Thus, currently, there is a policy bias in favour of allowing bids.

The public interest is a wide-ranging concept involving effective competition, foreign trade, prices, costs and employment. Pronouncements by two previous Trade and Industry Secretaries, Norman Tebbit and Peter Lilley, have made the possible effect on competition the key consideration when deciding whether or not to refer a bid, and hence it is the most important element of the public interest.

European merger control

Until 21 September 1990, the European Commission (EC) had no specific merger controls. Since then the EC has assumed the right to investigate those mergers which fall within the 1990 EC Merger Regulation. For this to apply, two conditions must be satisfied. There must be:

1 A concentration—two or more firms are acquired or merge.
2 A Community dimension—a concentration has a Community dimension where:
   (a) the combined aggregate *worldwide* turnover of all the undertakings is more than ECU 5000m (around £3.5 billion), and
   (b) the combined *Community-wide* turnover of at least two of the firms is more than ECU 250m (around £175 million).

However, not all bids which appear to have a Community dimension actually do. This is because of the 'two thirds' rule. A bid will not have a Community dimension where each of the parties achieves more than two thirds of their total Community-wide turnover within one and the same member state. In this case a bid will be investigated by the regulatory bodies of the individual member state concerned.

For example, the Hong Kong and Shanghai Bank bid for Midland Bank was looked at by the EC whereas the Lloyds Bank bid for Midland (before it was withdrawn) was referred to the MMC. Both bids constitute a 'concentration' under the EC Merger Regulation and both have a 'Community dimension'. However, the 'two thirds' rule differentiates between the bids. Thus:

1 Lloyds Bank has over two thirds of Community-wide turnover in the UK
  Midland Bank has over two thirds of Community-wide turnover in the UK

  ∴   UK regulation applies

2 Hong Kong and Shanghai Bank has less than two thirds of Community-wide turnover in the UK
  Midland Bank has over two thirds of Community-wide turnover in the UK

  ∴   EC regulation applies

The rules mean that the vast majority of UK mergers will remain within the remit of UK legislation. Both sets of regulations, however, are aimed at the same problem, which is the probable impact of a merger on effective competition. Provided firms are able to convince the investigating bodies (either the European Commission or the Monopolies and Mergers Commission) that effective competition is unlikely to be impeded then their proposed mergers are likely to be granted permission to proceed.

II NATIONAL MACROECONOMICS

Macroeconomics is the study of *aggregate variables* (i.e. variables that are aggregated or summed across all households or firms in the economy). Macroeconomists are typically interested in what determines the total level output of goods and services in the economy, the total level of consumption and investment, the level of employment, the level of interest rates, the overall level of prices or the rate of inflation etc. They believe that there are common factors which cause the variations in the above variables. For example, suppose interest rates rise and firms face higher borrowing cots. This will affect the output decisions of many firms and therefore total output in the economy. Each firm will adjust its output in a different way, but the interest rate is a common factor for all firms.

Many groups of people are interested in how aggregate economic variables such as inflation, investment, interest rates etc. are determined. For governments, they are vital in policy formulation, while for industrialists, they are essential for their production decisions. Financial market analysts are also interested in macroeconomics for similar reasons. Almost all participants in financial markets are directly or indirectly concerned about asset prices. We are all aware of the importance of asset prices (of shares, bonds etc.) for portfolio investment decisions. Indeed, many people are employed solely to forecast asset prices. Two of the most important aggregate variables that determine asset prices are:

1 Interest rates.
2 The profitability (earnings) of companies.

Macroeconomic analysis is essential in providing guidance on both of these. For interest rate determination, it is necessary to consider government economic policies, external factors (e.g. trade deficits) etc. The profitability of companies will be very closely related to the economy's output of goods and services (i.e. national income).

National macroeconomics is concerned with the study of these aggregate variables within the confines of a single national economy, and disregards the interactions between different national economies. National macroeconomics is sometimes called *closed economy macroeconomics*. This contrasts with *international macroeconomics*, or *open economy macroeconomics*, which takes into account the important influences that national economies have on each other. We discuss international macroeconomics in Part III.

In Chapter 5 we develop a simple macroeconomic model to examine how output, interest rates, employment, prices etc. are determined. The economy can be analysed by dividing it into two sectors, the *real sector* (which produces goods and services) and the *financial sector* (which channels the economy's savings into investment). Our main focus is to examine the inter-relationships between these sectors. That is, we examine how events in the financial markets, such as a rise in interest rates, affect the real sector, and vice versa.

In Chapter 6 we analyse the effects of monetary and fiscal policy, especially the effects on interest rates of the different ways of financing government expenditure. This will help explain why financial markets pay such close attention to variables such as the public sector borrowing requirement (i.e. the government's financial deficit) and the money supply figures published monthly by the Bank of England. These issues are essentially concerned with the constraints facing governments in respect of macroeconomic policy options open to it, i.e. with what economists call the government's budget constraint.

There is considerable disagreement among economists as to what causes macroeconomic fluctuations. Why do output, employment etc. vary so much from year to year? In Chapter 7 we outline the main reasons for their disagreement. These are essentially concerned with the efficiency of the price mechanism in establishing equilibrium in different types of markets, especially the labour market.

Finally, Chapter 8 is devoted to measuring economic performance, popularly known as national income accounting. This is intended to provide the actual counterparts to the theoretical variables considered in previous chapters.

5 The determination of national income: a simple macroeconomic model

The total output of goods and services produced in the economy (also known as *national income*) is determined by what consumers want to buy (*aggregate demand*) and by what producers want to supply (*aggregate supply*). The market for goods and services is known as the *real sector* of the economy; this is to distinguish it from the *financial sector*, which covers the markets for money and other financial assets, such as bonds and shares. Individuals spend part of their incomes on goods and services and the rest they save, usually in the form of (highly liquid and interest-earning) deposit accounts, bond holdings and share holdings.

We first analyse the demand side of the economy. What determines the level of aggregate demand and what are the main components of aggregate demand? To simplify the analysis, we will initially assume that the supply of output will always respond to changes in demand. The underlying assumption is that there is sufficient excess capacity in the economy to satisfy any increase in demand without putting any pressure on prices. The rationale for this assumption is that it enables us to hold all prices fixed and examine only quantity adjustments. This assumption is made purely for expositional purposes and will be relaxed later.

The economy is defined to be in *equilibrium* when *aggregate demand is equal to aggregate supply*. Equilibrium here means a situation where there are no forces tending to change the level of output. In Fig. 5.1 (p. 80) we depict this equilibrium as desired total expenditure (*E*, or aggregate demand) equal to total output of goods and services (*Y*). All points along the 45° *E* = *Y* line are in macroeconomic equilibrium.

5.1 The composition of aggregate demand

Total expenditure (*E*) (sometimes called *aggregate demand* or *AD*) in the economy can be separated into three main categories:

1 Private sector consumption expenditure (*C*).
2 Private sector investment expenditure (*I*).
3 Government expenditure (*G*).

Adding these together we get:

$$E = C + I + G \tag{5.1}$$

The reason for this particular way of decomposing aggregate demand is that in principle there are different factors determining each category. There are other ways of dividing total expenditure. For example one could divide it into retail versus wholesale. However, if the same factors affect retail and wholesale expenditures, then this division is not particularly useful for

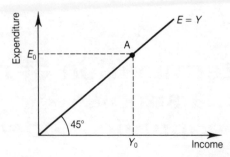

Figure 5.1   Equilibrium national income

economic analysis. In addition to the three categories listed above there is also net exports, but we leave our discussion of this category until Chapter 8.

5.1.1   Consumption

Each individual household's *consumption expenditure* on goods and services will depend on several factors, and there may be considerable variation between households. We are interested in aggregate consumption, that is, the consumption of all households aggregated together. Given that people work (and sacrifice leisure) to earn the income which enables them to acquire the goods that they wish to consume, it follows that a major determinant of consumption expenditure will be income. Higher income permits higher consumption. However, in general, not all income is spent on current consumption. Some income will be *saved* for future consumption. And, in general, the amount saved will rise as income rises. At very low income levels, consumption will be financed from past savings (this is known as *dissaving*), and then as income rises consumption will rise.

In addition to income, consumption will also depend on interest rates and the availability of credit. These determine whether people choose to consume their income in the current period, or devote more to future consumption (i.e. save more now). For example, in the late 1980s, the relaxation of credit restrictions in the UK housing market together with falling interest rates resulted in large increases in the personal sector's consumption expenditure, financed by the withdrawal of wealth held in housing (a process known as housing equity release). For our present purpose it is sufficient to treat consumption as a function of income, since income still determines the ability to repay loans taken out to finance consumption. We also know from our study of microeconomics that prices are a very important determinant of demand. But in this chapter we are assuming that prices are fixed, so that for the moment, prices will not be a determinant of consumption expenditure. As we said above, we shall relax this assumption later.

We can write a specific linear relationship between consumption and income as

$$C = a + bY \tag{5.2}$$

where a is a constant and b is the proportion of increments in income devoted to consumption. This relationship is sometimes called a *model of consumption behaviour* because it models or explains consumption in terms of a linear function of income. It is also known as the *consumption function*. The parameter b is referred to as the *marginal propensity to consume*, while the parameter a is known as *autonomous* or *subsistence consumption*, that is, the component of consumption that does *not* depend on the level of income. Given that some income is saved, b will typically

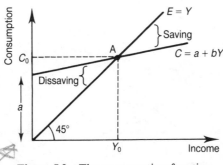

Figure 5.2 The consumption function

be less than unity. If $b = 0.8$, this implies that for every £1 increase in income, £0.80 is spent and the rest is saved.

Figure 5.2 illustrates this function and shows the level of consumption at different levels of income. At income level Y_0, consumption is C_0. At any income level less than Y_0, consumption expenditure is greater than income. Some consumption is financed from past savings. Positive saving occurs when income exceeds Y_0.

5.1.2 Investment

We define *investment* as any current activity that increases the economy's ability to produce output in the future. In other words, *investment is the addition to the economy's productive capital stock*. In this general definition we would like to include not only *physical investment* (i.e. building of plant and equipment, business construction, housing construction etc.) but also *investment in human capital* (i.e. education and training); however, because it is difficult to measure investment in human capital, macroeconomists tend to ignore this type of investment. Investment also includes physical *inventory accumulation* by firms (i.e. stocks of finished goods which have not yet been sold to final consumers). We can also distinguish between *gross investment* and *net investment*. Gross investment measures the total expenditure on investment during the year. But this does not measure the net addition to the economy's physical capital stock. This is because as capital is used in the production process, it deteriorates in efficiency and eventually has to be scrapped. Alternatively, technological progress can render the existing capital stock obsolete. The capital stock therefore declines year by year, and the amount by which it does so is known as *depreciation*. The net addition to the economy's physical capital stock is known as net investment. Net investment is therefore equal to gross investment *minus* depreciation. The excess of gross investment over net investment is therefore the amount of new investment necessary to keep the net capital stock constant. Only net investment adds to the economy's capital stock.

To begin with, we shall assume that investment demand is autonomous; that is, it does not depend on any of the factors we have looked at so far. In particular, it does not depend on current income. It could, for example, be determined by what business people expect future demand conditions to be. We will examine the effect of interest rates on the level of investment after we have introduced a financial sector (i.e. a money market) in which equilibrium interest rates are determined. At present, we let I be a fixed constant determined outside our model.

5.1.3 Government expenditure

The government spends money on *goods and services* (e.g. roads, hospitals, teachers, doctors, civil servants etc.) and on *transfer payments* (e.g. to pensioners and the unemployed). The

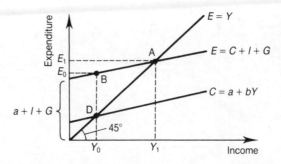

Figure 5.3   Determination of equilibrium national income

expenditure on goods and services can be divided into *public consumption expenditure* (e.g. teachers and doctors) and *public investment expenditure* (e.g. roads and hospitals). The level of government expenditure is determined by government policy. The government may alter G in order to change national income, but that is a policy objective. However, to the extent that the government has entered into prior commitments (e.g. to guarantee unemployment benefits to the unemployed), the level of national income or economic activity can in turn affect government expenditure. For example, in times of recession (low economic activity) the level of unemployment rises, and this will automatically raise government expenditure, since unemployment benefits will be paid to more people. Unemployment benefits are a form of transfer payment, since no service or goods are required in return. Only direct spending by the government on goods and services is included in G, and not transfer payments, which will be spent by pensioners and the unemployed etc. on consumption and hence are included in C.

5.1.4   Determining equilibrium income

Combining all the elements of demand we can now analyse the determination of equilibrium income. Our earlier definition of equilibrium was $E = Y$, and we assumed that supply (Y) responds to changes in demand (E). In Fig. 5.3 we show this equilibrium relationship in terms of all the components of aggregate demand. At income level Y_0, there is *excess demand*, equal to the vertical distance from B to D. That is, at income Y_0, desired expenditure is E_0. Since $E_0 > Y_0$, suppliers will supply more output. Since Y rises towards Y_1 desired expenditure also rises: recall that C is an increasing function of Y. Notice, however, that desired expenditures rise less than proportionately. That is, the excess demand gap is narrowing. At point A, income and expenditures are equal ($E_1 = Y_1$), and so Y_1 is the equilibrium level of national income.

5.2   The expenditure multiplier

Suppose the government decides to spend an extra £100 on goods and services. When it pays for those goods and services, the £100 becomes income in the hands of those who sold the goods and services to the government. This is known as an *injection* in the *income–expenditure process* (or *multiplier process*), a process by which changes in expenditure (or demand) lead to changes in income (or supply) which lead to further changes in expenditure and so on. Via the consumption function, some of the income (a proportion of it equal to b) is used for consumption expenditure. This, in turn, raises someone else's income and they again spend part of it on consumption. This process is not endless, since in each round of the income–expenditure process some of the extra income is saved. Saving represents a *leakage* in the income–expenditure process. The important point to note here is that, as a result of a one-off increase (i.e. injection) in desired expenditure (in our example it is G, but it could equally well be investment expenditure or export expenditure), the rise in income at the end of the process is *greater than* the initial rise in expenditure. This feature is known as the *expenditure multiplier*: there is a government expenditure multiplier, an investment expenditure multiplier and an export expenditure multiplier, one for each type of injection.

An example of the multiplier

To keep the analysis simple, we will consider an increase in investment of £100, but assume that there is no government sector.

Suppose initially that we are in equilibrium, with:

$$Y = £1000$$

$$C = £900$$

$$I = £100$$

where C is determined by the consumption function $C = 100 + 0.8Y$, that is, $a = £100$ and $b = 0.8$.

Consider the effect of an increase in I of £100 to $I = £200$. The new equilibrium level of income can be determined by what happens in each round of the income–expenditure process. In the first round, the increase in I leads to an immediate increase in demand and hence in excess demand $(E - Y)$ of £100 in the first instance. This increase in demand will be met by firms selling part of their inventories of finished goods (in this case investment goods such as plant and equipment), so there will be no pressure for prices to rise. This will raise income by £100. This is because the sale of £100 of investment goods means an increase of £100 in the income of the suppliers of those goods. In the second round, consumption will rise by £80 since $C = £100 + 0.8(£1100)$, which implies second round consumption of $C = £980$), and so on. In Table 5.1 we trace the effects on C and Y in each round (see also Fig. 5.4, p. 84).

For an initial increase in investment of £100, income ultimately rises by £500. The process stops when $Y = £1500$, $C = £1300$ and $I = £200$. At these values, we are again in equilibrium with income equal to expenditure. The value of the multiplier is 5, since a £100 increase in investment has led to a five-fold increase in income. Instead of calculating what happens in each

TABLE 5.1   Multiplier effect when investment increases by £100

	Consumption (C)	Investment (I)	Income (Y)	Aggregate demand (E)	Excess demand (E − Y)
Initial equilibrium	900	100	1000	1000	0
Round 1	900	200	1000	1100	100
Round 2	980	200	1100	1180	80
Round 3	1044	200	1180	1244	64
Round 4	1095.2	200	1244	1295.2	51.2
Round 5	1136.16	200	1295.2	1336.16	40.96
	⋮	⋮	⋮	⋮	⋮
Final equilibrium	1300	200	1500	1500	0

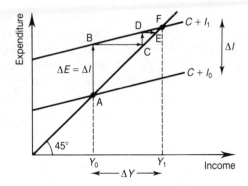

Figure 5.4   The expenditure multiplier: an increase in investment

round of the income–expenditure process until it stops, there is a direct way of deriving the multiplier. This involves finding the solution for equilibrium income (Y).

Our equilibrium condition is $Y = C + I = E$. Substituting the consumption function for C into the equilibrium condition gives

$$Y = a + bY + I \tag{5.3}$$

By rearranging terms, we get

$$Y - bY = a + I \tag{5.4}$$

and

$$Y(1 - b) = a + I \tag{5.5}$$

Dividing both sides of the equation by $(1 - b)$ yields

$$Y = \frac{1}{1 - b}(a + I) = \frac{1}{1 - b}a + \frac{1}{1 - b}I \tag{5.6}$$

To find the change in Y, denoted ΔY, when I changes by a particular amount ΔI, we write

$$\Delta Y = \frac{1}{1 - b}\Delta I \tag{5.7}$$

where $1/(1 - b)$ is known as the *multiplier* and we assume that the change in autonomous consumption is zero ($\Delta a = 0$). To check whether this gives us the same answer as in Table 5.1, we substitute in the value for b (0.8), which gives a value for the multiplier of

$$\frac{1}{1 - 0.8} = 5 \tag{5.8}$$

In the above example, the only leakage is savings. In practice there are two other important leakages: taxation and import spending. Taxes reduce the amount of income available for consumption. As a result, in each round of the income–expenditure process, less is being passed on. Import spending results in an increase in income for foreigners and not for domestic residents. In the UK, once account is taken of all the leakages, the value of the multiplier is about 1.5. There is some evidence that the value of the multiplier fell significantly after the 1973 oil crisis due to higher expenditure on oil imports.

The income–expenditure process can be used to explain economic booms and slumps (or recessions). A boom can be caused by an increase in autonomous investment or government expenditure that leads to a multiplier expansion in national income. In contrast, a slump can be caused by a reduction in autonomous investment (particularly reductions in inventory investment, sometimes called *de-stocking*, which is one of the main causes of recessions in the UK in the post-war period) or in government expenditure, leading to a multiplier contraction in national income. *Re-stocking* by firms is one of the first signs that a recession is over.

5.3 Equilibrium in the real sector: the IS schedule

Our analysis of the real sector has so far made no mention of money or interest rates. In particular, we have assumed that desired expenditures depend only on income. The question we now consider is how money affects aggregate demand. In the financial sector (i.e. the money market), the demand for and supply of money determine interest rates. One major link between the money market and the real sector is via interest rates. The main component of aggregate demand that depends on interest rates is investment. We can now generalize our above assumption that the amount of investment is a fixed quantity, independent of the cost of borrowing funds to finance investment.

There are essentially two reasons for this. First for firms that borrow funds for investment, the interest rate is the price of borrowing. A higher interest rate reduces investment demand since marginal investment projects are no longer profitable to undertake. Second for firms that finance investment out of retained profits, the interest rate still represents the required rate of return, since they could always earn this rate of return by depositing their funds in the money market instead of reinvesting the funds in additional capital in their companies. For these reasons, investment expenditure will be inversely related to the level of interest rates. A rise in interest rates reduces investment. This relationship is illustrated in Fig. 5.5, where investment is shown as a downward-sloping function of the rate of interest, i.e. $I = f(r)$.

Lower investment will in turn reduce aggregate demand and thereby lead to lower output. This link between higher interest rates and lower output can be illustrated by a downward shift of the desired expenditure schedule ($E = C + I + G$) in Fig. 5.3 together with a movement to the left on the horizontal axis of Fig. 5.5. It can be shown more conveniently using the *IS schedule* which is derived in Fig. 5.6 on p. 86 (IS refers to Investment = Savings).

In Fig. 5.6 we consider the effect of a rise in interest rates, from r_0 to r_1 (Fig. 5.6(a)). The initial equilibrium is at point A in all three diagrams. The level of investment is I_0, when $r = r_0$. This, combined with C_0 and G_0, determines desired expenditure at $C_0 + I_0 + G_0$ (Fig. 5.6(b)).

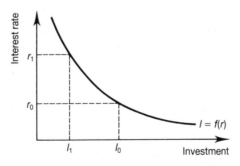

Figure 5.5 Investment and interest rates

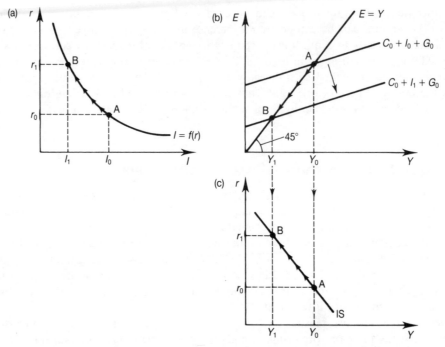

Figure 5.6   Goods market equilibrium: IS schedule

In Fig. 5.6(c) the economy is in equilibrium at the combination of income and interest rates given by Y_0 and r_0.

When interest rates rise to r_1, investment falls to I_1 (Fig. 5.6(a)) causing the entire aggregate expenditure schedule to shift downwards (to $C_0 + I_1 + G_0$) (Fig. 5.6(b)). Income falls to Y_1 via the multiplier process working in the negative contractionary direction. As demand falls, suppliers reduce output; otherwise they would build up inventories of goods which cannot be sold. In Fig. 5.6(c) the new combination of r and Y is shown at point B. Points A and B lie on the IS schedule, which shows combinations of r and Y for which the real sector is in equilibrium, that is, along $Y = E$ in Fig. 5.6(b).

Along $Y = E$ in Fig. 5.6(b), income equals desired expenditure. In the absence of government expenditure, desired expenditure is $E = C + I$. In equilibrium therefore $Y = C + I$, or equivalently, $I = Y - C = S$, where S (the difference between income and consumption) is desired savings. So an alternative characterization of equilibrium in the real sector is that *desired investment* equals *desired savings*; this explains why the curve in Fig. 5.6(c) is known as the IS schedule. The IS schedule is downward sloping in $r - Y$ space because, beginning at a point such as A on the IS schedule, an increase in interest rates reduces investment, which in turn requires a reduction in income to reduce savings to restore equality between investment and savings at another point, such as B on the IS schedule, to the left and above the initial point. Since $C = a + bY$, this means that $S = Y - C = -a + (1 - b)Y$, so that a fall in investment following an increase in interest rates requires a fall in Y to induce an equivalent reduction in savings and hence re-establish equilibrium in the goods market.

An important determinant of how large a reduction in income there is when interest rates rise is the interest sensitivity of investment. The more interest-elastic investment expenditure is (i.e. the flatter the curve is in Fig. 5.5), the bigger the reduction in income for a given rise in

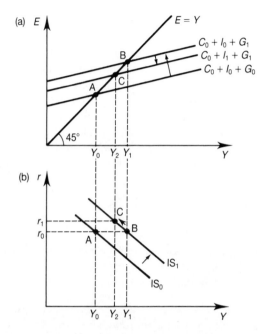

Figure 5.7   A shift in the IS schedule

interest rates. In terms of the IS schedule in Fig. 5.6, the slope becomes flatter as the interest elasticity of investment expenditure rises, but the IS schedule is always downward-sloping in $r - Y$ space.

At any given interest rate, if there is an autonomous change in an autonomous component of expenditure, such as government expenditure, then the entire IS schedule will shift. Figure 5.7 shows the effects of an increase in government expenditure from G_0 to G_1. Holding interest rates constant, the expenditure schedule shifts from $C_0 + I_0 + G_0$ to $C_0 + I_0 + G_1$ in Fig. 5.7(a). Equilibrium income increases via the multiplier process from Y_0 to Y_1 (i.e. from A to B along the 45° $E = Y$ line). In Fig. 5.7(b) this leads to a *shift* in the IS schedule from IS_0 to IS_1 (from A to B). However, if the increase in government expenditure also resulted in an increase in interest rates from r_0 to r_1, then investment expenditure would fall from I_0 to I_1 (see Fig. 5.6(a)). In Fig. 5.7(a) this leads to the expenditure schedule shifting from $C_0 + I_0 + G_1$ to $C_0 + I_1 + G_1$ (i.e. from B to C along the $E = Y$ line). In Fig. 5.7(b) there is a *movement along* the IS_1 schedule from B to C. Equilibrium income falls back from Y_1 to Y_2.

5.4   Financial sector assets and the demand for money

Next we turn to the financial sector. This is the sector dealing with *financial assets*, such as money, bonds and shares. Individuals also hold wealth in the form of *real assets*, such as houses, furniture and antiques; but holdings of real assets do not usually have much effect on the economy (although there are times when they can, such as the late 1980s when housing equity release was prevalent). We will therefore concentrate our attention on financial assets.

The main income-earning financial assets are bonds and shares. *Bonds* are assets which pay an annual fixed coupon for a fixed number of years. If bonds pay a fixed coupon indefinitely, they are known as perpetual bonds. Bonds are issued by companies or governments to pay for their expenditure, usually their investment expenditure. Bonds issued by the UK government are known as *gilts*. *Shares* (or *equities*) are assets which pay an annual dividend indefinitely, or at least until a firm becomes insolvent. The dividend is not fixed, but varies depending on the profitability of the company issuing the shares, and can be zero if the company is making losses. Shares are issued by companies when they are first incorporated and the shareholders are the owners of the company. This contrasts with the holders of the company's bonds, who are merely creditors of the company. If they do not receive their coupon payments they can force the company into insolvency. This is not true of shareholders, who cannot force a firm into insolvency even if they do not receive dividends for a number of years.

To keep things simple, we will assume that there are only two financial assets, money and bonds. Individuals allocate their financial wealth between money and bonds so that

$$A = M^D + B^D \tag{5.9}$$

where

A = aggregate financial wealth or assets in the economy.
M^D = aggregate demand for money.
B^D = aggregate demand for bonds.

We can infer from this *wealth identity* that, once we have determined the demand for money, the demand for bonds is determined as a residual, since the level of aggregate wealth is given (i.e. $B^D = A - M^D$). Therefore we can concentrate on factors that determine the demand for money. To do this we need to examine the motives for holding money and the cost of holding money.

The primary motive for holding money is the *transactions motive*, i.e. for the purpose of purchasing goods and services. The volume of transactions made by all individuals in the economy will have some relation to aggregate income. Since income is equal to the total value of all goods and services produced, the demand for money is a function of the level of output of the real sector. Higher output raises the demand for money, since more transactions have to be paid for. However, holding money for transactions purposes entails forgoing interest income, since it cannot be invested at the same time. Many forms of money holdings nowadays pay interest and can also be used for transactions (e.g. bank and building society accounts). But it is usually the case that such accounts require a longer notice of withdrawal the higher the interest earned, i.e. they are less *liquid* and therefore less useful for financing immediate transactions. As interest rates rise, the *opportunity cost* of holding money increases and we would expect people to economize on money holdings that do not earn interest.

The other main motive for holding money is the *speculative motive*. If interest rates are low, asset prices will be high. This is because financial assets, such as bonds, which pay a fixed coupon payment, will have a high price if the rate of interest in the money market is low. To see this, we can consider a perpetual bond which pays a fixed coupon of £d per year indefinitely. If the price of the bond is P_B then the yield on the bond is $r_B = d/P_B$. For example, if $d = £10$ and $P_B = £100$ then the yield on the bond is 10 per cent. If the money market interest rate (r) is also 10 per cent, investors will be indifferent as to whether to invest in this bond or in the money market. If, however, money market interest rates fall to 5 per cent and are expected to remain at 5 per cent, the bond becomes the more attractive investment, since it pays a fixed coupon of £10 per year regardless of interest rates. Investors will switch from the money market into the bond, which will cause the price of the bond to rise. The price of the bond will rise to £200, at which point it too offers a return of 5 per cent. If the general level of interest rates is expected to remain at 5 per cent indefinitely, this is the end of the matter. But if 5 per cent is a low rate of interest compared with historical experience and if 10 per cent is the average long-run rate

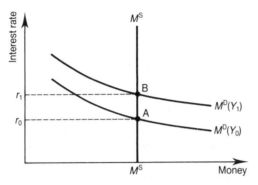

Figure 5.8   The demand for money

of interest, then investors will expect interest rates to rise again to 10 per cent. If this happens, investors will suffer huge capital losses on their bond holdings: investors who bought the bond at £200 will see the bond halved in value. Investors who expect interest rates to rise will therefore not want to hold fixed interest bonds at all. They will prefer instead to hold money in order to avoid the expected capital loss on the bonds. If interest rates do rise as expected, then investors will switch out of money into bonds. This is the speculative motive for holding money: investors are speculating on an increase in interest rates. The demand for money for speculative purposes will be negatively related to the level of interest rates: the lower the level of interest rates (in relation to long-term average values), the higher the demand for money. This is because investors are anticipating an increase in interest rates and wish to avoid capital losses on bond holdings, and so switch into money.

We can conclude from this analysis that the demand for money depends positively on the level of income and negatively on the rate of interest. This is shown in Fig. 5.8, where, for a given level of income, the demand for money, M^D, is downward-sloping with respect to the interest rate. The money supply is assumed to be fixed by the central bank, and therefore independent of both the interest rate and the level of income. The money supply curve M^S is therefore vertical in Fig. 5.8. At any given interest rate, a rise in income will raise the demand for money (i.e. lead to a *shift* of the demand for money function to the right). A change in interest rates will change the demand for money, but in this case it is a *movement along* a given money demand function. In Fig. 5.8, there are two different money demand functions for different levels of income. The higher level of income (Y_1) raises demand and, with a given supply, results in a higher interest rate (r_1).

The supply of money is determined in large part by the central bank. For our present purposes, we can treat the money supply as being *exogenously determined* and independent of the level of interest rates. In practice, the level of the money supply depends on the particular form of monetary policy that the central bank operates on behalf of the government. The banking system's behaviour with respect to loans also influences the supply of money. (These issues are discussed in more detail in Part III.)

5.5   Equilibrium in the financial sector: the LM schedule

Having examined the factors that determine the demand for money, we are now in a position to examine financial sector equilibrium. This will depend on the relationship between interest rates and the level of income. We will also consider how the real sector affects the financial sector.

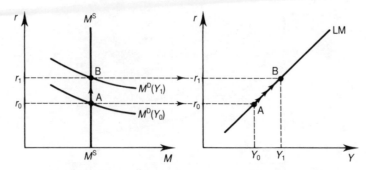

Figure 5.9   Money market equilibrium: the LM schedule

We know that the transactions demand for money depends on income. Therefore the real sector (which determines the level of income) affects the interest rate via the demand for money (which depends on the level of income). For a given supply of money, the higher the level of income, the higher the interest rate. The *LM schedule* in Fig. 5.9 shows combinations of r and Y for which the money market or financial sector is in equilibrium. Note that a change in the supply of money (i.e. a movement of the M^S curve) will shift the entire LM schedule (LM refers to Liquidity demand = Money supply). The LM schedule is upward-sloping in $r - Y$ space, because, beginning at any point on the schedule, an increase in interest rates reduces the demand for money, which, in turn, requires a compensating increase in income to increase the demand for money to restore equality between the demand for money and the fixed supply of money at another point on the schedule to the right and above the initial point.

The slope of the LM schedule depends on both the interest elasticity and the income elasticity of the demand for money. If the demand for money is not very interest elastic (i.e. an elasticity of less than unity) the resulting LM curve will be steep. A high income elasticity also makes the LM curve steep. The reason for this is that small changes in income lead to large shifts of the demand function, thereby resulting in large changes in the interest rate.

At any given interest rate, if there is a change in the supply of money, then the entire LM schedule will shift. Figure 5.10 shows the effect of an increase in the supply of money from M_0^S to M_1^S. The effect of the increase in money supply is to reduce equilibrium interest rates from r_0 to r_1. There is a movement along the money demand curve from A to B (see Fig. 5.10(a)). The increase in the money supply does not change aggregate income, which remains at Y_0. The LM curve shifts to the right from LM_0 to LM_1 (see Fig. 5.10(b)). The equilibrium point shifts from A on LM_0 to B on LM_1, with interest rates falling from r_0 to r_1 but income unchanges at Y_0.

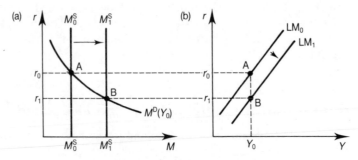

Figure 5.10   A shift in the LM schedule

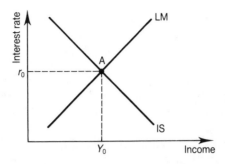

Figure 5.11   Macroeconomic equilibrium

5.6 Macroeconomic equilibrium

To summarize our results so far, we have two important relationships between the real and financial sectors:

1 A *change* in M^S leads to a *change* in r, which *changes I* and therefore *changes Y* (financial to real sector interactions):

$$\Delta M^S \Rightarrow \Delta r \Rightarrow \Delta I \Rightarrow \Delta AD \Rightarrow \Delta Y \qquad (5.10)$$

2 A *change* in Y leads to a *change* in M^D and therefore a *change* in r (real to financial sector interactions):

$$\Delta Y \Rightarrow \Delta M^D \Rightarrow \Delta r \qquad (5.11)$$

Here AD = aggregate demand and $\Delta A \Rightarrow \Delta B$ means '*changes* in A will lead to *changes* in B'.

Both the real and financial sectors will be in equilibrium when the rate of interest is at a level where desired expenditures equal output. This unique level of output is also equal to the level of income at which the demand for money equals the supply of money at the same rate of interest. In Fig. 5.11, this equilibrium is at the point of intersection of the IS and LM curves (point A). At this combination of income and the rate of interest, there is no tendency for anything to change; individuals are in equilibrium in their allocation of wealth between different assets (money and bonds) and in their allocation of income between different types of expenditure (*C, I* etc.). This is known as the *IS/LM model* of macroeconomic equilibrium.

5.7 Summary

1 The real sector deals with the markets for goods and services in the economy. The total output of goods and services is determined by the interaction between aggregate demand and aggregate supply. The economy will be in equilibrium when aggregate demand is equal to aggregate supply.

2 Aggregate demand is equal to the sum of private sector consumption expenditure, private sector investment expenditure and government expenditure.

3 Consumption expenditure can typically be expressed as an increasing linear function of total income. There will be a minimum level of consumption, known as autonomous or subsistence consumption, that does not depend on income. Above this minimum level, consumption

increases in proportion with increases in income, a proportion which is known as the marginal propensity to consume.

4 Investment is the addition to the economy's capital stock during the year. It includes not only purchases of new plant and equipment etc., but also the accumulation of stocks of finished goods. Gross investment is the total addition to the economy's capital stock. But every year, part of the existing capital stock becomes obsolete (this is known as depreciation). Net investment is the net addition to the economy's capital stock, after taking into account depreciation.

5 The government is engaged in public consumption expenditure (e.g. on the salaries of teachers, doctors and civil servants) and public investment expenditure (e.g. on building roads and hospitals). These constitute direct spending by the government on goods and services. It is also engaged in transfer payments to pensioners and the unemployed.

6 Equilibrium national income is given by the level of income at which total expenditure (which is an increasing function of income) equals total output.

7 The income–expenditure process is the process by which changes in expenditure (i.e. aggregate demand) lead to changes in income (i.e. aggregate supply). Increases in government expenditure, investment expenditure or export expenditure are injections in the income–expenditure process. They lead to multiplier expansions of income that are greater than the initial size of the injection. This is because an increase in expenditure is equivalent to an increase in income in the hands of the recipient of that expenditure. Part of the increase in income will go into additional expenditure and part of it will be saved. This additional expenditure is in turn equivalent to additional income, which generates further expenditure, and so on. At each stage in the income–expenditure process, there are leakages in the form of savings, taxation and imports. These help to limit the size of the overall expenditure multiplier. An important assumption in this analysis is that the price level is fixed.

8 The IS schedule shows the combinations of interest rates and income for which the real sector of the economy is in equilibrium. The real sector is in equilibrium when desired savings and investment are equal. The IS schedule is downward-sloping in $r - Y$ space. This is because, beginning in equilibrium, a fall in interest rates will increase planned investment and this will require an increase in income to raise savings to restore equality between desired savings and investment.

9 A change in interest rates or income will lead to a movement along a given IS schedule. A change in an autonomous component of aggregate expenditure, such as government expenditure, will lead to a shift in the IS schedule. For example, a reduction in government expenditure will shift the schedule to the left.

10 The financial sector deals with the markets for financial assets, including money and bonds.

11 The demand for money arises from the following motives. The primary motive for holding money is the transactions motive: money is held to buy goods and services. The other main motive is the speculative motive: money is held to avoid capital losses on bond holdings when interest rates are low (and bond prices are high) and interest rates are expected to rise (and bond prices are expected to fall). In both cases, the demand for money increases as interest rates and hence the opportunity cost of holding money falls. A reduction in income, on the other hand, reduces the transactions motive and so reduces the demand for money.

12 The LM schedule shows the combinations of interest rates and income for which the financial sector of the economy is in equilibrium. The financial sector is in equilibrium when the demand for and supply of money are equal. The LM schedule is upward-sloping in $r - Y$ space. This is because, beginning in equilibrium, a fall in interest rates will increase the demand for money and this will require a reduction in income to induce a corresponding

reduction in the demand for money to restore equality between the demand for and supply of money, if the supply of money is fixed.

13 A change in interest rates or income will lead to a movement along a given LM schedule. A change in the money supply will lead to a shift in the LM schedule. For example, a reduction in the money supply will shift the schedule to the left.

14 Macroeconomic equilibrium occurs when the real sector and financial sector are simultaneously in equilibrium, i.e. at the interest rate and income level at which the IS and LM schedules intersect.

Exercises

1 What are the main components of aggregate demand?

2 Explain the terms 'autonomous consumption' and 'marginal propensity to consume'.

3 What are the main categories of investment expenditure?

4 Explain the difference between government spending on goods and services and government spending on transfer payments.

5 Explain the terms 'expenditure multiplier', 'injection' and 'leakage', giving an example of each term.

6 Consider the following macroeconomic model:

$$Y = C + I + G$$

$$C = a + bY$$

$$I = I_0$$

$$G = G_0$$

(a) Find the equilibrium level of national income.

(b) What is the formula for the multiplier?

(c) What is the value of equilibrium national income if $a = 200$, $b = 0.6$, $I_0 = 500$ and $G_0 = 300$?

(d) What is the corresponding value for the multiplier?

7 Suppose that $C = 0.8Y$, planned investment is 500 and that there is no government ($G = 0$).

(a) What is the equilibrium level of Y?

(b) If actual output is initially 2000, is this an equilibrium? If not, describe how equilibrium is reached.

8 Consider the following macroeconomic model:

$$Y = C + I + G$$

$$C = a + bY_d$$

$$I = I_0$$

$$G = G_0$$

$$Y_d = (1 - t)Y$$

where t is the tax rate, and disposable income Y_d is proportional to gross income Y. If the values of b and t are 0.7 and 0.2, respectively, what is the value of the expenditure multiplier?

9 What is the IS schedule? Why is it downward-sloping?

10 If consumption is given by:

$$C = a + bY$$

and investment is given by

$$I = h - kr$$

what is the equation for the IS schedule?

11 What is the LM schedule? Why is it upward-sloping?

12 If the demand for money is given by:

$$M^D = d + eY - gr$$

and the money supply is fixed at $M^S = M_0^S$, what is the equation for the LM schedule?

13 Explain how macroeconomic equilibrium is determined in the IS/LM model.

14 Using the information in Exercises 10 and 12, what is the equilibrium level of income and interest rates if $a = 0$, $b = 0.8$, $h = 7$, $k = 0.2$, $d = 0$, $e = 1$, $g = 2$ and $M_0^S = 20$?

15 Explain the difference between real assets and financial assets.

16 Explain the difference between bonds and shares.

Business application: Economic growth and consumer spending 1981–90

The period 1981–90 covers the upswing of the business cycle from the 1981 trough to the 1990 peak. For business to benefit from an expanding economy, it needs to know the sources of economic growth. Changes in expenditure—consumer, investment, government, exports and imports—will affect growth.

The largest component of aggregate demand is consumer spending, which accounts for just over 65 per cent of total expenditure, and during 1981–90 it rose by 40 per cent in real terms. However, it is too broad a term to be of use to business, and what is required is a more disaggregated breakdown. Different sectors will grow at different rates. Fast-growing sectors will yield higher profits and will attract new firms, whereas contracting and stagnant sectors will do neither. Understanding the performance of the different sectors will help firms to react to structural changes within the economy and to identify profitable opportunities. However, simply knowing that changes are taking place is not enough; it is also necessary to know why they are occurring.

Table 5.2 (p. 96) shows how consumer spending has moved during the upswing. The growing awareness of health issues is reflected in a number of sectors. First, in the wake of various health scares (e.g. cancer, cholesterol and 'mad cow' disease (BSE)), spending on tobacco, milk, cheese and eggs, and meat and bacon has declined. Firms operating in these sectors will find it difficult to maintain profitability, and diversification would be a sensible option. Second, the increases in medical spending reflect the rise in prescription charges as well as the growth of private health provision. The latter implies an unease about the ability of the NHS to provide the relevant treatment at the right time, and so private cover provides an alternative. Third, recreation, entertainment and education spending has increased. The biggest increases here relate to sports goods, which should improve health, and radio, TV and video, which unfortunately do not. In addition, there has been no change in spending on books and newspapers. Fourth, the increase in spending on fruit indicates a better diet. In contrast, the rise in spending on soft drinks, which tend to have high sugar contents, is a cause for concern.

Increases in household goods and services, mainly washing machines, cookers etc., reflect generally rising living standards. However, consumer durable goods have been an area in which UK firms have performed particularly badly over the last 10 years, with the result that most of this increase has been spent on imports.

Spending on cars, their running costs and air travel is the main reason for the increase in transport and communications. Again, much of the spending on cars is on imports, which represents another missed opportunity for UK business.

Perhaps, reflecting a greater interest in their appearance, the biggest increase in spending on clothes and footwear is in menswear.

In terms of the standard demand function, Table 5.2 shows the effects of changing tastes, income, the availability of substitutes and advertising. UK firms can use this type of information to identify changing patterns of consumption and hence plan to take advantage of these changes.

TABLE 5.2 Consumer expenditure 1981–90

Sector	Real change (%)
NHS payments and other medical expenses	+114
Soft drinks	+95
Transport and communications	+58
Recreation, entertainment and education	+57
Household goods	+48
Clothing and footwear	+47
Housing	+28
Fruit	+26
Food	+10
Alcohol	+6
Fuel and power	+2
Meat and bacon	−7
Milk, cheese and eggs	−9
Tobacco	−22
Total consumer spending	+40

6 Macroeconomic policy

Macroeconomic policy is concerned with the government's attempts to manipulate aggregate demand or aggregate supply in order to achieve a set of *macroeconomic policy objectives*. Historically in the UK, the main macroeconomic policy objectives have been low inflation, low unemployment, economic growth and a balance of overseas trade. However, since 1979, the overriding policy objective has been to control inflation, and this has been at the expense of the other objectives. The government might establish a set of *macroeconomic policy targets*, such as an inflation rate of less than 3 per cent, or an unemployment rate of less than 2.5 per cent, or a growth rate of 3.5 per cent per annum, or eliminating a balance of trade deficit within three years. To achieve these targets, it will need to use a set of *macroeconomic policy instruments*. In general, there will need to be one instrument for every target chosen; this is known as *Tinbergen's rule*, after the Dutch economist Jan Tinbergen. The main policy instruments are fiscal policy and monetary policy, and these are sometimes known as *demand management policies*.

6.1 Fiscal policy and crowding out

Fiscal policy is concerned with the effects of changes in government expenditure or changes in government taxation policy. Suppose the government undertakes an expansionary fiscal policy by increasing its own expenditure on goods and services (G); it could be on defence, roads, schools, hospitals etc. What is the effect of this on output (Y) and interest rates (r)? We ignore at this stage the issue of how this extra expenditure may be financed, although this is clearly important and will be considered later. For now, suppose it is financed from a windfall gain which the government has received (a good example is the discovery of oil in the North Sea and the resulting government revenue that accrued).

Higher government expenditure will raise aggregate demand (i.e. total desired expenditure), both directly via the increase in the government's demand for goods and services and also indirectly via the expenditure multiplier process. Since we are also assuming for the moment that there is spare capacity in the economy, this implies that output will rise to meet the increase in demand without any inflationary pressures. Firms will have to employ more workers to enable them to increase their output, and so unemployment will fall. We can consider the effects of higher demand on output and interest rates.

The higher aggregate demand will raise incomes and thereby increase the demand for money. Assuming there is no change in the supply of money (i.e. the case of a pure fiscal policy which is not financed by printing money), there will be excess demand in the money market which will raise the rate of interest (see Fig. 5.8, p. 89). However, investment expenditure is negatively related to the rate of interest. Therefore the higher interest rates will reduce investment expenditure and thereby lead to a reduction in aggregate demand (see Fig. 5.6, p. 86).

There are therefore two counteracting effects on aggregate demand as a result of a fiscal expansion. The first effect, that of increased government expenditure, is expansionary. The second effect, which is contractionary, is known as the *crowding out* of private sector expenditure as a

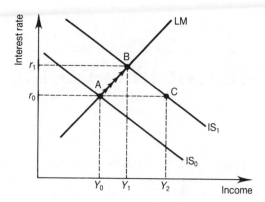

Figure 6.1   An expansionary fiscal policy

result of the increase in government expenditure. In the case of *complete crowding out*, the fiscal expansion will have no net effect on output. The increase in government expenditure is matched exactly by a reduction in private sector investment, as a result of the consequential increase in interest rates: the only effect is a redistribution of aggregate demand towards government expenditure and away from private sector investment expenditure. In most cases, however, there will be some net increase in aggregate demand.

The extent of crowding out depends on two factors:

1 *Income elasticity of money demand*
  When income rises, the extent to which the demand for money increases will determine how much interest rates rise. In terms of Fig. 5.8, the question is how much the demand for money curve shifts to the right when income increases. The higher the income elasticity of the demand for money, the greater will be the increase in interest rates when income increases.
2 *Interest elasticity of investment expenditure*
  Higher interest rates lead to lower investment expenditure. The more responsive investment expenditures are to interest rates, the greater will be the fall in investment, i.e. the larger the crowding out effect. Thus the second important factor is the interest elasticity of investment expenditure.

In Fig. 6.1 the effect of an *expansionary fiscal policy* is shown by the rightward shift of the IS schedule from IS_0 to IS_1. Beginning in equilibrium at point A (with interest rate r_0 and output Y_0), higher government expenditure will raise output at each interest rate. If the interest rate remained unchanged at r_0, the higher government expenditure and the higher private sector (consumption) expenditure which it induces would result in output increasing from Y_0 to Y_2 (point C). However, the increase in the demand for money and the consequential increase in the interest rate leads to a reduction in investment expenditure, which will lower the increase in output from Y_2 to Y_1 (point B). The case depicted in Fig. 6.1 is therefore one of partial crowding out: there is still a net expansion (Y_0 to Y_1). Note that, in our earlier analysis of the expenditure multiplier, we did not consider the monetary sector at all, and therefore omitted to take into account the effect of the rise in interest rates. The results derived earlier correspond with an increase in income to Y_2, which would be the effect of a fiscal expansion here as well if there was no rise in the interest rate and no crowding out of private sector investment by public sector expenditure.

6.2   Monetary policy and the liquidity trap

Any actions on the part of the government that change either the quantity of money in circulation or the rate of interest are defined as *monetary policies*. In some cases, the quantity of money or the interest rate are altered directly, while in other cases they change as a consequence of other (e.g. fiscal) policy measures. In this section, we consider only the effects of changes to monetary policy, and not how it is conducted. In a later chapter, we will consider both how the quantity of money is changed and the problems faced by the central bank in attempting to restrain monetary growth.

An *expansionary monetary policy* involves an increase in the supply of money or a reduction in the interest rate. In Fig. 5.9 (p. 90) we derived the combinations of Y and r for which the money market was in equilibrium. If the government increased the quantity of money in circulation, there would be an excess supply of money at the prevailing interest rate. The extra money would only be held willingly if interest rates were lower (see Fig. 5.10, p. 90). That is, the return on interest-bearing bonds would have to be lower for investors to be willing to hold fewer bonds and more money. In fact, one of the main mechanisms by which the supply of money is increased is via a reduction in the return on government bonds, which encourage savers to sell these bonds and hold money (since the opportunity cost of holding money is lower).

However, there is a limit to how far interest rates will fall when the money supply is increased. As interest rates continue to fall, bond prices rise to unprecedentedly high levels. Investors will believe that bond prices at these levels are unsustainable in the long run and so they will be unwilling to invest in bonds, since they expect interest rates to rise again shortly and therefore for bond prices to fall. Therefore, any further increases in the money supply will be held as money balances and not invested in interest-earning bonds, so there will be no market forces to reduce interest rates further. This means that at very low interest rates, the interest rate elasticity of the demand for money becomes infinite and the demand for money function becomes horizontal. This situation is known as the *liquidity trap*: the money stock is trapped unproductively in money balances and is not circulating around the economy, generating income as it does so.

In Fig. 6.2 the effect of an expansionary monetary policy is depicted as a movement of the LM schedule from LM_0 to LM_1. The initial equilibrium is at point A (with interest rate r_0 and output Y_0). The fall in the interest rate reduces the cost of borrowing for firms. This will raise investment and consequently output. The new equilibrium is at point B, where the interest rate is lower (r_1) and output is higher (Y_1). The immediate effect of the monetary expansion is to

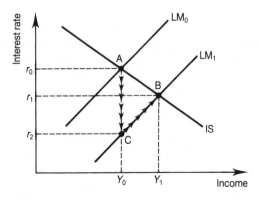

Figure 6.2   An expansionary monetary policy

lower the interest rate to r_2 at point C on the new LM_1 schedule. The money market will always clear before the goods market. The lower interest rate encourages investment. As investment rises, output will increase and raise the demand for money, which in turn would exert upward pressure on the interest rate. At point B, there is no further rise in the interest rate because the goods market is also in equilibrium. So the initial effect of the increase in the money supply is a reduction in the interest rate (which is necessary for the increase in money to be absorbed by those willing to hold the extra money in circulation), but no change in income. However, the lower interest rate encourages economic activity (especially investment) which in turn increases both income and the interest rate. Nevertheless, comparing Figs. 6.1 and 6.2, the final interest rate is lower with monetary policy than with fiscal policy.

6.3   Keynesian and monetarist macroeconomic policy recommendations

The biggest disagreements among economists occur over macroeconomic policy recommendations. Most economists would accept the desirability of the objectives of low inflation, low unemployment etc. But they disagree over how these objectives should be achieved. In particular, they disagree over the relative effectiveness of fiscal and monetary policies in achieving them. There are two main schools of economic thought concerning macroeconomic policy: the *Keynesian* school and the *monetarist* school. Keynesians are supporters of the British economist John Maynard Keynes, while monetarists are supporters of the American economist Milton Friedman.

The disagreements between these two schools centre around the sizes of three of the elasticities considered above: the income elasticity of the demand for money, the interest rate elasticity of the demand for money and the interest elasticity of investment expenditures. All these elasticities are estimated in macroeconomic models (such as the Treasury model or the London Business School model), but the different schools disagree over the structures of these models and hence over the size of the estimated elasticities. Keynesians believe that the income elasticity of money demand and the interest rate elasticity of investment are low, and that the interest rate elasticity of money demand is high. This means that the money demand curve is both flat and unresponsive to income changes, and that the investment expenditure curve is steep. Monetarists, on the other hand, believe that the income elasticity of money demand and the interest rate elasticity of investment are high, and that the interest rate elasticity of money demand is low. This means that the money demand curve is both steep and highly responsive to income changes, and that the investment expenditure curve is flat.

The extreme Keynesian and monetarist views of the macroeconomy are shown in Figs. 6.3 and 6.4, respectively. Keynesian economists believe that, since the money demand curve is flat and the investment expenditure curve is steep, the LM schedule will be flat and the IS schedule will be steep. This implies that fiscal policy (in the form of an increase in government expenditure moving the IS schedule from IS_0 to IS_1) will be effective in increasing national income from Y_0 to Y_1. In contrast, Keynesians believe that monetary policy will be ineffective, especially in the presence of a liquidity trap. Monetarist economists, on the other hand, believe that since the money demand curve is steep and the investment expenditure curve is flat, then the LM schedule will be steep and the IS schedule will be flat. This implies that monetary policy (in the form of an increase in the money supply moving the LM schedule from LM_0 to LM_1) will be effective in increasing national income from Y_0 to Y_1. In contrast, monetarists believe that fiscal policy will be ineffective, especially in the presence of crowding out.

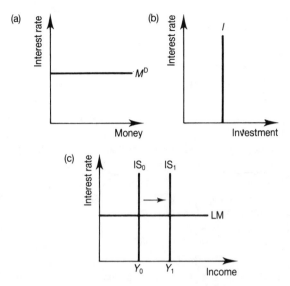

Figure 6.3 The extreme Keynesian view of the macroeconomy

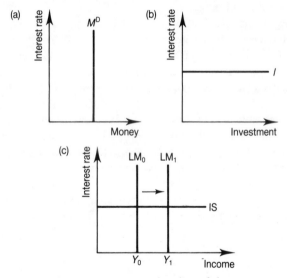

Figure 6.4 The extreme monetarist view of the macroeconomy

6.4 Financing government expenditure

The effects of monetary and fiscal policy considered above ignore the important question of how the government finances its expenditure. (In reality the government cannot rely on windfall gains.) More generally, we need to consider the *government's budget constraint*. This will then enable us to examine why economists pay considerable attention to the government's budget deficit. In the UK, the *public sector borrowing requirement* or PSBR (i.e. the government's *budget deficit* or *fiscal deficit*) is an important factor in determining asset prices, particularly the prices of government bonds.

There are, in principle, three ways of financing government expenditure (G):

1 Taxation (direct and indirect taxes, T).
2 Borrowing (selling government bonds, ΔB).
3 Monetary finance (increasing the supply of money, ΔM).

Note that direct taxes are taxes on income (income tax for individuals or corporation tax for companies), changes in the realized value of financial assets (capital gains tax) or transfers of wealth on the death of the original owner (inheritance tax); indirect taxes are taxes on various forms of consumer expenditure (e.g. value added tax, petroleum revenue tax and stamp duty). Note also that because bonds and money are asset stocks, borrowing and money finance involve *changes* in the stock of bonds and money outstanding, i.e. ΔB and ΔM, where B and M are respectively the stocks or levels of government bonds and money outstanding.

We can consider the effect of each of these methods on interest rates and output. But before doing so, a number of points should be borne in mind. We will still maintain our current assumption about spare capacity in the economy by taking prices to be fixed. Also, there is an additional source of finance in the UK at present, via the sale of state-owned assets, i.e. privatization. In the 1980s, the government received considerable sums from asset sales. We ignore this since it is at best transitory, and furthermore it could be argued that only certain types of government expenditure (namely, capital investment rather than current expenditure) should be financed from this revenue.

As a final point, Keynes argued that, on balance, government current expenditure should be financed from current taxation, while government capital expenditure should be financed by borrowing. Keynes did, however, recognize that market economies were characterized by fairly regular five year *business cycles* of boom and slump (or recession). In a boom, when tax revenues are buoyant and unemployment benefit payments are low, the government will be running a budget surplus, which can be used to pay off some of the National Debt. In a slump, on the other hand, tax revenues will be low, unemployment benefit payments will be high and the government will be running a budget deficit. Keynes argued that this *cyclical deficit* should be financed by temporary borrowing: it would be wrong to raise the income tax rate in a recession to eliminate the government's budget deficit. However, over the course of the business cycle, the government's budget should balance: it would be wrong to finance a *structural deficit* (i.e. a deficit that results from a government systematically spending more than it is prepared to raise from taxation) by either borrowing or printing money. This would not be regarded as 'sound public finance'.

6.4.1   Taxation

Suppose the government increases taxes in order to finance an increase in its own expenditure. Suppose also that the increase in tax revenue is exactly equal to the increase in expenditure, so that there is no change to the budget deficit. (The budget deficit is defined as the difference between government expenditure and taxation, i.e. the budget deficit $= G - T$; it is positive if $G > T$ and negative if $G < T$.) The higher government expenditure will increase aggregate demand (as in the fiscal policy example), whereas higher taxation will reduce the private sector's *disposable income*, which is defined as gross income *minus* income tax (i.e. $Y_d = Y - T$, where Y_d is disposable income and T is tax), and therefore its expenditure (especially consumption expenditure). The important question is whether there is any net increase in aggregate demand. In terms of our earlier decomposition of aggregate demand ($C + I + G$), G will rise and C will fall. But will G rise by more than C falls, so that there is a net increase in aggregate demand?

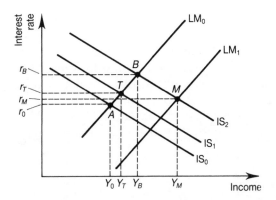

Figure 6.5 Financing government expenditure. *A*: initial position; *T*: tax finance; *B*: borrowing (debt finance); *M*: money finance

When taxes rise, the private sector will not in general reduce its expenditure by the same amount, but by less than the extra tax payments. This follows from the consumption function. When income increases, not all of it is spent, because some of it is saved. That is, the marginal propensity to consume is less than unity. It follows then that when disposable income falls (due to higher taxation), consumption will be reduced by less than the fall in income, and savings will also be reduced. (Recall that $C = a + bY$, where $b < 1$.) This implies that the reduction in consumption expenditure will be less than the increase in government expenditure.

There is therefore a net increase in aggregate demand. Higher demand must lead to higher interest rates. This is shown in Fig. 6.5 as the shift in the IS schedule from IS_0 to IS_1. The initial equilibrium is at point A and new equilibrium is at point T. There is no increase in the government's budget deficit $(G - T)$. This result (i.e. the increase in income from Y_0 to Y_T as a result of an increase in government spending fully financed by an increase in taxes) is known as the *balanced budget multiplier*.

6.4.2 Borrowing

If the government finances its extra expenditure by selling fixed-interest bonds to the private sector, there will be no direct change in the private sector's income. The private sector will invest some of its wealth in government bonds instead of in the money market or in a bank account. Therefore, there is no direct effect on private sector expenditure. The private sector's wealth holdings are merely reallocated towards government bonds and away from deposits.

To the extent that extra government borrowing raises interest rates, investment expenditure will fall. This is none other than the crowding out effect outlined earlier. Why do interest rates rise? Two explanations are usually offered. First, the higher private sector expenditure resulting from the higher government expenditure will raise the demand for money, which raises interest rates. Second, in order to borrow more funds the government has to offer lenders (in the private sector) an incentive in the form of lower prices for government bonds. This is exactly equivalent to offering higher interest rates.

In Figure 6.5 the effects on Y and r are given by the shift of the IS schedule from IS_0 to IS_2, and the new equilibrium is at point B. The expansion in output is larger than under tax finance because in this case there is no reduction in the private sector's disposable income. The interest rate is also higher, since a larger expansion in output will result in a greater shift in the demand for money. The higher interest rate also results in a greater crowding out of private sector expenditure.

In recent years, some economists have argued that government borrowing is merely equivalent to deferred taxation, since the only way in which the government can ultimately pay the future interest payments on its borrowings is through future taxation (a proposition known as *Ricardian equivalence* after the British economist David Ricardo who first invented the proposition). If this proposition holds and the private sector pays attention to the expected future tax liability, it may increase its savings and reduce its consumption expenditure now, and thereby cancel out any expansionary effects of higher government expenditure. Such an outcome requires a variety of fairly strong assumptions, and as yet this view does not appear to be accepted by most economists.

6.4.3   Monetary finance

The government may finance its extra expenditure by borrowing from the central bank. If the central bank does not finance this lending via an issue of bonds to the private sector, then the supply of money will have to increase to pay for the extra expenditure. (This is known as *monetizing* the budget deficit and sometimes as *inflation finance*.) A monetary expansion will reduce interest rates; this we showed earlier in Fig. 6.2. In the present case, the increase in the money supply finances higher government expenditure. In terms of Fig. 6.5, both the IS and LM schedules will shift to the right, to IS_2 and LM_1 respectively. The increase in government expenditure will raise interest rates and output to point B. This is identical to the case of borrowing, since the only difference here is that the lender is the central bank and not the private sector. If the central bank then increases the supply of money to pay for the additional government expenditure, the interest rate will fall and a further expansion of output takes place from point B. This additional expansion occurs through a rise in investment expenditure caused by the fall in interest rates. The final equilibrium is at M, with output increasing from Y_0 to Y_M.

To summarize: the essential consideration is what happens to the demand for funds in the economy. When the government raises its own demand for funds, interest rates will rise if this extra demand is to be met from the existing stock of finance available in the economy. With money creation, the stock of funds available is increased and therefore interest rates will fall (the possible inflationary consequences are considered in the next chapter).

6.5   The government budget constraint

The above discussion suggests that the government can finance a deficit either by borrowing (issuing bonds) or by increasing the money supply. The *government's budget constraint* is therefore given by

$$G - T = \Delta M + \Delta B \tag{6.1}$$

If the government is running a budget deficit $((G - T) > 0)$, then either $\Delta M > 0$ or $\Delta B > 0$ or both. If the government finances the deficit by borrowing (i.e. $\Delta B > 0$), then interest rates are likely to rise. With monetary finance (i.e. $\Delta M > 0$), interest rates may fall (but there may be higher inflation expected in the future, and this will have the effect of raising nominal interest rates as explained in the next chapter).

The government's budget constraint helps explain why financial markets pay close attention to the government's budget deficit and more importantly to any deficit expected in the future, since this is important for determining expectations about future interest rates. These, in turn, are critical for determining the prices of financial assets (as we saw above, the prices of financial assets such as bonds fall if interest rates rise). In a policy regime where the government is pre-committed to controlling the growth of the money supply (because it wants, in turn, to control inflation), the deficit can only be financed by borrowing. In that case, the size of the expected deficit is even more important for interest rates.

In principle, there is no necessary reason for *monetary targets* (i.e. targets restricting the growth rate of the money supply to $\Delta \bar{M}$, say, such as those that were in place in the early 1980s in the UK) to imply that there will be *fiscal deficit targets* as well. However, if the government is concerned about interest rates and crowding out, it may not want to issue too many bonds. In that case, there is a need to control the deficit as well. Of course, it could always finance higher expenditure via taxation, since this does not involve deficit finance, by definition. In the early 1980s, the government wanted to reduce taxation, especially income taxes, in order to provide incentives for its policy of promoting an *enterprise culture*. It also wanted to encourage private sector investment. Therefore, to avoid crowding out, the budget deficit had to be controlled. The government did this by sequentially reducing both the deficit and the level of the government's own spending as a proportion of national income.

In the late 1980s, and largely as a result of the Lawson boom in 1987–88, the UK government budget was in surplus (e.g. a £10 billion surplus in 1988). So the government began redeeming previously issued bonds, i.e. it began paying off the National Debt (so that $\Delta B < 0$). A PSBR (public sector borrowing requirement) was turned into a PSDR (public sector debt repayment). This does not happen very often in the UK, and by the early 1990s the government was again in deficit.

Finally, we note that although the framework outlined here suggests that borrowing raises interest rates, in the UK the relation between the PSBR and interest rates is at best a weak one. Budget deficits were falling for most of the 1980s, whereas interest rates have been fairly high. The explanations offered for this have to do with investment demand, restrictive monetary policies, and also relatively high US or German interest rates, which kept interest rates high in the rest of the world.

6.6 Summary

1 Macroeconomic policy deals with the government's attempts to use policy instruments, such as fiscal and monetary policy, to meet a set of macroeconomic policy targets, such as an inflation rate no higher than 3 per cent or an unemployment rate of less than 2.5 per cent.

2 Fiscal policy is concerned with the effects of changes in government expenditure or changes in government taxation policy. An increase in government expenditure, for example, will raise aggregate demand, both directly via the increase in the government's demand for goods and services and indirectly via the multiplier process. The IS schedule will shift to the right, and this will raise the levels of both income and interest rates. As interest rates rise, this will tend to crowd out private sector investment. In the case of complete crowding out, there will be a direct substitution of public expenditure for private expenditure, with no overall change in the overall level of aggregate demand.

3 Monetary policy is concerned with the effects of changes in the quantity of money in circulation or in the interest rate. An increase in the money supply (holding the price level fixed), for example, will shift the LM schedule to the right and this will generate an increase in aggregate demand if the extra money is spent. It may also reduce interest rates, which will induce an additional investment multiplier expansion of demand.

4 However, it is possible that in a liquidity trap (a situation where at sufficiently low interest rates, the interest rate elasticity of the demand for money becomes infinite) increases in the money supply are held idly in money balances, without either being spent or enabling a reduction in interest rates that would encourage investment expenditure.

5 Keynesian economists believe that the LM schedule is flat and that the IS schedule is steep. As a result, they believe in the efficacy of fiscal policy over monetary policy. Monetarist economists, on the other hand, believe that the LM schedule is steep and that the IS schedule is flat. As a result, they believe in the efficacy of monetary policy over fiscal policy.

6 Government expenditure can be financed in one of three ways: taxation (both direct and indirect), borrowing (typically by issuing government bonds or gilts) or by monetary finance (i.e. by printing money).

7 When the government finances its expenditure by raising income tax, there will be a government expenditure multiplier expansion of demand, but this will be partially offset by the effect of lower private sector disposable income reducing private sector consumption. The net effect on aggregate demand will be positive as long as the marginal propensity to consume is less than unity.

8 When the government finances its expenditure by borrowing, this will not change the private sector's disposable income; rather, the private sector's holdings of financial assets are reallocated towards government bonds and away from deposits or money market assets. The government may have to offer higher interest rates to attract these funds. To the extent that this raises the general level of interest rates, there will be some crowding out of private sector investment, which will tend to reduce the size of the borrowing-funded government expenditure multiplier. If Ricardian equivalence holds, so that the private sector takes into account the future tax liabilities underlying current increases in government borrowing, the private sector will reduce its current consumption in order to save for these future tax payments, in which case the increase in government expenditure is cancelled out exactly by reduced private sector consumption expenditure.

9 The final way for the government to finance its expenditure is to use monetary finance, otherwise known as printing money, monetizing the budget deficit or inflation finance. If the price level is fixed, monetary finance is the most expansionary of all forms of government finance. This is because an increase in the money supply will reduce interest rates and encourage private sector investment, which will provide an additional multiplier effect.

10 The government's budget constraint requires the government budget deficit $(G - T)$ to be financed by borrowing (ΔB) or printing money (ΔM).

Exercises

1 What is fiscal policy? What is the purpose of fiscal policy?

2 What is crowding out?

3 Use the IS/LM model to show the effect of an expansionary fiscal policy. Under what circumstances will fiscal policy be (a) effective in increasing output and (b) ineffective in increasing output?

4 Explain why Keynesian economists favour fiscal policy and why monetarist economists oppose it.

5 What is monetary policy? What is the purpose of monetary policy?

6 Use the IS/LM model to show the effect of an expansionary monetary policy. Under what circumstances will monetary policy be (a) effective in increasing output and (b) ineffective in increasing output?

7 What is the liquidity trap?

8 Explain the three main methods that the government can use to finance its expenditure.

9 Suppose the government reduces income taxes. Show in the IS/LM model the impact of the tax cut under two different monetary stances:
   (a) The government keeps interest rates constant through an accommodating monetary policy.
   (b) The money supply remains unchanged.
   Explain the difference in your results.

10 Use the IS/LM model to examine the effect of an increase in government expenditure financed by an increase in (a) taxation, (b) borrowing and (c) the money supply.

11 What is the government's budget constraint?

12 'The government's budget constraint is not a genuine constraint because it is possible to finance any level of budget deficit by printing sufficient money or by selling sufficient bonds.' Do you agree?

13 Compare and contrast the effects of fiscal policy and monetary policy in the IS/LM model.

14 Consider the following macroeconomic model:

$$Y = C + I + G$$

$$C = a + bY_d$$

$$I = I_0$$

$$G = G_0$$

$$Y_d = Y - T_0$$

where Y_d is disposable income and T_0 is tax revenue. The government raises government spending and taxation in equal amounts.
   (a) Is this a neutral (or balanced) budget for output?
   (b) If not, what is the net change in output and, hence, what is the balanced budget multiplier?

7 Macroeconomic fluctuations: output, unemployment, inflation and interest rates

The analysis of macroeconomic policies in the last chapter was conducted under the assumptions that the price level was fixed and that there was sufficient excess capacity in the economy for output (aggregate supply) to rise proportionately when aggregate demand increased. These assumptions are clearly not very realistic. The supply of output cannot keep on increasing indefinitely or at fixed prices. There are constraints on the capacity of the economy to produce output above what is called the *full employment level of output*. If not, many of the important questions relating to economic policy would either not arise, or would be uninteresting. In addition, the assumption of fixed prices ignores the ever-present problem of inflation. The questions that we now wish to ask are: 'Will output rise when demand rises?' and 'Will the rise in output be permanent or transitory?'. Depending on the answers, these questions have implications for the level of unemployment in the economy. Finally we ask: 'How are prices in the economy affected if aggregate demand is raised by government macroeconomic policies?'.

In short, we now have to introduce price effects into the analysis of macroeconomic policies, and consider whether expansionary macroeconomic policies can increase output or whether they simply lead to inflation. For this we begin with the determination of the price level via aggregate demand and aggregate supply. (*Inflation* is defined as a general increase in the prices of goods and services which raises the price level as measured by an index such as the retail price index (RPI); not all price rises are inflationary, e.g. temporary, seasonal increases in food prices are not inflationary.)

7.1 Aggregate demand

The simplest way to introduce flexible prices into the analysis is to examine the relationship between prices and aggregate demand. Suppose that, when aggregate demand is raised, say as a result of an increase in the nominal money supply, prices in the economy also rise. If prices have risen proportionately, the amount of real goods and services that can be purchased will not rise at all, and therefore a higher nominal supply of money will not necessarily result in a higher *real money supply* and therefore in higher *real aggregate demand*. Real demand or income (Y) is defined as the nominal demand or income (O) *divided by* the price level (P):

$$Y = \frac{O}{P} \tag{7.1}$$

Therefore the *rate of increase* (i.e. growth rate) of real income ($\dot{Y}$) is equal to the *rate of increase* in nominal demand or income ($\dot{O}$) *minus* the *rate of inflation* ($\dot{P}$):

$$\dot{Y} = \dot{O} - \dot{P} \tag{7.2}$$

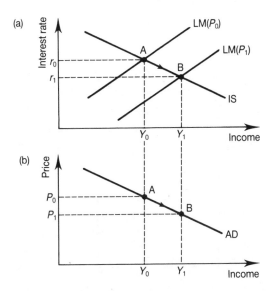

Figure 7.1 The aggregate demand schedule: (a) fall in prices with money supply fixed; (b) downward-sloping aggregate demand schedule

Real demand can only increase if the increase in prices is less than the increase in *nominal demand*, i.e. if $\dot{P} < \dot{O}$. For example, if the rate of inflation is 4 per cent and nominal demand is growing at 6.5 per cent, then the growth rate of real demand is 2.5 per cent per year.

Analogously, since people hold money for spending purposes, then, if prices rise, they will need to hold more money in order to maintain their level of purchases in real terms. This suggests that we should be concerned with the *real money supply*, the amount of goods and services that a given nominal supply of money can purchase. Similarly, we need to consider the *real demand for money*. The real supply of money is expressed as the nominal quantity of money *divided by* the price level. Thus the real money supply is M^S/P.

For a given nominal quantity of money, a lower price level will increase the real supply of money, which in turn will lead to lower interest rates, thereby increasing expenditure. In other words, *the aggregate demand schedule is downward-sloping with respect to the price level*. In contrast, the higher the price level, the lower the real money supply and the higher the interest rate. We know from our previous analysis that an increase in the interest rate reduces expenditure (especially investment expenditure).

In Fig. 7.1 this downward-sloping aggregate demand schedule is derived. Beginning with point A in Fig. 7.1(a), the money market equilibrium schedule $LM(P_0)$ is drawn for a given quantity of money and price level P_0. This corresponds with point A in Fig. 7.1(b), with income level Y_0 and price level P_0. If, for some reason, prices were to fall to P_1 and the nominal money supply remained unchanged, the real money supply would increase. In Fig. 7.1(a) this leads to a rightward shift of the LM schedule to $LM(P_1)$ yielding an interest rate of r_1 and an income level Y_1 at point B. Lower interest rates have increased investment expenditure and the equilibrium in the real sector is now given by a higher level of output at Y_1 further down the IS schedule. In Fig. 7.1(b) the new equilibrium is at B, with higher income Y_1 and a lower price level P_1. The points A and B in Fig. 7.1(b) lie on the aggregate demand schedule AD, which is drawn for a given nominal supply of money and a given fiscal policy stance.

Note that, in this derivation, the emphasis has been on the role of the interest rate in the transmission mechanism between the financial and real sectors. A change in the real money

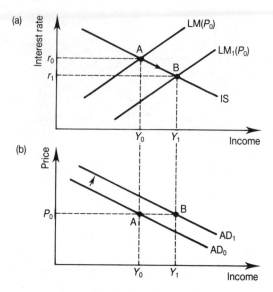

Figure 7.2 Monetary expansion and aggregate demand: (a) monetary expansion with prices fixed; (b) aggregate demand shift

supply reduces the interest rate and it is this lower interest rate that raises the demand for goods and services. It is quite possible for there to be a more direct effect on demand as a result of lower prices, via an increase in real wealth. Lower prices raise the value of real assets (i.e. M^S/P increases if P falls) and, by making people feel wealthier, tend to increase consumption, a process which is known as the *real balance effect* or *Pigou effect* (after the British economist A. G. Pigou). However, for expository purposes we will ignore the wealth effects on demand (and output).

7.1.1 Monetary policy and aggregate demand

Consider now the case of an increase in the money supply (an expansionary monetary policy) as depicted in Fig. 7.2. In this case, the LM schedule will shift to the right, lowering interest rates and raising aggregate demand (Fig. 7.2(a)). Assume that this occurs at a fixed price level (cf. Fig. 6.2, p. 99). In Fig. 7.2(b) we show this as the shift to the right of the entire aggregate demand schedule. Note the important distinction between an increase in the real money supply due to a lower price level (Fig. 7.1) and an increase in the real money supply due to an increase in the nominal quantity of money (Fig. 7.2). In the former case, we move along (down) a given aggregate demand schedule, and in the latter case, the new equilibrium is on a new aggregate demand schedule (AD_1).

7.1.2 Fiscal policy and aggregate demand

An increase in government expenditure or a reduction in taxation increases total desired expenditure. With increased government expenditure, the effect on aggregate demand is direct. With reduced taxation, the effect is indirect: lower taxes lead to higher disposable income, which will, in turn, increase aggregate demand by increasing consumption demand. In our previous analysis this was depicted as a rightward shift of the IS schedule, raising interest rates (leading to partial crowding out) and output (see Fig. 6.1, p. 98). In Fig. 7.3 we show that this is equivalent to a rightward shift of the aggregate demand schedule, since the fiscal expansion takes place at

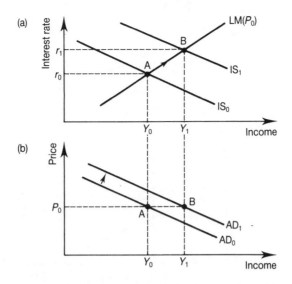

Figure 7.3 Fiscal expansion and aggregate demand: (a) fiscal expansion with prices fixed; (b) aggregate demand shift

a fixed price level (i.e. a move from A to B in Fig. 7.3(b)). The increase in demand this time is caused by the increase in government expenditure and private sector consumption expenditure (via the expenditure multiplier), although investment will have fallen as a result of the higher interest rate.

In terms of the aggregate demand diagrams (Figs. 7.2(b) and 7.3(b)) there does not seem to be any difference between monetary and fiscal expansions: both shift the AD schedule to the right. The difference is seen in the IS/LM diagrams where monetary expansions lower interest rates and fiscal expansions raise interest rates (Figs. 7.2(a) and 7.3(a)). Moreover, there is a major difference in terms of the composition of aggregate demand: investment is higher in the first case and lower in the second.

In addition to monetary and fiscal policy, other influences on demand will come from investment, consumption and the demand from foreigners (i.e. export demand). Therefore, in addition to the domestic price level we also need to consider our prices relative to foreign prices, which depend to some extent on the behaviour of exchange rates. We return to these issues in Part III on international macroeconomics.

7.2 Aggregate supply and unemployment

7.2.1 Long-run aggregate supply

Whether or not higher demand results in higher output depends on what happens to *aggregate supply*. To begin with, we note that in practice no economy can increase the supply of goods and services indefinitely. Resources required for production, such as labour and capital, are limited. For the purpose of macroeconomic demand policies, the important question is whether the economy is on this long-run output constraint or not. Further, if output can temporarily exceed this long-run capacity constraint, the important question is 'For how long?'. The most important macroeconomic policy consideration of all is whether

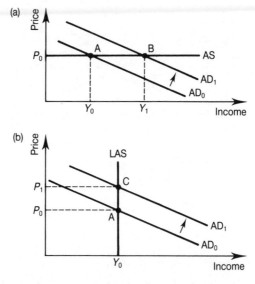

Figure 7.4 Output responses to aggregate demand shifts: (a) horizontal aggregate supply schedule (AS); (b) long-run vertical aggregate supply schedule (LAS)

a policy-induced increase in demand will generate higher output, or simply result in higher prices.

Our previous assumption of fixed prices is consistent with a horizontal aggregate supply schedule AS (see Fig. 7.4(a)). An increase in aggregate demand from AD_0 to AD_1 increases output and income from Y_0 to Y_1 at an unchanged price level P_0. The economy moves from A to B. However, if there is a long-run constraint on output given by the availability of resources in the economy, the *long-run aggregate supply schedule* (LAS) will be vertical (Fig. 7.4(b)). Any increase in aggregate demand will simply have the effect of raising the price level from P_0 to P_1, since output cannot increase above the full employment level, Y_0. The economy moves from A to C.

However, over time, through economic growth and technological developments, the capacity of the economy to produce output will increase. But this change is not a function of short-run changes in demand. We assume for simplicity that the long-run equilibrium is constant over the time horizon that we are considering.

If aggregate supply is fixed in the long run, this seems to suggest that all resources (including labour) are fully employed. However, we know that there are always some workers who are unemployed, at least temporarily. How can we explain this? To answer this, we have to consider how employment is determined in the labour market.

7.2.2 The labour market and unemployment

In the labour market, the number of workers that firms would like to employ will depend on the costs of employing them, which mainly depend on the real wage that they have to be paid. (The total cost of employing each worker is called the *unit labour cost* and this exceeds the real wage because of employers' National Insurance and pension contributions etc.—but we will concentrate our attention on the real wage paid to employees.) The *real wage* is given by the nominal wage (the money wage, W) *divided by* the price level (i.e. W/P). The higher the real wage, the fewer the workers that firms will want to employ. This is because it is profitable for firms to employ workers only up to the point where the real wage (which measures the marginal

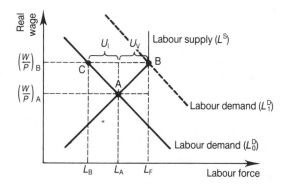

Figure 7.5 The labour market and unemployment. W: money wage; P: price level; W/P: real wage; U_I: involuntary unemployment; U_V: voluntary unemployment; L_F: full employment labour force

cost of employing additional workers) equals the value of the *marginal product* (or marginal benefit) of the last worker employed. The marginal product of each worker is the value of the additional output produced by that worker when he or she is employed in the production process.

When the other resources required in the production process (such as equipment and raw materials) are held constant, the marginal product of additional workers employed declines. Take the example of a typing pool in a busy office, and hold the number of word processing machines fixed at five, say. The sixth word processing operator (WPO) employed could still produce some output during the break times of the other WPOs, but would clearly not be as productive as the existing five WPOs. A seventh WPO would be even less productive. By the time the fifteenth WPO had been employed, everyone would be tripping over each other and total output produced might actually be lower than with fourteen WPOs; in this case, the marginal product of the fifteenth WPO is actually *negative*. No worker is going to be employed if his or her marginal product is less than his or her real wage. An increase in the real wage raises the marginal cost of labour above the marginal product of the last worker or workers employed. These workers are no longer profitable to employ and are likely to be fired.

In Fig. 7.5, the labour demand curve (L_0^D) is a downward-sloping function of the real wage (W/P): labour demand will fall as real wages rise. On the other hand, workers will be willing to work longer hours if the real wage rate per hour rises. Therefore labour supply (L^S) will rise as real wages rise. In the labour market, the intersection of labour demand (L^D) and labour supply (L^S) determines the equilibrium real wage. In Fig. 7.5 this is depicted as point A. *Labour market equilibrium* is defined as a situation where those workers who would like to work at the equilibrium real wage (i.e. $(W/P)_A$) are able to find jobs.

In other words, there is no *involuntary unemployment*. Involuntary unemployment occurs when someone who is willing to work at the equilibrium real wage is unable to find work. Those workers who are unemployed are not willing to work at the equilibrium real wage. They are still part of the *labour force*, since they are seeking work (possibly at a higher wage rate) and are therefore registered as unemployed. Thus in labour market equilibrium, we can still have some *voluntary unemployment*. In addition, there are always workers taking time off between jobs, as well as some who are retraining (this is known as *frictional unemployment*). The rate of unemployment that emerges in equilibrium is known as the *natural rate of unemployment*; it includes *voluntary unemployment* and *frictional unemployment*. If the full employment labour force is L_F, then the level of voluntary unemployment is U_V ($= L_F - L_A$) when labour demand is given by the schedule L_0^D in Fig. 7.5. The natural rate of unemployment is given by U_V/L_F.

The natural rate of unemployment is an equilibrium concept: it specifically refers to the situation in which the labour market is in equilibrium. In practice, actual unemployment may consist of both voluntary and involuntary unemployment. So the actual unemployment rate is not necessarily the natural rate. Many economists would argue that this distinction is not a useful one, since it is often difficult to ascertain in practice the proportion of actual unemployment that constitutes natural unemployment.

If the actual real wage is higher than $(W/P)_A$, then the labour market will be in disequilibrium with an excess supply of labour. Suppose that the actual real wage is $(W/P)_B$. At this real wage, L_F workers will be seeking work, but the demand for labour will be only L_B (see Fig. 7.5). The difference $(L_F - L_B)$ is the total number of unemployed. The total number unemployed can be divided between the involuntarily unemployed U_I $(=L_A - L_B)$ and the voluntarily unemployed U_V $(=L_F - L_A)$. The involuntarily unemployed are those who are willing to work at the lower equilibrium real wage $(W/P)_A$, but cannot find work because the going real wage $(W/P)_B$ is too high: in other words, their marginal products are less than the going real wage. The voluntarily unemployed are those who would willingly work at the going real wage, but not at the equilibrium real wage.

In most markets, when there is an excess supply of a good, the price will fall to clear the market. Experience shows that the labour market does not seem to behave like this; or if it does, it takes a very long time to do so. Unemployment has a habit of persisting for many years and the real wage at best responds very slowly to the excess supply of labour represented by the unemployed. A number of explanations have been put forward to explain both the nominal and real wage *rigidities* that have been observed in the labour market.

One possible explanation is *trade union bargaining*: trade unions seek to attain high real wages for their employed members, even if that means that some of their members become unemployed. Another possible explanation is called the *efficiency wage theory*. Employers wish to retain their best and most productive employees and therefore are willing to offer above-average wages to do this. Employers also recognize that they might alienate these workers and hence reduce their productivity if they attempt to reduce wages during a recession. *Implicit contract theory* provides another possible explanation. Employers often have an implicit contract with their employees to stabilize their incomes across the business cycle; so in a recession, real wages remain constant, but the least productive workers are fired. Yet another possible explanation is the *insider–outsider theory*. Existing employees (insiders) can demand high real wages because they recognize that potential replacement workers (outsiders) can be expensive to employ: they have to be trained and the insiders might refuse to cooperate with them; in addition, once they have been trained, they become insiders and will behave just like other insiders.

So it is possible to have high real wages and unemployment persisting for some time. Is there any solution to this problem? Keynesian economists believe that unemployment is due to insufficient aggregate demand. They believe that by increasing aggregate demand it is possible to shift the labour demand curve out from L_0^D to L_1^D in Fig. 7.5. The Keynesian equilibrium would be at point B with the equilibrium real wage at $(W/P)_B$, employment at the full employment level L_F and no unemployment. Keynesian-type involuntary unemployment occurs only if the actual real wage is above $(W/P)_B$.

On the other hand, supporters of the *natural rate hypothesis* (who are usually also monetarists) believe that government aggregate demand policies cannot reduce equilibrium unemployment. Rather, they believe that equilibrium unemployment can only be reduced by eliminating factors that impede the process of labour market clearing or increase incentives to supply more output. Examples of factors that tend to impede market clearing are restrictive labour practices, poor training and retraining, poor job and housing mobility, absence of child-care facilities, and minimum wage legislation. For example, the effect of minimum wage legislation is to make it difficult, if not impossible, for people with low productivities (such as unskilled, poorly educated or disabled people) to find jobs. The effect of the other factors is to reduce the marginal productivity of all workers. By removing restrictive practices, and improving training and job and housing mobility and so on, it is possible to increase the marginal productivity of workers and hence shift the labour demand curve to the right in Fig. 7.5 from L_0^D to L_1^D. Examples of disincentives to supply more output are high unemployment benefits and high taxes on earned income and interest on savings (which is sometimes known as unearned income). The effect of high unemployment benefits is to reduce the incentive of unemployed people to search for work. The effect of high income tax is to give a disincentive to provide greater labour effort or to reduce the attractiveness of savings which could be channelled into investment which, in turn, would increase the capital stock and hence the productive capacity of the economy.

7.2.3 Short-run aggregate supply and the Phillips curve

In order to explain why output fluctuates from year to year, it must be the case that, in the short run, it is possible to increase output above the long-run equilibrium level. This is achieved through additional overtime being worked by employees, and by retired people and people at home with children etc. re-entering the workforce. In other words, we are not always on the long-run aggregate supply schedule.

Suppose the government increases the supply of money in order to raise aggregate demand in the economy. Firms would experience an increase in demand for their goods, and would be willing to produce more, knowing that they can also raise their prices. They would attempt to employ more labour, both by offering more overtime work and by taking on more workers by offering higher money wages to those who are unemployed. Thus in the short run, output would rise, unemployment would fall and there would also be some increase in prices.

In Fig. 7.6, beginning at point A on the *long-run aggregate supply schedule* (LAS), the increase in demand is shown as the shift from AD_0 to AD_1. Output increases to Y_1 at point B on the *short-run aggregate supply schedule* (SAS$_0$). Prices will rise to P_1, which is necessary for firms to be willing to supply more output (recall that a competitive firm's supply curve is its upward-sloping marginal cost curve above minimum average cost). However, the rise in prices will have reduced real wages, since the money wage will not have risen proportionately in the short term. The reason for this is that additional workers taken on by the firm are producing less than existing workers. This is because the labour demand curve is downward-sloping with respect to the real wage.

However, workers will be keen to negotiate for higher money wages to restore their real wages to previous levels. As money wages rise, firms will be forced to raise prices even further,

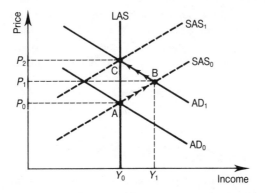

Figure 7.6 Short-run and long-run aggregate supply

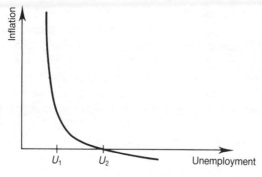

Figure 7.7   The Phillips curve

until a new equilibrium is reached at point C. In effect, the workers' demand for higher money wages will raise costs and shift the short-run aggregate supply schedule to SAS_1. The previous level of output Y_0 can now only be produced at higher money wages, since prices have risen. Furthermore, since prices have risen to the full extent of the demand increase, real wages will be the same as at point A.

Why is there no permanent rise in output? Those workers who were unemployed at point A were only willing to work for higher real wages. Firms would only be able to offer them higher real wages if productivity had increased. An increase in the nominal quantity of money does *not* induce a real change in economic conditions and does *not* change labour productivity. Therefore when the economy is at full capacity (i.e. at the full employment level of output), any increase in aggregate demand will go straight into inflation and will not induce a permanent increase in real output or a permanent reduction in employment.

In reality, this effect seems to happen at less than full capacity (i.e. at less than full employment). There appears to be a rate of unemployment which economists call the *non-accelerating inflation rate of unemployment* (or NAIRU) and attempts to use monetary or fiscal policy to reduce unemployment below this rate simply lead to accelerating inflation and no permanent reduction in unemployment. We can show this using the *Phillips curve* (named after the New Zealand economist Bill Phillips) which shows a downward-sloping relationship between inflation and unemployment: see Fig. 7.7. (The Phillips curve is an empirical relationship between inflation and unemployment: Phillips found that over long periods, inflation and unemployment pairs for the same year plot very close to this curve.) In Fig. 7.7, U_1 shows the NAIRU and U_2 shows the *zero-inflation rate of unemployment*. Any attempts to use demand management policies to reduce unemployment below U_1 will simply lead to accelerating inflation and no permanent reduction in unemployment. Above U_2, the level of unemployment is so high that wages and therefore prices start falling. In other words, there is negative inflation or *deflation*: this occurred in the 1920s and 1930s, for example. Between U_1 and U_2, it is possible for the government to use demand management policies to reduce unemployment, but inflation will be creeping up all the time. Supporters of the natural rate hypothesis argue that the NAIRU coincides with the natural rate of unemployment, but not all economists accept this. Many Keynesian economists would argue that the NAIRU is lower than the natural rate of unemployment.

7.3   Fluctuations in output

We are now in a position to analyse the effects of *economic disturbances* (or *shocks*) on output and prices. There are a variety of shocks that can occur, both on the demand side and the supply side. For instance, there might be:

1 Unexpected shocks to spending: for example, the amount of investment undertaken by businesses at any given interest rate might rise as a result of increased confidence about future business prospects.
2 Unexpected shocks in the money market: for example, the amount of money demanded at any given interest rate might fall as a result of a financial innovation, such as the introduction of interest-bearing chequing accounts.

Spending or money market shocks will in turn shift the aggregate demand schedule. At first, real output will rise or fall. Later as price adjustment occurs, real output will return to equilibrium and the price level will move to a permanently different level if the shock was *permanent* or back to its original level if the shock was *transitory*.

Prices may change unexpectedly as well. When that occurs, real output will change at first. Then price adjustments will return the economy to its original equilibrium. However, neither the price level nor real output will change in the long run as a result of price shocks.

7.3.1 Supply shocks

Consider the rise in the price of oil (as for example occurred in 1973/4 and 1978/9). The rise in the oil price raises the costs of production for firms. These costs have to be passed on to consumers in the form of higher prices. The short-run aggregate supply curve will move to the left from SAS_0 to SAS_1 as in Fig. 7.8. The new short-run equilibrium will be at point B, where output is lower (Y_1) and prices are higher (P_1) than at the original point A (Y_0 and P_0 respectively). Aggregate demand falls as higher prices reduce the real money supply and raise interest rates. Lower output implies lower employment.

In the long run, higher unemployment would tend to reduce money wages, thereby reducing real wages even further. If this happens, the economy could move back to Y_0. However, since the price of oil has risen permanently, firms would try to economize by using less oil, and this could reduce the productivity of labour, in turn reducing the demand for labour and employment. Potential output (LAS) could be reduced permanently. LAS_0 could shift to LAS_1 and potential output could be reduced from Y_0 to Y_2 and the price level could be permanently higher at P_2: the long-run equilibrium would be at a point such as C. Note that the cause of the permanent reduction in output is the increase in the price of oil relative to the price of other goods. The

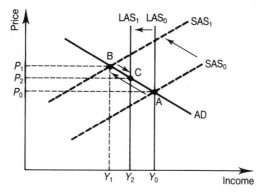

Figure 7.8 Supply shocks

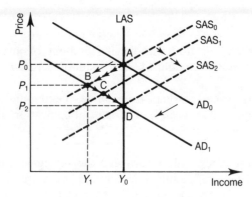

Figure 7.9   Demand shocks

only way firms could supply the previous level of output at the old price (P_0) would be if they were able to reduce other input costs proportionately. Supply shocks in general require permanent reductions in real wages for output to be restored to its potential level.

7.3.2   Demand shocks

A good example of a demand shock would be an unanticipated monetary contraction, which might be part of a wider disinflationary policy being pursued by the government. In the 1980s, the UK government pursued a restrictive monetary policy to reduce inflation and also to reduce the growth of demand generally in an attempt to reduce the trade deficit. The policy was one of successive reductions in the growth of the money supply, and was known as the *medium term financial strategy*. The aim was to reduce the rate of inflation rather than the price level. In order to reduce the price level, it is necessary to reduce the level of the money supply. However, the essential mechanisms are the same, so we shall consider it in terms of a reduction in the level of the money supply (which is easier to analyse in our graphical framework).

In Fig. 7.9 we begin with the economy initially in equilibrium at point A. The policy change is announced and the money supply is reduced at the same time. This leads to a reduction in aggregate demand. In the short run, firms will not be able to reduce prices (since they will have contracted workers and suppliers at fixed wages and prices). So, given the reduced level of demand, they are forced to reduce output to Y_1 along SAS_0. Money wages will not have changed, whereas prices have fallen to P_1, as firms are forced to reduce prices to prevent unwanted inventories of finished goods building up in the face of lower demand; firms may be making losses at this point. With money wages unchanged, real wages have risen. Firms respond by cutting costs and reducing employment. Involuntary unemployment will increase. The pressure of unemployment will tend to reduce money wages gradually, thereby moving the short-run aggregate supply curve to the right, to SAS_1. Firms begin to take on more workers. Also, falling prices increase the real money supply and therefore raise demand. If wages are sufficiently flexible downwards, full equilibrium is restored at Y_0, when money wages have fallen to a level where firms are operating on SAS_2 at point D and prices have fallen to P_2.

7.3.3   Macroeconomic policy responses

Another important area of disagreement among macroeconomists is the speed with which prices adjust and equilibrium is restored to the long-run level of output. Some economists (monetarists, and a recent variant known as *new classical economists* (whose intellectual leader is the American economist Robert E. Lucas), so named after a group of pre-Keynesian economists known as classical economists) argue that market adjustment is fairly rapid, so that there is no role for government demand management policies. Others (Keynesians) view the price mechanism as working very slowly, so that deviations of actual output away from potential or full employment output can persist for considerable time periods. Keynesians believe that the most important determinant of the level of output is the level of real or effective aggregate demand. They believe that recessions (when actual output is less than potential output and there is high unemployment) are largely caused by insufficient aggregate demand. These two groups (or schools) disagree essentially about the efficiency of the price mechanism. The following summarizes their viewpoints.

A: Models with flexible prices (monetarists, new classical economists)

1 The price level fluctuates immediately to keep the aggregate demand for output equal to potential output. The economy is therefore always on the vertical long-run aggregate supply schedule. Involuntary unemployment of labour and other resources does not occur; any unemployment is voluntary.
2 Potential or full employment output is determined by the capital shock and by the number of workers available, neither of which shifts very much from year to year.
3 The aggregate demand schedule determines only the price level.

B: Models with slowly adjusting or sticky prices (Keynesian economists)

1 Actual output does not necessarily equal potential output. The price level is fixed or slowly adjusting (economists call this *sticky prices*) and output is equal to aggregate demand at that price.
2 When demand shifts, actual output shifts in the same direction (known as the *principle of effective demand*).
3 The model with sticky prices is more successful in explaining short-run fluctuations in output than the model with flexible prices, which assumes instantaneous market clearing.

Keynesian economists therefore believe that there is a role for *macroeconomic demand management* (or *stabilization*) *policies* (especially fiscal policies) to increase or stabilize aggregate demand whenever actual output falls short of potential output, as a result of an economic shock, say. This is because they believe in the expenditure multiplier, which after all was a Keynesian invention; the multiplier only works if prices are fixed or slowly adjusting. Indeed, Keynesians believe that if actual output is less than potential output, this is because aggregate demand is too low. In contrast, monetarists and new classical economists believe that the economic system is very efficient in re-establishing equilibrium once a shock has put the system out of equilibrium. They believe that macroeconomic demand policies merely add noise to the process of re-establishing equilibrium, i.e. to the 'natural' processes of market clearing. In other words, they believe that there is no role for macroeconomic stabilization policies. Instead, they favour *microeconomic supply-side policies* which either reduce impediments to market clearing (e.g. removing minimum wage legislation or restrictive labour practices) or increase incentives to supply more output and investment (e.g. reducing taxes on incomes and savings). They argue that in the long run, output can only be increased if the long-run aggregate supply schedule shifts to the right or that the non-accelerating inflation rate of unemployment is reduced.

7.4 Inflation

In the above analysis, increases in aggregate demand through monetary expansions led to higher price levels; money increases did not change output in the long run. Increases in the money supply are often identified as an important cause of inflation. We briefly outline here the *quantity theory of money*, which is the basic theory underpinning both monetarism and the monetarist explanation of inflation.

Consider first the *equation of exchange* (also called the *quantity equation*), which is an identity:

$$M^S V \equiv PT \tag{7.3}$$

where
M^S = nominal supply of money.
V = velocity of circulation of money (the number of times each £1 circulates through the economy in one year).
P = aggregate price level.
T = total number of transactions taking place in the economy in any given time period (say, one year).

To see why this is an identity (i.e. why it must always hold), think of the right-hand side as analogous to a firm's sales revenue (the number of transactions (units sold) *times* the price of each unit). For the economy as a whole, PT is simply nominal national income, i.e. the total number of units of output produced *times* the average price at which each unit is sold (or O). All of these sales have to be paid for with money, and since one unit of currency can finance more than its own value in terms of sales, the total sales revenue (nominal income) must be equal to the total money stock *times* the number of times money changes hands. Every time a £1 coin changes hands, £1 of expenditure and £1 of nominal income are simultaneously created. Therefore, the total number of pounds in the economy *times* the number of times each pound changes hands (which equals V, the velocity of circulation of money) must by definition equal the economy's total income.

The number of transactions (T) is related to the level of real income Y. Higher real income would lead to more transactions. Thus for simplicity we can replace T with Y. Therefore we can write $M^S V = PY$. In addition, we assume that in the long run Y (real income) grows at a constant rate. Suppose we also assume that V is approximately constant from year to year. Then it is clear that the only way P can rise is as a result of a rise in M^S. Similarly, persistent increases in P (i.e. *inflation*) can only be caused by persistent increases in the money supply. All this depends crucially on the assumption of a constant V. Therefore we have to investigate what a constant V means.

We have defined V as the speed or velocity of circulation. In order to explain under what circumstances this will be constant, we use the equation of exchange to derive a demand for money function, and then show that a constant velocity is exactly equivalent to a constant (i.e. unchanging) demand for money function. In equilibrium, the demand for money is equal to the supply of money. Dividing both sides of the equation by PV and assuming $M^S = M^D$ implies

$$\frac{M^D}{P} = \frac{Y}{V} \tag{7.4}$$

i.e. the real demand for money is a positive function of (i.e. positively related to) income and a negative function of (i.e. negatively or inversely related to) velocity.

Suppose the quantity of money (M^S) is held fixed. Under what conditions could prices rise?

Clearly the only way would be via a fall in Y or a rise in V. In other words, with a fixed nominal money supply, the real quantity of money will change if prices change, and from the above equation, it should be clear that something on the right-hand side will have to change as well. A rise in V is just another way of saying a fall in the demand for money. If money is changing hands faster, then on average people must be holding less. Conversely, a fall in velocity implies a rise in the demand for money. If, on average, people are holding less money, then on average they must be spending more, which implies rising prices. It is for this reason that a stable demand for money is a necessary precondition to show that inflation is caused *only* by increases in the supply of money.

If the velocity of circulation is stable, then its rate of change over time (denoted $\dot{V}$) will be zero. The quantity equation can be expressed in terms of rates of change over time as follows:

$$\dot{M}^S + \dot{V} = \dot{P} + \dot{Y} \tag{7.5}$$

where $\dot{M}^S$ is the rate of change of the money stock etc. (e.g. $\dot{M}^S = 10$ per cent growth per annum). If we impose $\dot{V} = 0$ (i.e. stable velocity) and rearrange this equation, we get:

$$\dot{P} = \dot{M}^S - \dot{Y} \tag{7.6}$$

which says that the rate of inflation or the rate of change of the price level ($\dot{P}$) is equal to the rate of growth of the nominal supply ($\dot{M}^S$) *minus* the rate of growth in real output ($\dot{Y}$). So if $\dot{M}^S = 10$ per cent and $\dot{Y} = 2$ per cent, then the rate of inflation would be 8 per cent. Therefore any monetary expansion in excess of the long-run growth in real output is likely to lead to inflation. This equation could also be used for calculating the expected rate of inflation in terms of the expected or announced growth in nominal money and the expected real growth rate in the economy.

The velocity of circulation of money has been the subject of extensive research among economists, and it is not yet settled as to whether it can be taken to be stable. The problem is that in the short run, it clearly is not stable. It is also affected by a variety of structural changes in the payments mechanism, by de-regulation in financial markets and by increased competition between financial institutions (e.g. in the late 1980s there was increased competition between banks and building societies in the UK). These changes are known as *financial innovations*. Rapid financial innovation leads to many close substitutes for cash (which are generally interest-bearing, unlike cash, such as high-interest money market deposit accounts) and these close substitutes tend to reduce the velocity of circulation of cash.

In the 1980s in the UK, rapid financial innovation did indeed reduce the velocity of circulation of money. Other near-money assets, particularly those that arose out of the increasing competition between banks and building societies, provided good substitutes for the transactions motive of money and this reduced the speed with which ordinary money circulated around the economy. Where velocity is non-constant, the inflation rate is determined by the following equation:

$$\dot{P} = \dot{M}^S - \dot{Y} + \dot{V} \tag{7.7}$$

With velocity falling ($\dot{V} < 0$), the inflation rate will be lower than that predicted from difference between the growth rate in the nominal money supply and the long-run growth rate in real output. During the 1980s, the nominal money supply grew by an average 14.7 per cent per year and the average annual growth rate in real output was 2.24 per cent. However, the average annual inflation rate was 7 per cent, implying that velocity was decreasing at an average rate of 5.5 per cent per year during the decade.

7.5   Inflation and interest rates

Finally in this chapter, we examine the relationship between inflation and the level of interest rates. Consider an investor's decision to lend £100 for one year (i.e. invest in a one-year bond) at a 5 per cent rate of interest per annum (i.e. the bond pays a fixed annual coupon of £5) when there is no inflation. This then represents the real return from forgoing access to £100 for the length of the loan. That is to say, at the end of the period, the investor will have £105, and will be better off by £5 than at the time he or she made the loan. In other words, he or she has £5 more real purchasing power at the end of the year than at the beginning of the year. This 5 per cent return is known as the *real interest rate*. Throughout our analysis so far, it is the real rate of interest we have been considering, because we have assumed that prices are fixed and therefore that there is no inflation.

Suppose now that there is inflation and that it is expected to be 10 per cent over the length of the investment period. The investor would not now be willing to lend at 5 per cent since the return of £5 (on £100) would not compensate for the rise in prices, i.e. the *loss of purchasing power*. In order to maintain a 5 per cent real return, the investor would want to charge 5 per cent *plus* 10 per cent to compensate for inflation, i.e. 15 per cent. Thus inflation would lead to a rise in the *nominal interest rate* if the investor is concerned to earn a constant real rate of interest of 5 per cent. The borrower will in principle be willing to pay the higher rate, since inflation will also increase the nominal return on the capital investment that is being financed with the loan or bond.

The relation between expected inflation and the nominal rate of interest is known as the *Fisher equation* (after the American economist Irving Fisher). As an approximation, the Fisher equation is:

$$r = \rho + \dot{P} \tag{7.8}$$

where

r = nominal rate of interest.
ρ = real rate of interest.
$\dot{P}$ = expected rate of inflation.

In words, the Fisher equation states that the nominal interest rate that borrowers pay and lenders receive will exceed the real interest rate by the *expected rate of inflation*. When the expected inflation rate is zero, $r = \rho$ and the nominal and real interest rates are the same.

The opportunity cost of holding money is therefore equal to the nominal rate of interest. This follows because if an individual holds cash for one year, the expected opportunity cost to him or her of doing this is the real interest ρ forgone by not investing the cash in the bond *plus* the reduced purchasing power that he or she suffers by not using the cash to buy goods that are expected to rise in price by the expected inflation rate ($\dot{P}$). If the real rate of interest is 2 per cent per annum and the expected inflation rate is 8 per cent per annum, then the opportunity cost of holding cash is 10 per cent of the value of the cash for each year that the cash is held. In other words, the opportunity cost of holding cash is the nominal interest rate forgone by holding a non-interest bearing nominal asset instead of investing in an interest-earning bond. (It is *not* equal to the real interest rate.) We can compare this with the opportunity cost of holding a non-interest-bearing real asset, such as an antique. Suppose that the antique does not generate an income but that its value increases in line with the inflation rate, $\dot{P}$. Now the opportunity cost of holding the antique is the *real interest rate* of 2 per cent forgone by not investing in the interest-earning bond. This is because the investor in the antique gets compensated for the inflation rate of 8 per cent, but not for the real interest earned on the bond.

TABLE 7.1   Inflation and opportunity costs

Asset	Value at beginning of year (£)	Value at end of year (£)	Rate of return	Opportunity cost
Bond	100	110	$r_B = \rho + \dot{P} = 10\%$	$r_B - r_B = 0\%$
Antique	100	108	$r_A = \dot{P} = 8\%$	$r_B - \rho = 2\%$
Money	100	100	$r = 0\%$	$r_B - r = \rho + \dot{P} = 10\%$

This is illustrated in Table 7.1. (Note that the opportunity cost is always measured against the return on the highest-yielding asset available, in this case the bond.)

7.6   Summary

1 In earlier chapters, we assumed that the price level was fixed. This was justified by also assuming that there was sufficient spare capacity in the economy that any increases in demand could be satisfied without putting pressure on prices. But in reality, there are constraints on the capacity of the economy to produce output above the full employment level of output. Attempts to do so will lead to inflation.

2 Inflation is defined as a general increase in the price of goods and services which raises the price level, as measured by, say, the retail price index.

3 Real aggregate demand in the economy is defined as nominal aggregate demand divided by the price level. Real demand will only increase if the increase in nominal demand exceeds the inflation rate. The aggregate demand schedule is downward-sloping with respect to the price level. This is because a lower price level increases the real value of the money supply, which reduces the interest rate. This in turn increases investment, which is one of the main components of aggregate demand.

4 An expansionary monetary policy has the effect of shifting both the LM and aggregate demand schedules to the right and lowering interest rates. An expansionary fiscal policy has the effect of shifting both the IS and aggregate demand schedules to the right and raising interest rates.

5 The most important question relating to macroeconomic policy is whether a policy-induced increase in aggregate demand will result in higher output or simply result in higher prices. The answer depends on the slope of the aggregate supply schedule. If the aggregate supply schedule is horizontal, an increase in aggregate demand will lead to an equivalent increase in output and income with no change in the price level. This is equivalent to the assumption that there is sufficient spare capacity to satisfy the increase in demand at existing prices, and in this case we will get the full multiplier effect operating. However, there will generally be a long-run constraint on output given by the availability of resources in the economy. In this case, the long-run aggregate supply schedule will be vertical at the level of full employment output.

6 Over time, as a result of economic growth and technological progress, the capacity of the economy to produce output will increase and the long-run aggregate supply schedule will shift to the right. However, this change will not be a consequence of short-run changes in aggregate demand.

7   In the labour market, the demand for labour by firms is a downward-sloping function of the real wage (the nominal wage divided by the price level). The demand for labour increases as the real wage falls. This is because firms will only be willing to employ additional workers if the real wage exceeds their marginal product, that is, the value of their contribution to the production process, and the marginal product declines as more workers are added to the production process (and if there is no corresponding increase in capital equipment etc. to support their efforts). The supply of labour, on the other hand, will increase as the real wage increases, since workers will be willing to work longer the higher the real wage. Labour market equilibrium is defined as a situation where those workers who would like to work at the equilibrium real wage (where the demand for and supply of labour intersect) are able to find jobs.

8   Even in labour market equilibrium, there will be some workers who are unemployed. There will be some workers who are not willing to work at the equilibrium real wage but would be willing to work at a higher real wage and are registered as unemployed: this is called voluntary unemployment. Also there will be workers taking time off between jobs: this is called frictional unemployment. The unemployment that emerges in labour market equilibrium is called natural unemployment. But there is no involuntary unemployment, so that there is no one willing to work at the equilibrium real wage who is unable to find work.

9   If the actual real wage is higher than the equilibrium real wage, then total unemployment includes both voluntary and involuntary unemployment. Unemployment levels above the natural level can persist for many years as a result of labour market rigidities, trade union bargaining, efficiency wage deals, implicit contracts or insider–outsider considerations.

10 Keynesians believe that unemployment results from insufficient aggregate demand and argue that aggregate demand should be increased if unemployment is to be reduced. Supporters of the natural rate hypothesis (which states that unemployment cannot be reduced below the natural rate by boosting aggregate demand without causing accelerating inflation) argue that the best way to reduce unemployment is to reduce the factors which inhibit labour market clearing or which reduce the incentive to provide greater labour effort or capital to the productive process.

11 Although the long-run aggregate supply schedule may be vertical, the short-run aggregate supply schedule is positively sloping. This is because firms would be willing to supply more output in the short run if they could sell the additional output at higher prices. The higher prices would have the effect of initially reducing real wages and this would enable firms to take on extra workers to produce the extra output. However, the higher prices would lead workers to demand higher money wages. This raises costs to firms and causes the short-run aggregate supply schedule to shift upwards. Real wages return to their original level and there is no long-run increase in output above the full employment level of output.

12 The Phillips curve shows a downward-sloping relationship between inflation and unemployment. For unemployment rates above the zero-inflation rate of unemployment, prices will be falling (i.e. inflation will be negative). For unemployment rates below the non-accelerating inflation rate of unemployment (or NAIRU), inflation will be accelerating.

13 Shocks to aggregate supply (e.g. oil price increases) or aggregate demand (e.g. unanticipated monetary contractions) will change the level of output or the price level. The output and price levels will be sustained at their new levels if the shock is permanent, or return to their original levels if the shock is transitory.

14 Monetarists (and their successors, new classical economists) believe that markets clear very rapidly, i.e. prices adjust very quickly to restore equilibrium. They believe that the economy is always at or near full capacity output, with unemployment at its natural level and no involuntary unemployment. They also believe that the economy will move rapidly back to

equilibrium following an economic disturbance or shock. The only government policies that they support are microeconomic supply-side policies which reduce the impediments to market clearing or which increase incentives to supply more output. Keynesians, on the other hand, believe that some markets, particularly the labour market, do not clear very rapidly. This is because prices are sticky or slowly adjusting. As a result actual output, which is determined by aggregate demand, can be less than potential output. In particular, in a recession aggregate demand is low and unemployment is high. Keynesians therefore prefer macroeconomic demand management or stabilization policies (especially fiscal policies) to keep the level of aggregate demand close to potential output.

15 The simplest theory explaining inflation is the quantity theory of money. This states that the inflation rate equals the excess growth rate of the money stock over the real growth rate of the economy, plus the rate of change of the velocity of circulation of money. If velocity is constant, inflation will result whenever the money stock increases at a greater rate than the rate at which the economy grows.

16 There is also a relationship between inflation and nominal interest rates. Via the Fisher equation, the nominal interest rate equals the real rate of interest plus the expected inflation rate. This means that the opportunity cost of holding money is the nominal interest rate: people who hold non-interest-bearing cash deposits not only forgo the real return on interest-bearing assets, but they also lose purchasing power as a result of inflation.

Exercises

1 What is the full employment level of output?

2 What is the difference between nominal and real aggregate demand?

3 Why does the aggregate demand schedule slope downwards with respect to the price level?

4 The economy is at full employment. Now the government wants to change the composition of demand towards investment and away from consumption, without, however, raising aggregate demand above the full employment level. What is the required policy mix? Use the IS/LM model to show your policy proposal.

5 Since expansionary monetary and fiscal policies both shift the aggregate demand schedule to the right, does it really matter which of the two policies is used?

6 What is the marginal product of labour and why does it decline as more labour is applied to the production process?

7 Explain how equilibrium in the labour market is determined. How is it possible to have unemployment at the equilibrium real wage?

8 What is the natural rate hypothesis? How do supporters of this hypothesis believe that unemployment can be reduced?

9 Discuss some of the explanations for unemployment that have been put forward.

10 Explain how it is possible for the aggregate supply schedule to be (a) upward-sloping in the short run, and (b) vertical in the long run (both with respect to the price level).

11 What is the Phillips curve?

12 What are the sources of macroeconomic shocks? Provide two examples of (a) demand-side shocks and (b) supply-side shocks, and examine their possible effects on output and the price level.

13 Examine the different types of policy responses to macroeconomic shocks favoured by (a) Keynesian economists and (b) monetarists.

14 What is the quantity equation? Analyse the role of the quantity equation in explaining the causes of inflation.

15 What is the Fisher equation?
16 Explain why the opportunity cost of holding money balances is equal to the nominal rate of interest.
17 If nominal income grows at 8 per cent per annum, the money supply grows at 12 per cent per annum and prices grow at 6 per cent per annum, calculate (a) the growth rate in real income, (b) the growth rate in the real money supply and (c) the rate of change in the velocity of circulation of money.

Business application: Unemployment—searching for jobs

There has been much discussion about the possible causes of, and increases in, unemployment. Factors such as structural changes to the economy, the recession, attempts to increase productivity and competitiveness, technological advances, pay rises and labour market imperfections, such as relatively high unemployment benefits, union power and the existence of minimum wages, have all been offered as explanations. In addition, there is the debate about the extent to which unemployment is voluntary or involuntary.

Assuming that firms are trying to take on labour and that workers are looking for jobs, both parties would benefit if they knew the most commonly used sources of employment information. Firms would find the type of worker they wanted more quickly and search unemployment would be reduced. Rigidities, or imperfections, in the labour market would therefore be lessened. Better information would reduce unemployment without inducing any upward pressure on wages, since those looking for work would be willing to do so at the going real wage rate.

Table 7.2 draws from the preliminary results of the 1989 Labour Force Survey published in the *Employment Gazette*, April 1990. It shows that, overall, jobcentres and newspapers are by far the most popular sources of employment information. However, the jobcentre is more frequently used by men (37 per cent), with newspapers more commonly used by women (some 40 per cent). The preference for newspapers is most obvious with married women, 45 per cent of whom favour this source. Although less important, the survey also shows that men are more likely to apply direct or to ask friends, colleagues etc. The response of women to these methods does not depend on marital status.

The ability to find the type of worker required will depend on where the information is placed. Part-time work may be more attractive to married women than to other potential workers, and if firms want this type of employee, newspaper advertising will be most effective, particularly since visiting a jobcentre may be difficult. However, non-married women, who probably do not have family commitments, do not distinguish between jobcentres and newspapers in their search for employment. In contrast, men prefer the jobcentre, possibly because payment of unemployment benefit depends upon actively seeking work and the Department of Social Security is less likely to be convinced by a claim that reading a newspaper constitutes a serious attempt to find work.

TABLE 7.2   Methods of looking for work by the unemployed (%, 1989)

Main method of looking for work	All	Men	Women	Married women	Non-married women
Jobcentre	32	37	25	18	32
Newspapers	31	25	40	45	32
Direct application	8	9	7	7	7
Ask friends etc.	10	11	7	7	7
Answering advertisements	11	10	12	14	10

If firms are seeking unskilled or semi-skilled workers, jobcentres may be the most effective source, given that most of the unemployed are likely to belong to these categories. In addition, advertising in local papers, or possibly even the tabloid newspapers, may be worthwhile. The use of broadsheet newspapers is more suitable if the objective is to attract graduates, professionals or senior management, as also is the use of professional publications. Local papers, particularly if they have large readerships, may also be useful for these categories as well as being effective in finding skilled workers.

The pattern of employment search has changed during the 1980s. Between 1984 and 1989, the use of newspapers as the main source of employment information rose from 23 per cent to 31 per cent, whereas the preference for jobcentres fell from 37 per cent to 32 per cent. Answering advertisements, direct application and asking friends etc. have also become less popular, which suggests that firms are having to be more positive in their quest for labour.

Thus firms will have more success in finding the desired type of labour—male, female, skilled, unskilled, full-time, part-time—if they use the most effective sources, and this requires knowing where the unemployed look for job information.

8 Measuring economic performance: national income accounting

In this chapter, we look at the different measures of the economic activity that takes place during some given time period, typically one year. This procedure is known as *national income accounting*. The most frequently used measure of economic activity is the level of total income per year. In order to obtain some measure of income, we look at the activities of the various sectors of the economy. In Chapter 5 we found that the main elements of aggregate demand are consumption (by the private sector households), investment (by private sector firms), government expenditure (public sector consumption and investment) and net exports (foreign sector).

8.1 The circular flow of income

Consider first a very simple framework, where there is no government and no foreign sector (later we will introduce both these sectors). In this simple case we can analyse an economy which comprises only *households* and *firms*. Households supply all the *factors of production* (labour, capital, buildings, raw materials etc.) to firms which produce goods and services. This output is sold to households who are the only consumers of all the goods and services produced. In return for supplying factors of production (or factor services), households receive factor incomes (wages, salaries, rents, profits etc.). All this income is then spent on goods and services which households purchase from firms. In this simple framework we have made one crucial assumption, which is that firms are owned by households, i.e. households own all the shares (equity) in the firms (foreign-owned firms will be considered later). Figure 8.1 summarizes the two main types of flow between households and firms: first flows of goods and services, and second flows involving payments, i.e. expenditure on goods and services and earnings received by all the factors of production.

From Fig. 8.1 there are three different ways of measuring total income:

1 Total value of goods and services produced.
2 Total factor earnings (income from employment + income from self-employment + profit from companies + interest income + rental income).
3 Total expenditure.

Under the assumptions implicit in this simple framework all three ways should yield the same answer. This is because:

1 First, since all income is spent, factor incomes = total expenditure.
2 Second, since all output is sold, total expenditure = total output.
3 Third, since households own all firms and all factors of production, total output = factor incomes.

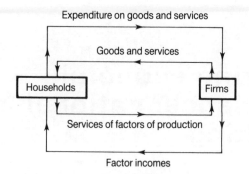

Figure 8.1   Circular flow of income

This simple framework outlines the basic principles involved in *national income accounting*. (It also explains why, in the last three chapters, we have used the terms *national income, output* and *expenditure* interchangeably.) In practice, there are many additional complications which need to be incorporated. For example, we need to account for both a government sector and a foreign sector. In addition there are also the effects of price changes and depreciation of capital (a factor of production) as a result of producing output. In what follows we incorporate all these features.

8.2   Measuring national income

The output produced by domestic factors of production is known as the *gross domestic product* (GDP). This is the output produced by those factors of production that are based in the domestic economy. The output of firms that are foreign-owned is part of GDP to the extent that the output is produced domestically. The profits accruing to foreign firms will be treated as income earned by foreigners from investments in the UK economy (i.e. by shareholders residing in other countries). Similarly, income generated from foreign assets owned by UK residents will also need to be incorporated. This is done later.

8.2.1   Value-added measures of income

In practice, not all of the output produced by firms is sold directly to households. Some firms produce intermediate goods which become the inputs used by other firms. Therefore if we added up all the output of all firms we would be double counting to some extent, since the output of firms producing intermediate goods would be counted once as their own final output and a second time as part of the value of output produced by other firms.

For this reason, national income accounting uses the concept of *value added*. For each firm we measure its output as:

$$\text{Total value of output} - \text{Total value of inputs} = \text{Value added} \qquad (8.1)$$

GDP is then equal to the sum of the value added of all firms in the economy.

8.2.2   Investment and saving

Also in practice, households do not spend all of their factor incomes on the output produced by firms. Instead they *save* some of their income. The question then arises: what happens to the total value of output produced by firms? They only receive some of the factor incomes via consumption expenditure. Total expenditure, however, must still equal total output. The extra expenditure is *investment*. Firms have to spend money on capital goods (plant and equipment produced by other firms) since this is necessary for the production of consumer goods. For this reason, total factor incomes will be the sum of the output of consumer goods and the output of capital goods. Writing this out in terms of factor earnings and total expenditure, we have the following:

$$\text{Factor earnings} = \text{Consumption } (C) + \text{Savings } (S) \tag{8.2}$$

$$\text{Total expenditure} = \text{Consumption } (C) + \text{Investment } (I) \tag{8.3}$$

It follows from the above that *savings* equals *investment*, i.e. $S = I$. Note that this is an accounting identity. Recall from Chapter 5 that we defined macroeconomic equilibrium as a situation where *desired savings* are equal to *desired investment*. By definition, *actual savings* always equals *actual investment*, but only in equilibrium will desired savings equal desired investment. Out of equilibrium, desired savings will not equal desired investment, and output (and income) will adjust until actual and desired savings equal actual and desired investment.

8.2.3   Inventories

If firms do not manage to sell all of their output during the year, they will be holding stocks (i.e. *inventories*) which for the purpose of national income accounting are treated as additions to their capital stock. That is, inventories are regarded as capital expenditure or investment. The reason for this is that there would otherwise be no record of this output, since it is not being passed on to any household or firm. To the extent that aggregate demand is less than expected, the increase in inventories will be unplanned and involuntary, i.e. firms will experience an unplanned and involuntary increase in investment. In this way, actual investment can exceed desired investment. When, in subsequent periods, the goods are sold and the stocks are run down, this is treated as negative investment, since the goods were not produced in that period but instead sold from inventories. Firms will run down their inventories until actual investment again equals desired investment.

It is clear from this that it must be the case that actual savings always equals actual investment. This is because actual investment is defined to equal planned investment in plant and equipment *plus* actual inventory accumulation of unsold goods. Savings is defined as that part of income, and hence output, not consumed:

$$\text{Savings} = \text{Output} - \text{Consumption} \tag{8.4}$$

Investment (including inventory accumulation) is defined as that part of expenditure, and hence output, not equal to consumption expenditure:

$$\text{Investment} = \text{Output} - \text{Consumption} \tag{8.5}$$

Hence, by definition, savings equals investment.

We can illustrate this with a simple example. Suppose that output is 100, consumption is 80 and planned investment is 15. Clearly savings is 20 and inventory accumulation 5. Planned investment plus inventory accumulation is 20, which equals savings as required. Suppose instead that planned investment was 25 instead of 15. Total demand during the year at 105 exceeds output by 5. The additional demand is satisfied from drawing down inventories by 5. But again planned investment (25) plus net inventory accumulation (-5) equals savings, as required.

But these do not represent equilibrium positions. In the first case, aggregate supply is 100 but aggregate demand is only 95. Equilibrium will be established by a multiplier contraction of income and output. If we assume a marginal propensity to consume of 0.8, then income and output will fall to 75, resulting in equilibrium consumption of 60, actual and planned savings of 15, actual and planned investment of 15, and inventory accumulation of zero. In the second case, aggregate supply is 100 and aggregate demand is 105. Equilibrium will be established by a multiplier expansion of income and output. If we again assume a marginal propensity to consume of 0.8, then income and output will rise to 125, resulting in equilibrium consumption of 100, actual and planned savings of 25, actual and planned investment of 25, and inventory accumulation of zero.

8.3   The government sector

What are the various activities of the government? Governments raise revenue via different forms of taxation. The two main classes are *direct taxation* (T_d) and *indirect taxation* (T_i). Direct taxes are those that are levied on incomes (i.e. wages, rents, interest and profits), and indirect taxes are taxes on expenditures (e.g. value added tax (or VAT), excise duties on tobacco and alcohol, petroleum revenue tax, etc.). Revenues from these taxes finance two main types of government expenditure. First, there is *expenditure on goods and services* (G), which involves the government in directly employing people (e.g. civil servants, soldiers, teachers, doctors etc.) and purchasing goods (e.g. stationery, school books, bandages, bullets etc.). In addition, governments also conduct public investment programmes (e.g. schools, roads, bridges, hospitals, tanks, ships etc.). Second, governments make transfer payments (B), for which no goods or services are required in return. These payments are dependent on the status of the recipients, e.g. unemployment benefits, old age pensions, various social security payments (such as income support and housing benefit), debt interest to holders of government bonds etc. These transfer payments represent pure redistributions from taxpayers to certain categories of people, and do not represent the real use of economic resources as with G.

Of the four items of government activity identified, not all will add to national income. Only government expenditure on goods and services (G) results in factor incomes. The remaining three, T_d (direct taxation), T_i (indirect taxation) and B (transfer payments), all involve the redistribution of national income. Suppose the government raises direct taxation and uses the proceeds to finance a higher level of unemployment benefits. Both T_d and B will rise, but the amount of economic activity will not have changed directly. There will be indirect effects on economic activity if the marginal propensity to consume of the recipients of unemployment benefits is greater than that of those who are taxed. In other words, there may be a multiplier effect from the redistribution of purchasing power between those in work and those out of work.

Incorporating the government sector, our measure of GDP becomes:

$$\text{GDP at market prices} = C + I + G \tag{8.6}$$

This is a measure of income from the expenditure side. *GDP at factor cost* (i.e. factor earnings) takes account of indirect taxation (T_i). Expenditure taxes imply a difference between what consumers pay for goods and services (*market prices*) and what producers actually receive (*factor cost prices*). The opposite would be true in the case of subsidies. Treating T_i as indirect taxes net of subsidies (T_i is also known as the *factor cost adjustment*), we have:

$$\text{GDP at factor cost} = C + I + G - T_i \tag{8.7}$$

To summarize, the three measures that we started with are:

$$\text{GDP at factor cost} = Y = C + I + G - T_i \tag{8.8}$$

$$\text{Factor incomes} = \text{Output} = \text{Expenditure} \tag{8.9}$$

When we include the government sector, the private sector's *disposable income* will be

$$\text{Disposable income} = Y + B - T_d \tag{8.10}$$

and its savings will be

$$\text{Savings} = (Y + B - T_d) - C \tag{8.11}$$

From the above, factor earnings will be used up in the following way:

$$Y = C + S - B + T_d \tag{8.12}$$

and from the expenditure measure we get (see (8.7)):

$$Y = C + I + G - T_i \tag{8.13}$$

It follows therefore that:

$$C + S - B + T_d = C + I + G - T_i \tag{8.14}$$

or

$$S + T_d + T_i = I + G + B \tag{8.15}$$

That is,

$$\text{Leakages} = \text{Injections} \tag{8.16}$$

It is always the case that total leakages from an economy equal total injections into the economy. Rewriting in terms of sectoral balances, we get:

$$S - I = G + B - (T_d + T_i) \tag{8.17}$$

That is, the *financial surplus of the private sector* $(S - I)$ is equal to the *financial deficit of the public sector* $(G + B - (T_d + T_i))$. (Note that the introduction of the government sector implies that private sector savings are no longer identically equal to private sector investment, even when investment includes net inventory accumulation.)

8.4   The foreign sector

Most countries trade with other countries, by *exporting* some of their goods and services to other countries and by *importing* goods and services from other countries. When we include the foreign sector (exports and imports), our measure of national income will now be:

$$Y = C + I + G + X - Z \tag{8.18}$$

where

$$X = \text{exports}$$
$$Z = \text{imports}$$

and

$$NX = X - Z = \text{net exports (or } trade\ surplus \text{ or } trade\ balance\text{)} \tag{8.19}$$

Note that exports are part of domestic output $(+X)$ and imports are not $(-Z)$. Another way of looking at the equation is to rewrite it as:

$$Y + Z = C + I + G + X \qquad (8.20)$$

This says that total output or aggregate supply (which equals domestic output *plus* imported goods) equals total expenditure or aggregate demand (which is the sum of consumption expenditure, investment expenditure, government expenditure and export expenditure).

Exports are an injection into the expenditure process and imports are a leakage. Therefore, writing the leakages/injections identity with the foreign sector we have:

$$S + T_d + T_i + Z = I + G + B + X \qquad (8.21)$$

or

$$S - I = G + B - (T_d + T_i) + (X - Z) \qquad (8.22)$$

The *financial surplus of the private sector* $(S - I)$ has to equal the *financial deficit of the public sector* $(G + B - (T_d + T_i))$ plus the *trade surplus* $(X - Z)$. Therefore, for a given public sector deficit, a trade deficit corresponds to insufficient private sector savings.

8.5   Gross national product and national income

GDP is defined as the output produced by domestic factors of production. However, domestic residents also receive income from their ownership of foreign factors of production, such as land and factories (i.e. from *direct investment* abroad). Domestic residents also receive investment income from foreign holdings of financial assets, such as bonds and shares (i.e. from *portfolio investment* abroad). Similarly, foreigners might own some domestic factors of production and domestic financial assets. Profits from these would add to their income. Therefore to get a measure of total income that includes the foreign sector (known as *gross national product* or *GNP*), we add the net income received by domestic residents from abroad:

$$\text{GNP} = \text{GDP} + \text{Net property income from abroad} \qquad (8.23)$$

Note that 'property income' here comprises all types of income (interest, profits, dividends etc.).

In the process of producing output each year, part of the economy's capital stock gets old and dilapidated. In order to keep the productive capacity of the economy constant, we would have to replace that part of the capital stock. To get a measure of the net increase in the capital stock every year, and therefore of the net income produced by net investment expenditure, we need to subtract the amount of *depreciation* of the capital stock during the course of the year. Therefore we end up with *national income* (*NI*):

$$\text{National income} = \text{GNP at factor cost} - \text{Depreciation} \qquad (8.24)$$

8.6   Nominal and real GNP

If we wanted to compare the level of output that the economy produced this year with the level in previous years (which itself is a measure of *economic growth*), we would want to look at the quantity of goods and services produced and not just the money value of that output (i.e. the value of the output measured in current prices). This is because a higher level of GNP could result from higher prices (inflation) or from higher levels of production. In order to measure

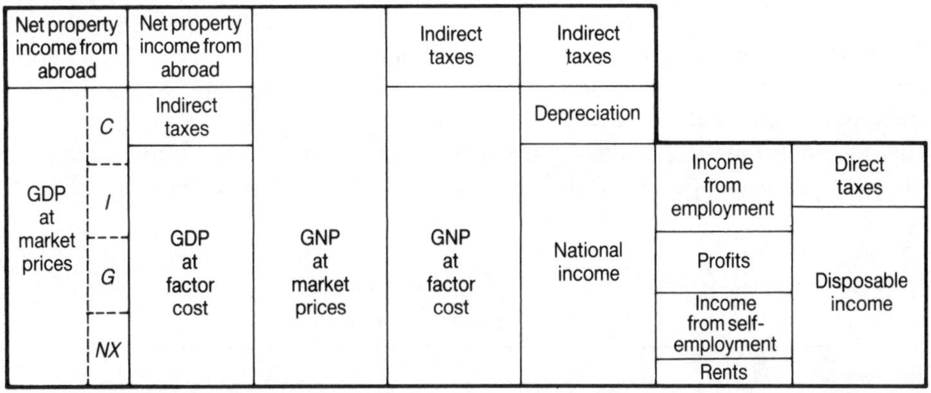

Net property income from abroad	Net property income from abroad		Indirect taxes	Indirect taxes			
GDP at market prices — C	Indirect taxes			Depreciation			
	I	GDP at factor cost	GNP at market prices	GNP at factor cost	National income	Income from employment	Direct taxes
	G					Profits	Disposable income
						Income from self-employment	
	NX					Rents	

Figure 8.2   National income accounting definitions

real output, we divide *nominal* output (*GNP at current market prices*) by the price level (to give *GNP at constant prices*, also called *real GNP*). The measure of the price level used for this is called the *GNP deflator*. This is a price index of all goods in the economy. The *retail price index* (RPI), which is the popular measure of inflation, includes only selected items (albeit a large number) because it is used as an indicator of changes in the *cost of living*. (For example, in the UK the RPI does not include luxury items such as fur coats, but does include tobacco and alcohol since these are both important expenditure items in the average household's budget.) Therefore, real GNP is equal to GNP at market prices *divided by* the GNP deflator:

$$\text{Real GNP} = \frac{\text{Nominal GNP}}{\text{GNP deflator}} \qquad (8.25)$$

If the GNP deflator is based on 1985 prices (i.e. takes the value 1.00 in 1985) then real GNP is said to be based on constant 1985 prices.

The real growth rate of national income ($\dot{Y}$) between two dates is calculated as follows:

$$\text{Real growth rate of GNP } (\dot{Y}) = \frac{\text{Real GNP}_1 - \text{Real GNP}_0}{\text{Real GNP}_0} \qquad (8.26)$$

where the subscript 0 refers to the earlier date and the subscript 1 refers to the later date.

Figure 8.2 provides a summary of national income accounting definitions and Table 8.1 (pp. 136–137) shows the UK national accounts for 1991.

8.7 Summary

1 National income accounting deals with different ways of measuring the circular flow of income. Households supply all the factors of production (labour, capital etc.) to firms, which produce all the goods and services purchased by households from the earnings derived from supplying the factors of production (wages, interest etc.). There are therefore three different ways of measuring total income:
   (a) The total value of goods and services produced.
   (b) Total factor earnings.
   (c) Total expenditure.

2 The output produced by domestic factors of production is called gross domestic product (GDP). GDP is equal to the sum of the value added of all the firms in the economy. This avoids double counting the value of intermediate goods which are used as inputs in the production of final goods.

3 Not all factor income is consumed during the year; some of it is saved. Similarly, not all expenditure is consumption expenditure; some of it is investment expenditure. Therefore, by

TABLE 8.1   UK national accounts 1991

(a) *Gross domestic product*

GDP at market prices = $C + I + G + X - Z$

	£ millions
Consumption expenditure	368,091
Investment expenditure (including inventory accumulation)	90,433
Government expenditure	121,488
Export of goods and services	136,013
Total final expenditure	716,025
less Imports of goods and services	(140,661)
GDP at market prices	575,364

GDP at factor cost = GDP at market prices − Factor cost adjustment

GDP at market prices	575,364
less Factor cost adjustment	(79,730)
GDP at factor cost	495,634

(Note: Factor cost adjustment = Net indirect taxes = Taxes on expenditure − Subsidies)

(b) *Gross national product and national income*

GNP at market prices = GDP at market prices + Net property income from abroad

	£ millions
GDP at market prices	575,364
plus Net property income from abroad	1,580
GNP at market prices	576,944

GNP at factor cost = GNP at market prices − Factor cost adjustment

GNP at market prices	576,944
less Factor cost adjustment	(79,730)
GNP at factor cost	497,214

National income = GNP at factor cost − Depreciation

GNP at factor cost	497,214
less Depreciation	(64,342)
National income	432,872

TABLE 8.1   *Continued*

(c) *National income and disposable income*

National income = Income from employment + Profits + Income from self-employment + Rents

	£ *millions*
Income from employment	330,865
Profits of companies (*less* stock appreciation)	62,761
Income from self-employment	22,220
Rents	17,026
National income	432,872

Disposable income = National income − Direct taxes

National income	432,872
less Direct taxes (*less* transfer payments)	(87,185)
Disposable income	345,687

(d) *Nominal GNP and real GNP*

Real GNP (constant 1985 prices) = Nominal GNP (current prices)/GNP deflator (1985 = 1.0)

	£ *millions*
Nominal GNP (current prices)/GNP deflator (1985 = 1.0)	576,944
	÷1.409
Real GNP (constant 1985 prices)	409,471

(e) *Growth rate of real GNP*

	£ *millions*
Real GNP in 1985	358,729
Real GNP in 1991	409,471
Annual growth rate of real GNP	2.36%

definition, savings are equal to investment. Inventories of finished goods are counted as investment for national income accounting purposes.

4 The government sector also makes an appearance in the national income accounts. First, the government raises direct taxes (which are taxes on factor earnings) and indirect taxes (which are taxes such as VAT on expenditures on goods and services). Second, the government is involved in expenditure on goods and services (e.g. civil servants' salaries, school books and road building), and in making transfer payments (e.g. unemployment benefits and pensions). Only direct government expenditure on goods and services results in factor incomes. Direct taxation, indirect taxation and transfer payments involve the redistribution of income. The effect of indirect taxes is to create a distinction between GDP at market prices (which is what consumers pay) and GDP at factor cost (which is what producers receive). The private sector's disposable income is the sum of factor earnings and transfer payments less direct taxes.

5 The foreign sector also makes an appearance in the national income accounts as a result of imports and exports. The effect of the foreign sector is to add net exports (i.e. exports minus imports, or the trade surplus) to total expenditure.

6 In terms of sectoral balances, the financial surplus of the private sector $(S - I)$ equals the financial deficit of the public sector $(G + B - (T_d + T_e))$ plus the trade surplus $(X - Z)$.

7 Gross national product (GNP) equals GDP plus net property income from abroad. Net property income from abroad equals the income from both direct investment (ownership of capital, land etc.) and portfolio investment (ownership of bonds, shares etc.) received from abroad by domestic residents, less property income owing to overseas residents from their direct investment and portfolio investment in the UK.

8 National income equals GNP at factor cost less depreciation, i.e. the amount by which the economy's capital stock depreciates during the course of the year.

9 Real GNP (at constant prices) equals nominal GNP (at current market prices) divided by the GNP deflator.

Exercises

1 Explain the three different ways of measuring national income.
2 Explain the significance of 'value added' in national income determination.
3 Explain the difference between gross domestic product and gross national product.
4 Explain the difference between gross national product and national income.
5 Explain the difference between nominal and real GNP.
6 From the following data on the house building industry, calculate its contribution to GDP (assuming that all the produce of the last four producers is bought by the house builder):

	Sales	Purchases of intermediate goods
House builder	5000	1900
Window producer	200	100
Roofing tile producer	300	200
Timber producer	400	300
Brick producer	1000	800

7 You are given the following components of GNP:

Income from employment	600
Direct taxes	350
Transfer payments	50
Consumption expenditure	550
Depreciation	100
Indirect taxes	230
Subsidies	30
Investment expenditure	250
Income from self-employment	100
Government expenditure	150
Rents	100
Exports	350
Imports	100
Net property income from abroad	100
Profits	220
Stock appreciation	20

Calculate:
(a) GDP at market prices.
(b) GDP at factor cost.
(c) GNP at market prices.
(d) GNP at factor cost.
(e) National income from both the expenditure side and income side.
(f) Disposable income.
8 You are given the following data:

Year	GNP at current market prices	GNP deflator
1988	120.5	1.00
1989	132.6	1.08
1990	139.2	1.17
1991	152.7	1.28
1992	155.7	1.34
1993	172.3	1.43

(a) Calculate real GNP between 1988 and 1993 in 1988 prices.
(b) Calculate the annual growth rates in both nominal and real GNP between 1988 and 1993.
     Comment on your results.

Business application: The impact of the recession

Although there is no official definition of a recession, it is generally accepted that one occurs when output (as measured by real GNP) falls for at least two consecutive quarters. For an economy to be in the recovery stage, output would have to rise for two consecutive quarters. According to this definition, the UK economy experienced two recessions in the 1980s and 1990s: the first from 1979 Q4 to 1981 Q2, and the second from 1990 Q2 to 1991 Q4.

Recessions do not hit all parts of the economy equally; in this sense they are not homogeneous in nature. The worst-hit sectors during the 1979–81 recession were in manufacturing: textiles and clothing, metals and other minerals, other manufacturing and engineering. Overall manufacturing output fell by some 15 per cent. The service sector did much better, with output down just 1 per cent. Indeed, some sub-sectors, such as financial and business services, actually expanded. The differing impacts on the manufacturing and service sectors resulted in a geographically uneven recession, with London and the South East relatively immune whereas the rest of the country was more badly affected.

The 1990–91 recession was different, with the service sector, and hence the South East, hit harder this time. Given the shakeout in manufacturing that took place during the 1979–81 recession, it could be argued that only the most efficient and most competitive firms remain and that they would be better able to cope with the recession. In addition, the 1990–91 exchange rate was much lower than it was in 1979–81 and so, notwithstanding the world slowdown, exports should have performed reasonably well. These factors, plus the dependence of the service sector on domestic demand, suggest that this sector, rather than the manufacturing sector, should have been harder hit in 1990–91. However, as Table 8.2 shows, this is not the case.

Manufacturing output fell less sharply during 1990–91, whereas the service sector suffered a larger decline than in 1979–81. However, parts of the manufacturing sector were hit very hard, with metals, textiles and clothing, engineering and construction experiencing the largest falls in

TABLE 8.2 Output changes by sector, 1990 Q2–
1991 Q4

Sector	Change (%)
Manufacturing	−7.9
Services	−2.1
Energy and water	+3.0
Metals	−16.5
Chemicals	+1.5
Engineering	−7.8
Construction	−12.3
Distribution, hotel and catering	−4.9
Food, drink and tobacco	+8.0
Textiles	−11.6
Transport and communication	−2.3

TABLE 8.3   Regional unemployment, 1990 Q2–1991 Q4

Region	Change in unemployment (%)
South East	+120
East Anglia	+100
West Midlands	+72
East Midlands	+73
North	+29
North West	+38
Yorkshire and Humberside	+48
Scotland	+18
UK	+64

output. In contrast, food, drink and tobacco and chemicals in the manufacturing sector and energy and water have increased their output.

Throughout the 1980s, sectors such as engineering, food, drink and tobacco, other manufacturing and chemicals achieved relatively low trend growth rates. Others, such as transport equipment, textiles and metals actually suffered a downward trend in output. Thus it appears that the UK's traditional manufacturing base is continuing to contract and the process of de-industrialization is showing no sign of ending.

The extent to which there were regional differences in the impact of the 1990–91 recession is examined in Table 8.3, which shows how regional unemployment has changed. There do appear to be regional differences, with the South East, East Anglia and the East and West Midlands suffering above average increases in unemployment. Industries such as mechanical, instrument and electrical engineering, cars and commercial vehicles are extremely important to the Midlands' economies and were all hit hard by the recession. In contrast, the economies of East Anglia and the South East are regarded as being heavily dependent on the service sector, and yet these suffered the highest increases in unemployment. One explanation for the large increase in unemployment, but the relatively small fall in the service sector's output, is that firms have shed labour in an attempt to cut costs in order to remain competitive. Hence productivity in this sector has probably risen sharply.

The 1990–91 recession was therefore similar to that of 1979–81 with the manufacturing sector being hit relatively harder than the service sector. Many parts of the manufacturing sector have seen output falling as has some of the service sector. However, in terms of unemployment, the largest increases have occurred in the regions most closely associated with the service sector.

III INTERNATIONAL MACROECONOMICS

International macroeconomics (or *open economy macroeconomics*) deals with the effects that one national economy can have on another national economy. In national macroeconomics, we examined how the national income of one country could be determined in isolation from what was happening in other countries. This is valid only if the country in question did not engage in international trade or international capital movements (i.e. was a closed economy). It is also valid, curiously enough, for the 'world economy' which is itself a 'closed' economy. But it is not valid for most countries in the world today. Most countries are open to world trade and many countries allow the free movement of capital into and out of their economies. For example, the UK has been completely free of capital controls since 1979.

International trade and capital movements can have important influences on both the level and composition of national income. In addition, the exchange rate, which measures the price of one country's currency in terms of another country's currency, also has an important role to play. The role of the exchange rate differs depending on whether a country operates a regime of fixed or floating exchange rates. As a result, macroeconomic policies can have completely different effects from those predicted in a closed economy. In the same way, the interest rate has a new role to play in an open economy. All these factors are of interest to the international macroeconomist.

Chapter 9 looks at open economy macroeconomics in general terms. In particular, we are interested in determining national income in an open economy when there are international trade and capital flows. We look at the role of the real exchange rate on the level of international competitiveness in determining imports and exports, and the role of interest rate differentials in determining international capital flows. We also look at macroeconomic policies in an open economy and how the effectiveness of these differs depending on whether exchange rates are fixed or floating.

Chapter 10 examines exchange rate determination in some detail. We look at the three main models of exchange rate determination: the purchasing power parity model, the monetary model and the portfolio balance model.

In Chapter 11 we examine the money supply process in the UK. There are two main models of money supply determination: the money multiplier model and the flow of funds model. The first model examines the role of the banking system in the money creation process. The second approach is more general and looks at all the sources of monetary growth, including the government and the international sector. This chapter ends with an examination of the conduct of monetary policy.

Finally, in Chapter 12, we examine the European Monetary System and one of its most important components, the Exchange Rate Mechanism (or ERM). The UK joined the ERM on 8 October 1990 but was forced to leave it on 'Black Wednesday', 16 September 1992.

9 Open economy macroeconomics

In this chapter, we examine the effects of international transactions and exchange rate changes on the domestic economy. In particular, we incorporate international considerations into our analysis of macroeconomic policy. As will be seen later, monetary and fiscal policies can have significantly different outcomes from those in our earlier analysis when they are considered in the context of alternative exchange rate regimes.

We consider first the determination of national income when there are international transactions in goods and services. Then we consider how the exchange rate is determined in terms of the demand for and supply of domestic currency. The important issues here are the effect of central bank intervention in the foreign exchange market, the determination of the *real exchange rate* (also known as the *terms of trade*), and the effect of the real exchange rate on the competitiveness of domestically produced goods. Monetary and fiscal policies are then analysed under alternative exchange rate regimes. Finally, we consider the role of the forward exchange rate in equalizing interest rate returns across countries (a concept known as *interest rate parity*), emphasizing the role of expectations in markets for financial assets.

9.1 National income determination in the open economy

There are two main types of international transactions. First, there are transactions in goods and services, which are part of international trade and classified as *current account transactions*, and second, there are international transactions in financial assets (e.g. treasury bills, shares, bonds, syndicated loans, trade credits etc.) which are classified as *capital account* transactions.

9.1.1 Current account

We will begin with macroeconomic equilibrium in domestic goods, where demand for domestic goods $(E = C + I + G)$ is equal to supply (Y). With international trade, some of the output produced in the domestic economy is consumed by the residents of other countries (i.e. exports (X)), and some of the domestic economy's consumption is produced by the residents of other countries (i.e. imports (Z)). Imports and exports constitute the domestic economy's *current account* or *trade account*. Therefore we now write our equilibrium condition as:

$$Y = C + I + G + X - Z \tag{9.1}$$

The difference between the last two terms $(X - Z)$, is *net exports* or the *trade surplus* $(NX = X - Z)$. The above is simply an identity. It does not say anything about the determinants of exports and imports. Note that X is an injection into the economy (like investment and government spending) and Z is a leakage (like savings and taxation). This means that an alternative version of the equilibrium condition is:

$$I + G + X = S + T + Z \tag{9.2}$$

Since aggregate demand (or desired expenditures) depends on domestic income (Y), the demand for imports will also depend on domestic income. As income rises, imports will rise (i.e. there is a *marginal propensity to import* out of increased income). Similarly, the income of foreigners will determine their demand for our exports. In addition, *relative prices* will also influence both exports and imports. The higher the prices of domestic goods are relative to the prices of goods produced in other countries, the more we tend to import. This will also reduce our exports, since foreigners will find British goods more expensive relative to their own goods. Relative prices essentially determine our *international competitiveness*. Denoting the income level in the rest of the world as Y^*, the above discussion implies that exports and imports are determined as follows:

$$X = f(Y^*, \text{competitiveness})$$
$$Z = f(Y, \text{competitiveness})$$

(9.3)

This simply means that exports of UK goods are determined by (i.e. are a function of) overseas income and the level of competitiveness of UK goods relative to overseas goods. Similarly, imports of goods from overseas depend on (i.e. are a function of) UK income and competitiveness. An increase in competitiveness will raise exports and reduce imports, and thereby lead to an improvement in the trade balance.

9.1.2   Capital account

Capital flows between countries result from domestic residents buying foreign financial assets and vice versa. Investors will be concerned mainly with the rates of return available in different countries. Thus, whether we have a net capital inflow or a net capital outflow will depend on our interest rate relative to the interest rates in other countries. If financial assets across countries are *perfect substitutes*, in the sense that they are identical in terms of their main characteristics (e.g. risk, term to maturity, tax treatment etc.), and, in addition, if there are no barriers to capital flows (such as exchange controls), then we would expect to see a substantial and persistent capital outflow if our interest rate was lower than the interest rate in other countries. Conversely, if our interest rate was higher, we would experience a substantial and persistent capital inflow. But persistent capital inflows and outflows are not sustainable in the long run because no country's capital stock is infinite. This suggests that, in this case of *perfect capital mobility*, interest rates would be equalized across countries in equilibrium in order to prevent these capital flows. In practice, of course, we do not observe this, since foreign and domestic financial assets are generally only *imperfect substitutes*. This is because residents in the UK tend to prefer to hold UK securities even if they are offering lower yields (and the same is true of the residents of other countries). Therefore interest rates can differ to some extent, and the size of actual capital flows (i.e. the *change* in the capital stock of financial assets) will depend on (i.e. be a function of) the size of the difference between domestic and foreign financial assets:

$$\Delta K = f(r - r^*)$$

(9.4)

where

ΔK = capital flow ($\Delta K > 0$ for capital inflow and $\Delta K < 0$ for capital outflow).

r = domestic interest rate.

r^* = foreign interest rate.

There will be capital inflows if $r > r^*$ and capital outflows if $r < r^*$.

The degree of capital mobility between countries has important implications for economic policy. With a high degree of capital mobility, the domestic interest rate cannot diverge significantly from world interest rates. With perfect capital mobility, as we have said, we have to have $r = r^*$. This imposes constraints on the government's ability to pursue expansionary policies. For example, fiscal expansions which tend to raise domestic interest rates will result in capital inflows, but worsen the current account. (The policy implications of having a high degree of capital mobility are discussed in more detail in Section 9.4.)

9.2 The balance of payments

9.2.1 The foreign exchange market

In the last section, we argued that one of the main factors determining exports and imports was the level of competitiveness of goods produced in the UK. Competitiveness is determined by the relative prices of goods produced in the UK to those of goods produced overseas. These prices are denominated in their respective local currencies (e.g. British sterling, US dollars, German marks, French francs, Japanese yen etc.). The exchange rate between currencies will determine how different national prices compare with each other. It is therefore important to consider how the exchange rate is determined, since exchange rate changes will affect the level of competitiveness.

We can explain how the exchange rate is determined in terms of the demand for and supply of sterling. When foreigners want to buy either British goods or British financial assets they need to acquire sterling, since all transactions in the domestic economy have to be conducted in domestic currency. This creates a demand for sterling. Similarly, when British residents want to buy US goods or US assets they create a demand for dollars. This demand for dollars is equivalent to a supply of sterling to the foreign exchange market.

We define the exchange rate e as the \$/£ exchange rate, i.e. as the foreign price of domestic currency (e.g. \$1.75 per £). Thus an *appreciation* of the exchange rate (an increase in e) implies a rise in the dollar price of sterling. Conversely, a *depreciation* implies a fall in the dollar price of sterling. (Note: some economists define e as the £/\$ exchange rate, i.e. as the domestic price of foreign currency (e.g. £0.57 per \$), in which case an appreciation of sterling would imply a fall in e.)

In Fig. 9.1, the demand curve for sterling (D_0) is downward-sloping, indicating that, as e falls, the demand for sterling rises, since British goods become cheaper. The supply curve of sterling (S) is upward-sloping, since a rise in e will reduce the price of the dollar, thereby making US goods cheaper. In Fig. 9.1, the equilibrium exchange rate is e_0. At any given exchange rate, if there is an increase in the demand for sterling, the demand curve might shift to D_1, and the equilibrium exchange rate rises to e_1.

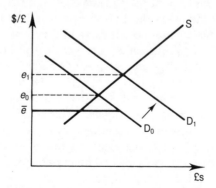

Figure 9.1   The foreign exchange market

If a country's central bank (which in the UK is the Bank of England) wants to maintain a *fixed exchange rate* at, say, $\bar{e}$, it could simply advertise a buying price at $\bar{e}$, which implies that no one would sell sterling below this price since the central bank would always be willing to pay at least $\bar{e}$ (see Fig. 9.1). Similarly, it could advertise a selling price at $\bar{e}$ to stop sterling rising above this level. This used to be the form in which exchange rates between the world's major currencies were fixed under the Bretton Woods system, which operated between the end of the Second World War and the early 1970s. Nowadays, there are no advertised buying or selling prices. Instead, the authorities intervene when the exchange rate is rising above or falling below some desired level. At $\bar{e}$, there is an excess demand for sterling. The Bank would have to supply pounds in return for dollars, thereby increasing its foreign exchange reserves. If $\bar{e}$ was above the equilibrium price e_0, the Bank would be buying pounds and supplying dollars. The Bank can only maintain fixed exchange rates away from equilibrium levels as long as it has adequate *foreign currency reserves* (typically in the form of US dollars) to support its interventions in the foreign exchange market.

9.2.2   UK balance of payments

In order to understand the difference between fixed and flexible exchange rates, we will examine the accounting framework of the UK balance of payments. Table 9.1 gives a brief summary of the balance of payments in 1985 (when there was a current account surplus) and in 1991 (when there was a current account deficit).

The *current account* consists of the trade in goods (called *visible exports and imports*) *plus* the trade in services (called *invisible exports and imports*) such as banking, shipping, tourism, insurance etc. Together these make up the *trade balance* ($X - Z$). In addition, transfer payments between countries (e.g. foreign aid, the UK's budget contribution to the European Community) and the net flow of property income from abroad (interest, profits, dividends) are included in the current account. Table 9.1(a) shows that there was a current account surplus of £3 billion in 1985.

The *capital account* records transactions in financial assets. Table 9.1(a) shows that capital inflows into the UK in the form of sterling bank deposits or purchases of British government bills and bonds and UK company shares amounted to £12.4 billion in 1985. The outflow of capital from the UK to buy factories or shares in companies abroad at £15.2 billion exceeded the inflow of capital into the UK. Included in capital outflows are trade credits. Trade credits arise when producers do not demand immediate payment for goods (i.e. they make temporary loans to the purchaser). For example, suppose a UK producer exports goods worth £10,000 but does not get paid immediately. On the current account, the value of the exports is recorded immediately as £10,000 under visible exports. On the capital account, we enter −£10,000 to show the credit extended (i.e. the capital outflow). When the current and capital accounts are added together, the monetary inflow to the UK is zero. The money comes in only when the exporter is paid. Overall, the UK capital account was in deficit of −£2.8 billion in 1985.

In compiling these accounts not all transactions are recorded accurately. Some items are incorrectly measured, primarily because not all transactions are recorded in the official statistics. Adding together rows (1) and (2) and the adjustment in row (3), the *balancing item* required to measure (1) and (2) more accurately, we obtain the UK *balance of payments* in 1985 as £0.9 billion.

The final entry in Table 9.1(a) is *official financing*. This is always of equal magnitude and opposite sign to the balance of payments in the line above, so that the sum of all entries in Table 9.1(a) is always zero. Official financing measures the international transactions that the government must take to accommodate all other transactions shown in the balance of payments accounts. In order to understand the official financing item, we need to consider why we had a surplus in 1985.

TABLE 9.1   UK balance of payments

(a) 1985	£ billions
Visible exports	78.1
Visible imports	−80.1
Invisible exports	80.0
Invisible imports	−75.0
(1) Current account surplus	3.0
Capital outflows	−15.2
Capital inflows	12.4
(2) Capital account deficit	−2.8
(3) Balancing item	0.7
(4) Balance of payments 'surplus' ((1) + (2) + (3))	0.9
(5) Official financing	−0.9

(b) 1991	£ billions
Visible exports	103.4
Visible imports	−113.7
Invisible exports	116.2
Invisible imports	−112.2
(1) Current account deficit	−6.3
Capital outflows	−19.1
Capital inflows	27.9
(2) Capital account surplus	8.8
(3) Balancing item	−4.4
(4) Balance of payments 'deficit' ((1) + (2) + (3))	−1.9

9.2.3   The balance of payments under fixed and flexible exchange rates

Under *flexible exchange rates*, the demand for pounds will always equal the supply of pounds (e_0 in Fig. 9.1). All the negative items in the balance of payments create a supply of pounds, and all the positive items create a demand for pounds. The exchange rate adjusts to equate the supply of pounds to the demand for pounds. This implies that *under freely floating exchange rates, the balance of payments must always be equal to zero*:

$$\text{Balance of payments} = (X - Z) + \Delta K = 0 \qquad (9.5)$$

If there is a current account deficit, there must be a capital account surplus exactly offsetting it. This is because a current account deficit means that the revenues from our exports are insufficient to pay for all our imports. The rest $(Z - X)$ must, by definition, be financed with loans or credits from abroad. These loans or credits represent 'capital inflows' and lead to a capital account surplus exactly offsetting the current account deficit. To illustrate, suppose our imports are £100 million and our exports are only £80 million. We will have a current account deficit of £20 million. But because we have managed to import £100 million worth of goods, the overseas suppliers must have lent us £20 million to do so. Alternatively, we might have sold domestic assets worth £20 million to the overseas suppliers. In either case, there is a 'capital inflow' and hence a capital account surplus of £20 million.

If there is a balance of payments 'deficit', this must imply that the negative items are greater than the positive items. The supply of pounds must be greater than the demand for pounds. This excess supply of pounds indicates that domestic residents want to buy more foreign goods and assets than foreigners want to buy domestic goods and assets. The balance of payments 'deficit' is exactly equal to the excess supply of pounds. In other words, a balance of payments 'deficit' reduces the UK money supply by the same amount. Similarly, a balance of payments 'surplus' increases the UK money supply by the same amount.

Under freely floating exchange rates and in the presence of a balance of payments 'deficit', a depreciation of sterling will only be prevented if the central bank intervenes in the foreign exchange market to buy up the excess supply of sterling by running down reserves of foreign currency. In the balance of payments, this is shown as *official financing*. In other words, official financing represents the amount of central bank intervention in the foreign exchange market to maintain sterling above the equilibrium value.

Under *fixed exchange rates*, the central bank has an explicit policy of targeting the exchange rate. In this case, the exchange rate is, by definition, not going to adjust in the presence of any disequilibrium in the foreign exchange market. That is, if there is any excess supply of sterling, the central bank will buy sterling with its reserves of foreign currency. An excess supply implies a balance of payments 'deficit', which can be sustained as long as the country has sufficient reserves of foreign currency to finance it.

9.2.4   Official financing

Table 9.1(a) indicates a balance of payments 'surplus' for 1985. This implies that in 1985 the UK acquired £0.9 billion of foreign exchange reserves to offset the balance of payments 'surplus' shown as £0.9 billion in the second last line of Table 9.1(a). Thus from Table 9.1(a), we can deduce that, although the UK was officially pursuing a floating exchange rate regime in 1985, the Bank of England did in fact intervene in the foreign exchange market in order to stabilize it. On average, it was buying foreign exchange and selling pounds, thus maintaining the exchange rate at a slightly lower level than would have been observed under a completely free float. Thus one way of gauging the extent of intervention is to look at changes in the level of foreign currency reserves.

Since 1986, however, the balance of payments statistics are reported in a different way. There is no longer a breakdown of the balancing item and official financing. The two are presented as the balancing item only. This, of course, implies that one can no longer gauge the extent of central bank intervention in the foreign exchange market directly. The new balancing item includes both the measurement (statistical) problems mentioned earlier and also how the deficit or surplus was financed. In order to judge how much intervention there was over a particular period, we need to consider by how much official reserves have changed over that period. These, however, also include other items, such as subscriptions to (or repayments from) the International Monetary Fund (IMF) etc., so an accurate measure of central bank intervention is no longer possible to obtain.

The 1991 balance of payments accounts are shown in Table 9.1(b).

9.2.5   The balance of payments constraint

For the balance of payments to be equal to zero, we need the sum of the current account and the capital account to be equal to zero. Under flexible exchange rates, when there is a trade deficit, the capital account must be in surplus, otherwise the exchange rate would have depreciated. We can sustain a trade deficit, but only by maintaining high interest rates to generate a capital account surplus.

Often in the UK when the trade figures are first released and they show a substantial deficit the immediate response is seen in the financial markets with lower prices and higher yields for fixed-interest securities (e.g. government bonds or gilts). This is easily explained using our framework. Given the trade deficit, market participants are expecting higher interest rates in order to generate the required capital account surplus. The only other way would be if the government let sterling depreciate in order to reduce the trade deficit by reducing imports and increasing exports. However, this would raise import prices and lead to higher inflation (particularly if the imports are used as raw materials in the production of domestic goods so that higher import prices are passed on in the form of higher prices for final goods), which the government also likes to keep under control. This is one of the reasons why sterling does not depreciate consistently when trade deficits are announced.

9.3   Competitiveness: the real exchange rate

Whether a depreciating exchange rate improves the trade deficit (i.e. increases exports and reduces imports) depends on what happens to relative prices, and not on the nominal exchange rate (e) alone.

The *real exchange rate* measures relative prices in a common currency. Formally, it is defined as:

$$\text{Real exchange rate} = \frac{eP}{P*} \tag{9.6}$$

where

$$P = \text{domestic price level.}$$
$$P* = \text{foreign price level.}$$

Figure 9.2 (p. 152) illustrates this with the use of a simple example. Suppose initially the exchange rate (e) is \$2/£1 and the price of a good in the US is \$40. In order to be competitive with US producers, a UK producer's price would have to be £20, since: e *times* UK price = US price. With e = \$2/£1, converting the UK price of £20 into dollars gives \$40. This conversion into a common currency gives the real exchange rate, which is simply a comparison of relative prices between US and UK producers. The real exchange rate is defined as the ratio of domestic to foreign prices, when both are expressed in a common currency. The real exchange rate above is expressed using US dollars as the common currency. A real exchange rate of 1 implies that foreign and domestic prices are equal.

If the UK now has 20 per cent inflation and the UK price of the good rises to £24 (but there is no increase in prices in the US), there will be a rise in the real exchange rate to 1.2. That is, the ratio of domestic to foreign prices has risen. Thus if the nominal exchange rate is still \$2/£1, the UK producer will lose competitiveness. However, if the nominal exchange rate depreciates by the difference in the inflation rates, the real exchange rate will remain constant. Thus in the example in Fig. 9.2, as long as the nominal exchange rate depreciates to 1.67 (i.e. $1 \times 40/24$), the real exchange rate remains constant. The nominal exchange rate which adjusts sufficiently to maintain a constant real exchange rate is known as the *purchasing power parity* (*PPP*) *exchange rate*. It refers to the rate at which the purchasing power of a currency with respect to

US price $= P^* = \$40$

Nominal exchange rate $= e = \$2/\pounds1$

Competitive UK price $= P = \dfrac{P^*}{e} = \dfrac{40}{2} = \pounds20$

Real exchange rate $= \dfrac{eP}{P^*} = \dfrac{2 \times 20}{40} = 1$

$\downarrow$

UK inflation $= 20$ per cent; US inflation $= 0$ per cent

$\downarrow$

US price $= P^* = \$40$

New UK price $= P = \pounds24$

New real exchange rate $= \dfrac{eP}{P^*} = \dfrac{2 \times 24}{40} = 1.2$

$\Rightarrow$ Loss of competitiveness in UK

$\downarrow$

Purchasing power parity exchange rate

$\qquad = $ Real exchange rate $\times \dfrac{P^*}{P}$

$\qquad = 1 \times \dfrac{40}{24} = 1.67$

$\Rightarrow$ Nominal exchange rate must fall to 1.67 to keep real exchange rate constant and restore UK competitiveness

Figure 9.2   Competitiveness: the real exchange rate

a foreign currency is held constant. We return to a more detailed examination of PPP exchange rates in the next chapter.

In Table 9.2 we examine the behaviour of the real and nominal exchange rates between the UK and the US. Given the nominal exchange rate in 1976, 1985 and 1991, and the relative price indices, we can calculate the real exchange rate (in 1976 prices) as eP/P^*. For example, the last row of Table 9.2 shows that the nominal exchange rate in 1985 had to be 1.43 for the real exchange rate to be constant. Although both countries have experienced inflation between 1976 and 1985, UK inflation was higher, thereby requiring a nominal rate depreciation for UK producers to remain as competitive as they were in 1976. The actual nominal rate in 1985 (at 1.30) had depreciated more than enough (it should have fallen to only 1.43), and as a result sterling was *undervalued* relative to 1976. In comparison with 1976, the 1991 nominal exchange rate had depreciated, but this time sterling was *overvalued* relative to 1976. For competitiveness to remain at the 1976 level, the nominal rate would have to be 1.28. Note that in determining whether a currency is overvalued or undervalued, the relative retail price indices are only one particular indicator. Since not all goods in retail price indices are traded goods, our calculations above are only an approximation of the PPP exchange rate. As an alternative to using retail

TABLE 9.2 Nominal and real exchange rates in the UK

	1976	1985	1991
Nominal $/£ rate ($e$):	1.81	1.30	1.77
Prices (1985 = 100):			
UK (P)	42	100	141
US ($P*$)	53	100	126
Real $/£ rate:	1.43	1.30	1.98
PPP nominal rate:	1.81	1.43	1.28
(assuming 1976 constant			
real exchange rate)			

$$\text{Real exchange rate} = \frac{eP}{P*}$$

PPP nominal rate = Nominal rate required to keep real
exchange rate constant

Example:

$$\frac{e_{1976} \times P_{1976}}{P^*_{1976}} = \text{Real rate}_{1976} = 1.43$$

PPP nominal rate:

$$e_{1985} = \frac{1.43 \times P^*_{1985}}{P_{1985}} = 1.43$$

$$e_{1991} = \frac{1.43 \times P^*_{1991}}{P_{1991}} = 1.28$$

prices, one could use unit labour costs, since this is directly related to the costs facing producers and will affect their pricing decisions.

In Fig. 9.3 we illustrate the effects of changes in the real exchange rate. As the real exchange rate increases, UK prices increase relative to US prices. UK goods become more expensive, thereby reducing the demand for them, and at the same time, UK consumers will find that imports are cheaper. Thus the higher the real exchange rate, the larger the trade deficit, which is why the NX ($=X-Z$) schedule is downward-sloping, indicating that the higher the real exchange rate, the greater will be the trade deficit. Where the NX schedule crosses the vertical

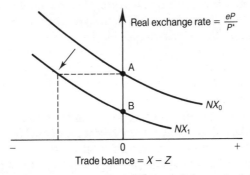

Figure 9.3 The real exchange rate and the trade deficit

axis, we can find the real exchange rate at which the trade deficit is zero. Along the NX schedule, the level of government expenditure and other domestic demand elements are held constant. A rise in government expenditure raises demand, national income and therefore imports. At any given real exchange rate, the trade balance worsens. The NX schedule shifts from NX_0 to NX_1. For equilibrium ($NX = 0$), the real exchange rate has to be lower (i.e. fall from A to B). Essentially, higher demand has to be offset by a reduction in relative prices, such that a higher proportion of total demand is directed towards domestically produced goods.

9.4   Macroeconomic policy in the open economy

In our earlier analysis of monetary and fiscal policies in the IS/LM framework, we found that both monetary and fiscal policies were successful in expanding demand in the economy (at least when prices were slow to adjust). The main difference between the two policies was the effect on interest rates. Fiscal policy raised interest rates via crowding out, whereas monetary policy reduced interest rates unless the economy was in a liquidity trap. These mechanisms are still present in monetary and fiscal expansions in an open economy, but there are important additional constraints.

First, in the presence of capital flows, a change in domestic interest rates will affect the capital account of the balance of payments. Under some circumstances, it may not be possible to sustain domestic interest rates at levels that are significantly different from other countries' interest rates. Second, by influencing exchange rates, capital flows will affect domestic demand, since the real exchange rate is an important determinant of domestic demand through its effect on exports and imports. This effect will not be present under fixed exchange rates, by definition, but in this case we have to consider the consequences for the money supply, since central bank intervention to maintain a particular exchange rate will make the money supply *endogenous* (i.e. outside the central bank's control), rather than *exogenous* (i.e. fixed by the central bank) as we have been assuming up to now.

We will examine monetary and fiscal policies under both a fixed exchange rate regime and a flexible exchange rate regime. Throughout the analysis we assume that capital is *perfectly mobile* internationally. Specifically, this implies that domestic interest rates cannot diverge from world interest rates (i.e. there are no exchange controls and so domestic and foreign assets are perfect substitutes and must therefore yield the same return). This is clearly an extreme assumption and is made here for analytical purposes only. Nevertheless, during the 1980s and 1990s the world has moved closer to having perfect capital mobility than it has ever done in the past. When capital is not perfectly mobile our results will be somewhat modified, but the general conclusions will still hold as long as there is a fair degree of capital mobility. Initially we also treat prices as fixed in order to examine the effects on real aggregate demand. In order to examine the effects of fiscal and monetary policy under fixed and floating exchange rates, we will use a variant of the IS/LM model known as the *Mundell–Fleming model* after the two American economists who developed it.

9.4.1   Fixed exchange rates

To maintain a fixed exchange rate, the central bank will from time to time have to intervene in the foreign exchange market. When there is an excess supply of pounds, the central bank will buy pounds and sell foreign currency to prevent a fall in the value of sterling. The supply of pounds in circulation will fall and foreign exchange reserves will fall. The money supply will fall. Conversely, when the central bank sells pounds to stop the currency appreciating, the money supply will rise. If, for example, there is a balance of payments 'surplus', foreign currency will flow into the central bank, which will offer sterling in exchange. Therefore the supply of money is both the amount of pounds in circulation in the domestic economy (known as *domestic credit*) *plus* reserves. Higher reserves will raise the money supply. It is in this sense that the money supply is said to be endogenous. *The authorities cannot fix both the money supply and the exchange rate.*

Fiscal policy

In Fig. 9.4 we characterize the initial equilibrium as the intersection of IS_0 and LM_0 at point A. The horizontal line $BP = 0$ denotes external equilibrium. That is, the balance of payments is in equilibrium ($=0$). Under perfect capital mobility, domestic and foreign interest rates have to be equal ($r = r^*$), otherwise there would be net capital flows. Therefore any point not on the $BP = 0$ line cannot be a situation where the balance of payments is in equilibrium, since $r \neq r^*$.

An increase in government expenditure financed via borrowing will shift the IS schedule from IS_0 to IS_1, as demand in the domestic economy is increased as a result of the larger budget deficit. Interest rates rise as a result of the higher income generated, and the economy will move towards point B. The domestic interest rate rises to r_1. This will attract capital inflows since r_1 is greater than r^*. The demand for pounds will rise as foreigners attempt to buy more UK financial assets. Given a fixed exchange rate, the central bank must provide the extra pounds and take in the foreign currency. The effect is clearly to increase the UK money supply and to lower interest rates. In Fig. 9.4, this is shown as the shift of the LM schedule from LM_0 to LM_1. The economy will be in equilibrium again at point C.

What determines the extent of capital inflows and the increase in income from Y_0 to Y_1? Capital inflows will continue as long as domestic interest rates are higher than r^*. But the inflows themselves have the effect of lowering interest rates because they raise the UK money supply. When interest rates are again equal to r^*, capital inflows will stop. Because assets are perfect substitutes internationally, investors will be content to keep their capital in the UK because they are getting the same interest rate as they could get anywhere in the world, i.e. they will not withdraw their capital when the UK interest rate falls back to r^*. The net effect is to raise income to Y_1 with interest rates unchanged. A fiscal expansion in this case induces a monetary expansion as well. In terms of the balance of payments, there will be a trade deficit and a capital account surplus, but since the eventual equilibrium is again on the $BP = 0$ line, the balance of payments will again balance. The increase in income is determined by the size of the fiscal expansion. *But fiscal policy is super-effective in an open economy with fixed exchange rates.*

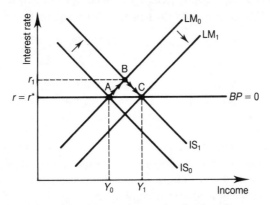

Figure 9.4   Fiscal expansion under fixed exchange rates

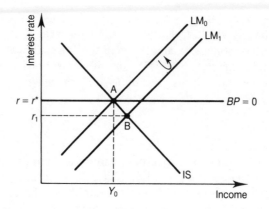

Figure 9.5   Monetary expansion under fixed exchange rates

Monetary policy

An increase in the supply of money shifts the LM schedule from LM_0 to LM_1, resulting in lower interest rates (point B in Fig. 9.5). This leads to capital outflows, since domestic interest rates are now lower than world interest rates. The central bank will have to buy pounds and reduce its foreign currency reserves to maintain the fixed exchange rate. This will reduce the supply of money, as pounds bought by the central bank will no longer be in circulation in the domestic economy. The LM_1 schedule will shift back to LM_0. Note that since the money supply is endogenous, the central bank cannot change the money supply independently of other countries under a fixed exchange rate regime.

There is no net increase in output, since there is no increase in real aggregate demand. The actual increase in the supply of pounds is offset by capital outflows (loss of reserves) which increase the money supply and consequently the inflation rate in other countries. Under fixed exchange rates then, all that has happened is that inflation has been exported. More importantly, countries which fix exchange rates sacrifice monetary independence. In other words, *monetary policy is totally ineffective in an open economy with fixed exchange rates.*

9.4.2   Floating exchange rates

When exchange rates are freely floating, there is no need for reserves, since the central bank does not intend to intervene in foreign exchange markets. The central bank does not have the obligation of providing foreign currency to people who want to buy foreign goods or foreign financial assets.

Fiscal policy

An increase in government expenditure financed by borrowing (so that the government's budget deficit increases) shifts the IS schedule from IS_0 to IS_1 in Fig. 9.6, raising the interest rate to r_1. The resulting capital inflow will lead to an appreciation of the exchange rate from e_0 to e_1, say. This raises the real exchange rate from $e_0 P/P^*$ to $e_1 P/P^*$. The demand for domestically produced goods will fall as imports become cheaper and exports become more expensive, i.e. there is a loss of competitiveness. The IS_1 schedule will move leftwards back towards the original IS_0 schedule as export demand falls. The reason why the economy moves back to the initial equilibrium point is that, as long as domestic interest rates are higher than world interest rates, capital inflows will continue and the exchange rate will keep on appreciating. This process can

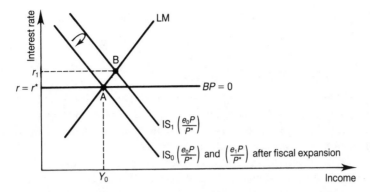

Figure 9.6 Fiscal expansion under floating exchange rates

only stop when domestic interest rates are again at r^*. The mechanism which is responsible for reducing interest rates is the reduction in demand, especially export demand.

There is thus no change in output, and the net effect is simply a trade deficit which is exactly equal in size to the government budget deficit. The above analysis implies that *fiscal policy is totally ineffective in raising output when exchange rates are freely floating and capital is perfectly mobile*. These conclusions are based on strong assumptions. In practice, domestic and foreign assets are unlikely to be perfect substitutes and there can therefore be some divergence between domestic and foreign interest rates. In terms of Fig. 9.6, this would mean the $BP = 0$ line is upward-sloping. A fiscal expansion in that case would not be completely ineffective.

Monetary policy

In the case of a monetary expansion (Fig. 9.7), the LM schedule moves to the right from LM_0 to LM_1, lowering interest rates to r_1 (i.e. a movement from A to B). This will actually increase competitiveness, as the resulting capital outflow leads to a depreciation of the currency from e_0 to e_1, say. The real exchange rate will fall, increasing the demand for domestic output, especially export demand. The IS curve shifts from IS_0 to IS_1, raising the interest rate to r^* again (i.e. a movement from B to C). As before, the system is driven back to equilibrium ($BP = 0$) via the exchange rate change, which will continue as long as r is less than r^*. The net effect of a monetary expansion is a capital account deficit and a trade surplus via the lower real exchange rate.

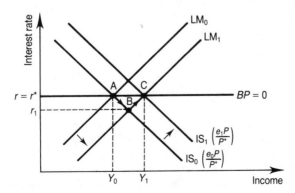

Figure 9.7 Monetary expansion under floating exchange rates

Output is higher due to the increase in competitiveness. *Monetary policy is super-effective in an open economy with floating exchange rates.*

9.4.3   Floating exchange rates and flexible prices

Our analysis so far has identified which policies are effective in raising demand under alternative exchange rate regimes. Demand increases are translated fully into output increases only if prices are fixed. When prices are not fixed, we need to consider the effects of rising prices that may result from expansionary government policies.

In Figure 9.8, we consider the case of a monetary expansion under floating exchange rates. Initially output rises to Y_1 and the real exchange rate falls from $e_0 P_0/P*$ to $e_1 P_0/P*$ (since $e_1 < e_0$) as in Fig. 9.7 (i.e. the economy moves from A to B to C). Suppose now domestic prices rise. There are two important channels through which output will be reduced:

1 The increase in domestic prices raises relative prices and reduces competitiveness, i.e. leads to a rise in the real exchange rate, which will lower the demand for domestically produced goods and increase the demand for foreign goods. In terms of Fig. 9.8, the IS_1 schedule will shift back to IS_0.
2 The increase in prices reduces the real money supply which will shift the LM_1 schedule back towards LM_0, raising interest rates. Higher interest rates will also cause an appreciation of the currency.

Both these effects are going on at the same time. The IS schedule will be shifting to the left, as will the LM schedule. The economy moves back to point A. The net effect is a higher price level, a lower nominal exchange rate (even though it is higher than at C), but no long-run change in the real exchange rate. That is to say, there are offsetting changes in e and P, so that $e_1 P_1/P* = e_0 P_0/P*$ (with $P_1 > P_0$ and $e_1 < e_0$). The nominal exchange rate initially falls and then rises, but not back to the original level.

The speed with which the economy moves from A to B to C and back to A again (especially the speed with which the economy moves from C to A) depends on the degree of flexibility of prices. If prices are highly flexible, so that the market mechanism is very efficient, the movement back to A will be very rapid. Government macroeconomic policies will be largely ineffective in moving the economy away from A except for short periods. This is the framework in which the monetarists and new classical economists believe. Keynesians, on the other hand, believe in

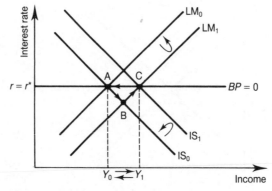

Figure 9.8   Monetary expansion under floating exchange rates and flexible prices

sticky or slowly adjusting prices. They believe that the movement between C and A is very slow. They therefore believe in the efficacy of macroeconomic demand management policies in taking the economy from A to C, since any tendency to move back from C to A will take many years. However, both monetarists and Keynesians accept the importance of supply-side policies in helping to shift point A (the full capacity point) to the right.

9.5   Interest rate differentials and exchange rate expectations

In the above analysis, we assume $r = r^*$ (i.e. that domestic and overseas interest rates are the same), which results from our assumption of perfect capital mobility. In practice, even when comparing otherwise similar countries, we sometimes observe significant differentials in interest rates. If we compared a three month US treasury bill with a three month UK treasury bill, it is difficult to explain why their interest rates should differ. There are no capital controls between the two countries and there is no real risk of either government defaulting. In order to explain these differentials, we need to specify not only interest income, but also any capital gains (or losses) arising from exchange rate movements.

Consider an example of a UK investor deciding on whether to invest £100 in the UK or the US. Suppose that interest rates are 5 per cent in the US and 10 per cent in the UK and the current spot exchange rate is $2/£1. Under this scenario the investor will know with certainty how much the investment (principal *plus* interest) will be worth in nominal terms. At the end of one year, the investor will have $210 if he or she invests in the US, and £110 if the money is invested in the UK. If the exchange rate in one year's time is still $2/£1, then clearly the investor will be better off with a UK investment, since the US investment is worth only £105 at the year end. Suppose however that sterling is expected to depreciate by 5 per cent over the next year. If expectations are realized, the $/£ exchange rate will then be $1.90 per £1 at the end of the year. At this rate, the dollar proceeds converted back into sterling will amount to exactly £110, since $210/$1.90 per £1 = £110. Another way of thinking about interest returns is to ask why, when interest rates differ significantly, anyone would want to hold the currency with the lower return (dollars in the above example). The answer must be because they expect it to appreciate against any currency offering a higher interest rate. In the above example, the dollar is expected to appreciate against sterling. So rather than just looking at interest rate differentials, we need to consider expected exchange rate changes.

The equalization of returns via expected exchange rate adjustments is known as *interest parity*:

$$r^* = r + \text{expected rate of appreciation of the domestic currency} \qquad (9.7)$$

Interest parity means that, in equilibrium, interest rates will be equal once we have taken into account the likely appreciation of the domestic currency. (Note that if $r > r^*$, the expected rate of appreciation of the domestic currency will be a negative number, since the currency is expected to *depreciate*.) If this were not the case, there would be an incentive for everyone to move into the currency offering the highest return, after taking into account exchange rate changes (this incentive is known as an *arbitrage opportunity*). However, as investors attempt to do this, the interest rate in the preferred country would fall and its exchange rate would appreciate until the incentive to transfer capital between countries had disappeared and interest parity has been restored. (We only have $r = r^*$ when exchange rates are expected to remain unchanged.)

One way of calculating the expected rate of appreciation of the domestic currency is to examine the difference between the spot and forward exchange rates. The *spot exchange rate* is the exchange rate for foreign currency to be delivered today, whereas the *forward exchange rate* is the exchange rate agreed today for foreign currency to be delivered at some future date, say in a year's time. In other words, it is possible to agree today the price of a transaction that will take place at some date in the future. This is the essence of a *forward contract*: it is a contract whereby the price is agreed today, but the transaction takes place in the future.

The relationship between spot and forward rates can be shown in the following illustration. (One frequent source of confusion with interest rates is that sometimes they are expressed as a percentage (e.g. 11 per cent) and sometimes they are expressed as a proportion (e.g. 0.11); whenever we see the expression $(1 + r)$, as below, we know that r is being expressed as a proportion, so that $(1 + r) = 1.11$ and *not* 12 even though r might be written as $r = 11$ per cent).

Suppose that £Y invested in the UK for one year yields

$$£Y(1 + r) \tag{9.8}$$

while £Y invested in the US for one year yields

$$\$Y(e)(1 + r^*) \tag{9.9}$$

where e is the spot exchange rate (measured in $ per £). Selling forward the year-end dollar proceeds into sterling at today's forward rate yields

$$\frac{£Y(e)(1 + r^*)}{E} \tag{9.10}$$

where E is the forward exchange rate (also measured in $ per £).

Interest parity implies that these two investments, (9.8) and (9.10), yield the same:

$$\frac{£Y(e)(1 + r^*)}{E} = £Y(1 + r) \tag{9.11}$$

Simplifying, we get

$$\frac{E}{e} = \frac{(1 + r^*)}{(1 + r)} \simeq 1 + r^* - r \tag{9.12}$$

or

$$\dot{E} = r^* - r \tag{9.13}$$

where $\dot{E} = (E/e) - 1$ is known as the *percentage forward premium* on the domestic currency, i.e. it is the percentage difference between the forward exchange rate and the spot exchange rate. Now $\dot{E}$ is often used as a measure of the expected rate of change of the exchange rate. The last equation states that *the expected rate of change of the exchange rate is equal to the interest rate differential between two countries if interest parity holds*. The equation can be rearranged to yield

$$r^* = r + \dot{E}$$

$$= r + \text{percentage forward premium on the domestic currency} \tag{9.14}$$

which is the same as Equation (9.7) if interest parity holds. (Note again that if $r > r^*$, the percentage forward premium will actually be a *percentage forward discount* which is subtracted from the right-hand side of this equation.)

Expectations of future exchange rate changes will to some extent be reflected in the *forward premium* (implying an anticipated appreciation of the domestic currency) or the *forward discount* (implying an anticipated depreciation of the domestic currency). In our example above, if the investor bought sterling forward (i.e. agreed to buy a given amount of sterling on a given future date at a price (exchange rate) agreed now), then given that the dollar proceeds of the investment are known with certainty, he or she would find that both investments offer exactly the same return. If they did not offer the same return, it would be possible to make riskless arbitrage profits. By writing a forward contract there is no uncertainty about the sterling value at the end of the year of the US investment. This equalization of returns when adjusted for forward exchange rates is known as *covered interest parity* (i.e. the sterling value of the US investment at the end of the year is protected or covered by a forward contract).

We can illustrate all this using the following example. Suppose that we observe the following:

UK interest rate (r) = 11 per cent
US interest rate (r^*) = 7 per cent
Spot exchange rate (e) = \$1.75 per £1
Forward (one year) exchange rate (E) = \$1.6869 per £1

Also suppose that a UK investor starts with £100 at the beginning of the year. He or she could invest in the UK for a year, ending up with £111 at the end of the year. Alternatively, the investor could exchange the £100 into dollars and invest in the US for one year. At the same time, the end of year dollar proceeds could be sold forward into sterling at the one year forward exchange rate. This would guarantee, or lock in, the sterling value of the end of year US investment, and hence protect it from *exchange rate risk*. This is the risk from not knowing at the beginning of the year what the end of year exchange rate will be and therefore what the sterling value of the US investment will be worth in sterling. We know what the US investment will be worth in dollars. It will be worth

$$100 \times 1.75 \times (1.07) = \$187.25 \qquad (9.15)$$

But the sterling value of the investment depends on the exchange rate ruling at the time. If the exchange rate is $e = \$2$ per £1, then the sterling value of the US investment is only £93.63 (i.e. 187.25/2), while if the exchange rate is $e = \$1.50$ per £1, the sterling value of the US investment is £124.83 (i.e. 187.25/1.50). This uncertainty over the sterling value of the US investment can be avoided completely if the dollar proceeds are sold forward at the beginning of year forward exchange rate. This locks in the sterling value of the dollar proceeds at £111 (i.e. 187.25/1.6869). This shows that in this example covered interest parity holds: any investment covered or hedged in the forward foreign exchange market will earn the same interest rate whether the investment is made in the US or in the UK.

However, suppose that we observe a one-year forward exchange rate of $E = \$1.60$ per £1. Every £100 invested in the US for one year with the dollar proceeds sold forward would be worth

$$\frac{100 \times 1.75 \times (1.07)}{1.60} = £117 \qquad (9.16)$$

at the end of the year. A smart investor could borrow £100 in the UK at $r = 11$ per cent, exchange it into dollars at the spot exchange rate $e = \$1.75$ per £1, invest the dollars in the US at $r^* = 7$ per cent while at the same time selling the dollars forward at $E = \$1.60$ per £1 and hence lock in a sterling value at the end of the year of £117. The investor has to repay the sterling loan of £100 plus interest of £11, a total repayment of £111. But the investor can take out a *riskless arbitrage profit* of £6 per £100 borrowed (i.e. £117 − £111).

However, as the Nobel prize-winning economist Milton Friedman once said 'There is no such thing as a free lunch'. The financial markets are very *efficient* and do not allow riskless arbitrage profit opportunities to last for very long. Something is clearly out of equilibrium in the above example and market pressures would rapidly restore equilibrium. If a large number of investors attempted to undertake these transactions, the following pressures would operate:

1 There would be an increase in borrowing in the UK, which would tend to raise UK interest rates.
2 There would be an increase in the purchases of spot dollars against sterling, which would tend to reduce e.
3 There would be an increase in lending in the US, which would tend to reduce US interest rates.
4 There would be an increase in the supply of forward dollars, which would tend to reduce the price of forward dollars against forward sterling, which is equivalent to an increase in E.

The final equilibrium might be:

UK interest rate (r)	= 11.5 per cent
US interest rate (r^*)	= 6.5 per cent
Spot exchange rate (e)	= $1.73 per £1
Forward (one year) exchange rate (E)	= $1.6524 per £1

when again covered interest parity holds.

Covered interest parity holds for most of the world's major currencies.

9.6   Summary

1 There are two main types of international transactions: current account transactions (which are international transactions in goods and services) and capital account transactions (which are international transactions in financial assets).
2 The current account surplus is defined as the difference between exports and imports; it is also known as the trade surplus or net exports. The demand for a country's exports depends on the level of income in the rest of the world, and on the relative prices or competitiveness of those exports. The demand for imports depends on the level of domestic income and again on the relative prices or competitiveness of those imports. An increase in competitiveness will raise exports and reduce imports and thereby lead to an improvement in the trade balance.
3 Capital flows between countries result from domestic residents buying foreign financial assets, and vice versa. There will be a net capital inflow into the domestic economy if domestic interest rates are sufficiently high relative to foreign interest rates. If there is perfect capital mobility, so that international assets are perfect substitutes for each other and there are no barriers to capital flows, then interest rates in all countries will be equalized, otherwise there will be substantial capital flows. If there is imperfect capital mobility, so that domestic and foreign assets are imperfect substitutes for each other and/or governments place restrictions on the extent to which their residents can hold foreign assets, then interest rate differentials can persist, within limits, without causing capital flows. But if interest rate differentials exceed those limits, then capital will flow from the lower to the higher interest rate economy.
4 Competitiveness is determined by the relative prices of goods produced in the UK and goods produced overseas, measured in a common currency using the exchange rates between the UK and overseas countries. The exchange rate is determined by the demand for and supply of sterling. The demand for sterling comes from people wishing to buy British goods or financial assets. The supply of sterling comes from people in the UK wishing to buy foreign

goods or financial assets. If the exchange rate is allowed to float, the equilibrium exchange rate will be determined by the intersection of supply and demand. If the government wants to fix the exchange rate, it will need to use foreign currency reserves to support the exchange rate at the chosen level.

5 The balance of payments is the sum of the current account, the capital account and official financing. If there is a current account deficit, this will be financed from a capital account surplus and official financing. Official financing measures the extent to which the authorities have intervened in the foreign exchange markets to stabilize the exchange rate. But by definition the balance of payments must always equal zero.

6 Competitiveness is measured by the real exchange rate. The real exchange rate is defined as the nominal exchange rate (measured in foreign currency units of domestic currency, e.g. $ per £) times the ratio of domestic to foreign prices. If the nominal exchange rate or the domestic price level rises, or the foreign price level falls, the domestic economy loses competitiveness relative to the foreign economy.

7 The purchasing power parity (PPP) exchange rate is the nominal exchange rate that keeps the real exchange rate (and hence competitiveness) constant whenever there are differing inflation rates between the domestic and foreign economies. When inflation in the UK is greater than inflation in the US, the PPP exchange rate will be falling. If the actual (nominal) exchange rate is higher than the PPP level, the exchange rate is said to be overvalued; if it is less than the PPP level, it is said to be undervalued.

8 The effects of fiscal and monetary policies in an open economy can be substantially different from those in a closed economy. The effects also differ depending on whether exchange rates are fixed or floating and on the degree of capital mobility. With fixed exchange rates and perfect capital mobility, fiscal policy is super-effective in increasing real income. This is because a fiscal expansion will (temporarily) raise interest rates which induces capital inflows which in turn increases the money supply which leads to a further increase in real income. The increase in income leads to a trade deficit which is financed by a capital account surplus. In contrast, monetary policy is completely ineffective in these circumstances. This is because a monetary expansion reduces interest rates, which induces a capital outflow which corresponds to an outflow of money equal in size to the monetary expansion. The implication is that the country is simply exporting inflation to other countries. A country cannot fix both its exchange rate and its money supply.

9 With floating exchange rates and perfect capital mobility, fiscal policy is ineffective in increasing real income. This is because a fiscal expansion will raise both interest rates and the exchange rate, which reduces competitiveness and in turn leads to a reduction in exports equivalent in size to the fiscal expansion. In other words, there is a trade deficit equal to the additional government expenditure. In contrast, monetary policy is super-effective in increasing real income. This is because monetary expansion lowers interest rates, which induces a capital outflow and a reduction in the exchange rate. This in turn leads to an increase in exports. The net result is higher real income and a trade surplus which finances a capital account deficit.

10 The effectiveness of macroeconomic policies in an open economy also depends on what happens to prices. Demand increases are translated fully into output increases only if prices are fixed. If prices are flexible, a monetary expansion when output is at its full employment level will eventually lead to a higher price level, a lower nominal exchange rate, but no long-run change in output or the real exchange rate.

11 With perfect capital mobility, interest rates adjusted for expected exchange rate changes will be equalized across all countries. This property is known as interest rate parity. Covered interest parity is the special case where interest rates are equalized after adjustment for the

difference between the forward and spot exchange rates. The evidence indicates that covered interest parity holds across the major exchange rates.

Exercises

1 Consider the following open economy macroeconomic model:

$$Y = C + I + G + X - Z$$

$$C = a + bY$$

$$I = I_0$$

$$G = G_0$$

$$X = X_0$$

$$Z = mY$$

where X = exports, Z = imports and m = marginal propensity to import. If $m = 0.2$ and $b = 0.7$, what is the value of the multiplier?

2 The UK's trading partners have a recession. What happens to the UK trade balance and the UK level of output?

3 Examine the role of competitiveness and interest rate differentials in international macroeconomics.

4 What factors determine the level of the nominal exchange rate?

5 How does a central bank maintain a fixed exchange rate?

6 What are:
   (a) The main components of the current account?
   (b) The main components of the capital account?

7 What is official financing and why does it exist?

8 What is the real exchange rate?

9 Which of the following increase a country's competitiveness?
   (a) A rise in the domestic price level.
   (b) A rise in the foreign price level.
   (c) A rise in the nominal exchange rate.
   (d) A rise in the real exchange rate.

10 (a) What is the purchasing power parity exchange rate?
   (b) Calculate the purchasing power parity exchange rate for 1994 if:

   Real $/£ exchange rate in 1986 = 1.47
   Price level in UK in 1994   = 199
   Price level in US in 1994   = 152

11 Contrast the effects of an expansionary monetary and fiscal policy on output and interest rates in (a) a closed economy and (b) an open economy with a fixed exchange rate and perfect international capital mobility.

12 Assess the following statement: 'Under floating exchange rates, monetary policy is more powerful than in a closed economy but fiscal policy is less powerful; the opposite is true under fixed exchange rates'.

13 Explain why the government cannot fix both the money supply and the exchange rate when there is international capital mobility. What advice would you have given to Chancellor of

the Exchequer Nigel Lawson in 1987 and 1988 when he attempted to target sterling to 3 Deutschmarks per £ and at the same time control inflation?

14 Explain why monetary policy is completely ineffective in increasing output when the following three hold simultaneously:
  (a) Flexible prices.
  (b) Floating exchange rates.
  (c) International capital mobility.

15 Suppose the economy is near full employment, but the trade deficit is thought to be too large and sterling is overvalued. Describe a change in monetary and fiscal policy that will keep the economy at full employment output, but will lower both sterling and the trade deficit. Compare your answer with the government's macroeconomic policy between 1990 and 1992.

16 (a) What is the forward exchange rate?
   (b) What is covered interest parity?

17 (a) If UK interest rates are currently 10 per cent per annum and US interest rates are 6 per cent per annum, what is the expected rate of depreciation of sterling over the next year?
   (b) If the spot exchange rate is 3 Deutschmarks per £ and the one-year forward exchange rate is 2.76 Deutschmarks per £, and UK interest rates are currently 14 per cent per annum, what is the current interest rate in Germany?

Business application: UK export performance

The UK has been running a visible trade deficit since 1983 and a current account deficit since 1987. It has also been a net importer of manufactured goods since 1983. On the more positive side, after many years of decline, the UK's share of world exports stabilized in the early 1980s and then increased slowly to around 9 per cent by the second half of the decade. But this is a far cry from the period just after the Second World War, when the UK accounted for 25 per cent of the world's exports.

There are many factors which determine the level of UK exports. First, de-industrialization, the relative and absolute decline in the manufacturing sector, is one reason for the poor export performance. The decline in manufacturing capacity creates a supply-side constraint which means that UK producers cannot meet domestic and overseas demand in times of rapid economic growth.

A second factor is the price competitiveness of UK exports. This is affected by movements in the exchange rate, relative inflation and relative unit labour costs. The UK tends to have higher inflation and higher relative unit labour costs than other countries, especially in Europe, and so tends to lose competitiveness over time. In addition, government policy between October 1990 and September 1992 was aimed at maintaining a fairly high exchange rate within the Exchange Rate Mechanism (ERM) thereby further harming competitiveness. These factors are important because estimates indicate that a 4 per cent decline in competitiveness reduces UK export volumes by 1 per cent.

A third factor affecting UK exports is product quality. This includes things such as design, delivery, reliability, after-sales service and marketing. Although improving, the UK has traditionally done badly in terms of non-price competition.

Fourth is the commodity structure of exports. Traditionally the UK has exported manufactured and semi-manufactured goods such as textiles, machinery and metals. However, these tend to be low value-added and attempts to switch to exporting high value-added products, such as electronics and consumer goods, have been relatively unsuccessful.

Fifth is the geographical structure of exports. The pattern of trade has changed, with the UK trading to an ever-increasing extent with the EC. This has meant a decline in the importance of trade with Commonwealth countries and even with the USA. Consequently, there has been a movement away from relatively low income per head countries towards high income per head ones.

For this geographical change to be successful, the countries to which we are exporting must have a relatively high income elasticity for UK exports or a high marginal propensity to import UK goods. If this was so, the faster these countries grew, the faster our exports would rise. Exporters should therefore target the countries which exhibit the highest income elasticities. Unfortunately, the income elasticity for UK exports as a whole is less than unity, although UK manufacturers have an income elasticity of around 1.5. Thus a growth in world incomes will have relatively little impact on UK exports. In contrast, the UK has a high marginal propensity to import and so any increase in domestic demand will simply suck in additional imports.

TABLE 9.3   UK export growth and international growth rates

Country	Real growth in GDP 1985–89 (%)	Real growth in UK exports 1985–89 (%)	Real growth in GDP 1989–91 (%)	Real growth in UK exports 1989–91 (%)
Germany	12.2	0.6	7.4	14.5
France	11.1	−0.8	5.0	6.8
Italy	13.4	7.8	5.1	16.7
Ireland	14.3	4.8	6.3	−1.2
Portugal	18.8	68.0	5.3	4.2
Spain	19.6	63.1	6.4	20.0
USA	14.3	−14.6	1.4	−18.2
Japan	18.4	69.8	10.4	−13.7

Periods of world growth are therefore likely to result in a worsening of the UK current account while a world downturn should improve it.

Table 9.3 shows the effects of other countries' growth rates on UK exports. Since 1989 was the year when most countries experienced their highest growth rates, 1985–89 represents increasing growth while 1989–91 covers the slowdown (falling growth, as opposed to negative growth, which is encountered during a recession).

In terms of size, the UK's largest markets are Germany, the USA and France. Unfortunately, exports to Germany were static while those to the USA and France actually fell. Overall, export performance was extremely poor during the upswing, with real exports growing faster than income for only three countries, Portugal, Spain and Japan. The improvement in exports to Japan is not as impressive as it appears since the UK sold less there than it did to its seven largest EC markets. The same applies to Portugal, which was an even smaller market than Japan. Within Europe, the UK had most success in the poorer parts of the EC and least success in the richest markets. This mirrors previous failings of exporting to high income per capita countries.

The UK does slightly better in the slowdown, with exports growing faster than income in three key markets, Germany, France and Italy. Exports to Spain continued to grow rapidly. However, stable or expanding growth is the norm and so these improvements are likely to be short-lived.

The figures confirm the decline in the importance of the USA, with real exports falling throughout the period. The fall in exports to Japan may reflect the difficulties involved in selling there, particularly if there is a move towards greater protectionism during a slowdown.

For the UK exporter, Italy, Spain and Portugal appear to offer the best prospects. However, Spain and Portugal are in the process of industrializing and so are unlikely to yield the export revenues needed to pay for the UK's imports. The inability to increase exports to the likes of Germany and France suggests that the UK has not solved the long-standing problems of its lack of competitiveness in terms of both price and non-price factors.

10 Exchange rate determination

In the last chapter we examined the effects of exchange rate changes on the domestic economy, without paying too much attention to the question of how the exchange rate itself is determined, apart from the simple notion of supply and demand for currencies. We need something more than this. In particular, we need to consider what factors determine the supply and demand for currencies. However, having said this, we will see that there is no single model that can fully explain exchange rates, nor any simple rule that can be employed for forecasting exchange rates. In this section, we consider some of the most popular models, bearing in mind that at best they can only identify some of the major influences on exchange rates.

That there exist no models that can consistently predict exchange rates accurately should not come as a surprise. First, foreign currency is a financial asset, and the exchange rate is correspondingly the price of a financial asset; as such it will be governed by investors' expectations about the future, which by definition is uncertain. Second, if the foreign exchange market is *efficient*, then the current price (the spot exchange rate) will fully reflect all publicly available information. If the current price of a financial asset fully reflects all publicly available information, then its price will only change in the future as a result of new information or 'news'. But news, by definition, is unpredictable (otherwise, clearly, it is not genuinely news). Therefore, as the exchange rate changes to reflect the new information, it will do so in a way that is completely unpredictable. *An efficient market is one where past prices are of no use in predicting future prices.*

Clearly, if publicly available information is not immediately reflected in current prices, then this condition would not hold. Past price movements could be used to predict future price movements. To illustrate, suppose that it was known that the exchange rate responded to changes in a particular variable by moving in the same direction and by the same percentage change (it does not really matter what this variable is). Suppose also that it took two days for the exchange rate to fully adjust, and that it moved 50 per cent of the full adjustment on each day. A change in the particular variable constitutes news. If it is announced that this variable has fallen by 1 per cent, we also know that the exchange rate will fall by 0.5 per cent immediately and by another 0.5 per cent on the second day. A smart investor could make money by selling sterling for dollars as soon as the fall in the particular variable is announced and buy the sterling back the next day (this strategy is known in the financial markets as a *trading rule*). The investor would be able to buy back pounds for 0.5 per cent less than they were sold for on the previous day. If the original exchange rate was $2/£1, it would fall to $1.99/£1 immediately and to $1.98/£1 on the second day. The investor could sell sterling at $1.99 on day one and buy it back on day two at $1.98, leaving the investor with the same number of pounds, but with a riskless profit of one cent per pound from the transaction. Note that the investor can only profit from the delayed reaction of the exchange rate to the announced change in the particular variable. The exchange rate adjusts immediately by half the percentage movement in this variable. No investor can exploit this change: it takes place too quickly. However, the investor can exploit the predictable change in the exchange rate between day one and day two. But there is a problem with this. If all investors attempted to exploit this trading rule by selling sterling on the day that the fall in the particular variable is announced, market pressures would lead to the exchange rate falling by the full 1 per cent immediately, and no investor would be able to move fast enough to exploit the trading rule. Indeed, it is clear that in an efficient market, there is no profitable trading rule that can be exploited, since prices move too quickly. It follows then that if the market is efficient, the best forecast of future exchange rates is the current rate (adjusted for current interest rate differentials). While we can be certain that future exchange rates will differ from the current exchange rate, there is no way in which in an efficient market that this difference can be exploited to make profits. It is in this context that the models presented here should be judged.

We consider three popular models of the exchange rate that have received most attention in the economics literature:

1 The purchasing power parity model.
2 The monetary model and the overshooting hypothesis.
3 The portfolio balance model.

We shall concentrate mostly on the second model, not because it is in any sense the best model, but because it highlights the importance of expectations and in that context the role of anticipated macroeconomic policies. To the extent that exchange rates can be explained by *economic fundamentals* (i.e. fundamental economic variables as opposed to irrational behaviour by speculators), the overshooting hypothesis and the portfolio balance approach are possibly the most useful. However, the short-term view of the exchange rate is often dominated by *chartism* (or *technical analysis*) which attempts to detect patterns in past exchange rate movements that will be repeated and hence are useful in making predictions about exchange rate movements. Chartism is very popular among the analysts in the foreign exchange market and suggests that in the short term the foreign exchange market may not be efficient. If the foreign exchange market is continually efficient, then chartism does not provide a reliable guide to future price movements.

10.1   The purchasing power parity (PPP) model

Stated very simply, the PPP model of exchange rates says that *the nominal exchange rate moves in a way that keeps the real exchange rate constant*. The simplest form of the PPP model suggests that the exchange rate adjusts until the same bundle of goods costs the same in all countries. This in turn implies that

$$P = \frac{P^*}{e} \tag{10.1}$$

(where e = foreign price of domestic currency, such as \$ per £), P is the domestic price level and P^* is the foreign price level. Stated in this absolute way, *the nominal exchange rate is equal to the ratio of the foreign price level to the domestic price level*, i.e. $e = P^*/P$. If there is a rise in the domestic price level which raises the relative price of British goods abroad, the nominal exchange rate e will have to fall (i.e. depreciate) to preserve $P = P^*/e$. In other words, the role of the exchange rate is simply to equate the price of UK goods to the price of equivalent foreign produced goods, with both prices measured in a common currency. This assumes that goods produced in different countries are perfect substitutes. Note that in this strong version of PPP (sometimes called the *absolute* or *levels version*), the nominal exchange rate moves in such a way as to keep the real exchange rate not only constant, but equal to one. The PPP model is sometimes known as an *international trade arbitrage model*, since trade flows in goods will occur if PPP does not hold between countries.

A second version of PPP states that *the rate of change in the domestic price level is equal to the rate of change in the foreign price level less the rate of exchange rate appreciation*:

$$\dot{P} = \dot{P}^* - \dot{e} \qquad (10.2)$$

or

$$\dot{e} = \dot{P}^* - \dot{P} \qquad (10.3)$$

where $\dot{e}$ is the rate of appreciation of the exchange rate, $\dot{P}$ is the rate of change of the domestic price level (i.e. the domestic inflation rate) and P^* is the rate of change of the foreign price level (i.e. the foreign inflation rate). This version of PPP (sometimes called the *relative* or *rates of change version*) states that *the rate of change in the exchange rate is equal to the difference between foreign and domestic inflation rates*. Thus, for example, if UK inflation is 5 per cent higher than US inflation, sterling would be expected to depreciate by 5 per cent to maintain constant purchasing power for holders of US dollars who wish to purchase UK goods.

As a result of its simplicity, the PPP hypothesis has had considerable appeal for a long time. However, there are a variety of problems with this explanation of exchange rate determination. First, it ignores capital flows between countries. In recent years, these have been so enormous that the influence of the capital account on the exchange rate could not possibly be offset by the relatively small net trade flows that occur on the current account. Capital flows can often be the dominant factor affecting the exchange rate over both the short and medium term. Second, not all goods and services are traded internationally (e.g. New York taxi services are not available in London and vice versa), and, strictly speaking, PPP implies that the exchange rate adjusts to equalize the prices of internationally traded goods. However, non-traded goods are also included in measures of the domestic price level, which implies that we should not expect PPP to hold exactly even in its relative version, i.e. in terms of differential inflation rates. Also, calculations of PPP-consistent exchange rates based only on traded goods appear to reject PPP, but can be useful as indications of overvaluation or undervaluation when assessing long-term competitiveness (as we saw above).

To summarize our discussion of PPP: there is very little evidence to suggest that exchange rates move rapidly to offset national inflation rate differentials. Many researchers have failed to find evidence for PPP even in the very long run. However, as some form of benchmark equilibrium exchange rate, it may often be used as a guide to possible paths for the current exchange rate.

10.2   The monetary model and exchange rate overshooting

10.2.1   The monetary model

In the early 1970s, the *monetary model* was by far the most popular approach to exchange rate determination, due mainly to its close association with *monetarism*, which was also in the ascendancy during that period.

The central tenet of the monetary model is that *the exchange rate is the ratio of national monies*, since by definition the exchange rate is the price of one currency in terms of another. Therefore:

$$e = M^*/M \qquad (10.4)$$

where M is the UK money supply and M^* is the US money supply. It followed then, so the theory claimed, that exchange rate behaviour could be explained by changes in relative money supplies. A rise in the UK money supply would immediately lead to a depreciation of sterling.

Equivalently, if the growth rate in the UK money supply ($\dot{M}$) is greater than that in the US ($\dot{M}^*$), there will be a depreciation of sterling:

$$\dot{e} = \dot{M}^* - \dot{M} < 0 \quad \text{if} \quad \dot{M} > \dot{M}^* \tag{10.5}$$

In its early formulation there were three fairly strong assumptions made:

1 *Stable velocities of circulation of money.* In common with closed economy monetarism, it was assumed that the demand for money was stable. Therefore a rise in the domestic supply of money led to a rise in the domestic price level. However, for many countries the evidence shows that the demand for money functions and hence the velocities of circulation of money are not stable.
2 *Purchasing power parity holds at all times.* (With stable demand for money functions, the PPP and monetary models are essentially identical.) Given the lack of evidence for PPP, this assumption was particularly unattractive.
3 *Flexible prices in goods markets.* This essentially implied that a monetary expansion would raise domestic prices immediately and thereby lead to an immediate depreciation of the currency. More importantly, since domestic prices would immediately rise by the percentage increase in the money supply, the exchange rate would also depreciate to its PPP level. If, however, prices did not adjust immediately, then clearly the exchange rate would not move immediately to its long-run PPP level.

10.2.2   Exchange rate overshooting

The monetary model was revived to some extent with the development of the *Dornbusch model* (after the German economist Rudiger Dornbusch) in the mid 1970s which specifically allowed for *sluggish price adjustment* in the goods market, which is a fairly realistic assumption for the goods market. This is in contrast with asset markets, where price adjustments are almost instantaneous. This approach could explain significant deviations of the actual exchange rate from the PPP exchange rate. Popularly known as the *overshooting hypothesis*, it could explain excessive jumps in the exchange rate in response to 'news', while at the same time letting the long-run exchange rate be determined by PPP. Many analysts in foreign exchange markets believe that overshooting effects are prevalent.

We will consider a model which has sluggish price adjustment and work out the consequences for the behaviour of the exchange rate in the short run and long run in response to changes in macroeconomic policy, specifically monetary policy changes. The overshooting hypothesis can also be extended to explain some of the *volatility in exchange rates* that is commonly observed.

There are three main assumptions in this model:

1 There are two domestic markets: an *asset market*, which determines the prices of financial assets, in particular the domestic interest rate (i.e. the return on domestic bonds) and the exchange rate, and a *goods market*, which determines the aggregate price level. Prices in the asset market adjust *instantaneously* to equate demand and supply. The exchange rate depends on domestic and foreign interest rates, which are the relevant returns on financial assets, namely domestic and foreign bonds. The exchange rate is said to be a *forward-looking variable* because expectations about future interest rates play a crucial role in determining a currency's price now. The goods market, on the other hand, is characterized by significant transaction costs, and therefore price adjustments in the goods markets are *sluggish* and the price level is a *backward-looking variable*. However, in the long run, higher demand will lead to higher prices, so that there are no long-run real effects from a monetary expansion.

2 *Interest parity* is assumed to hold. Interest rates on domestic and foreign financial assets (r and r^*) are equalized by the expected change in exchange rates ($\dot{e}$):

$$r = r^* - \dot{e} \qquad (10.6)$$

or

$$\dot{e} = r^* - r \qquad (10.7)$$

If r is greater than r^*, the reason why investors are still willing to hold foreign financial assets is because the domestic currency is expected to depreciate (i.e. $\dot{e} < 0$). (The foreign interest rate (i.e. the return on foreign bonds) is assumed to be exogenous, i.e. determined outside the model.)

3 The *international Fisher effect* is assumed to hold. Combining interest parity and PPP with the Fisher equation (which assumes that the nominal interest rate equals the real rate *plus* expected inflation) implies that, in the long run, real interest rates are equalized across countries (this is known as the international Fisher effect). The Fisher equation implies that for the domestic economy

$$r = \rho + \dot{P} \qquad (10.8)$$

and for the foreign economy

$$r^* = \rho^* + \dot{P}^* \qquad (10.9)$$

where ρ is the real rate of interest in the domestic economy and ρ^* is the real rate of interest in the foreign economy (therefore, *the real rate of interest is the difference between the nominal rate of interest and the inflation rate*). Combining this with interest parity

$$r = r^* - \dot{e} \qquad (10.10)$$

gives

$$\rho + \dot{P} = (\rho^* + \dot{P}^*) - \dot{e} \qquad (10.11)$$

Combining in turn with relative PPP

$$\dot{e} = \dot{P}^* - \dot{P} \qquad (10.12)$$

implies

$$\rho + \dot{P} = (\rho^* + \dot{P}^*) - (\dot{P}^* - \dot{P}) \qquad (10.13)$$

which reduces to

$$\rho = \rho^* \qquad (10.14)$$

i.e. long-run interest rates are equalized across countries.

If the three assumptions hold, then *in the long run, the rate of change of the exchange rate is equal to the difference between foreign and domestic inflation rates*. If foreign and domestic inflation rates are equal, then both nominal and real interest rates will be equal. It is only when inflation rates differ that nominal interest rates differ (by the inflation rate differential), but real interest rates will still be the same in all countries, so investors will earn the same real interest rate, regardless of which country they invest in.

Asset market equilibrium

In Fig. 10.1(a) we represent the asset market equilibrium as combinations of the domestic price level and the nominal exchange rate for which the real exchange rate is constant. For simplicity, we assume that the foreign price level is constant and equal to unity. Therefore the hyperbola

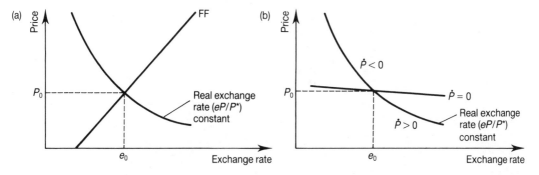

Figure 10.1 (a) Asset market equilibrium and (b) goods market equilibrium

in the figure represents all the combinations of P and e for which the real exchange rate (eP/P^*) is constant (with $P^* = 1$). (In other words, it is the graph of the equation $P = 1/e$.) The asset market equilibrium schedule FF is upward-sloping and drawn for a given nominal money supply. With a fixed money supply, a higher price level will reduce the real money supply and raise the interest rate. A higher interest rate causes an exchange rate appreciation. An increase in the money supply shifts FF to the left, since, at any given price level, the real money supply is higher and therefore the interest rate and the exchange rate will be lower. A fall in the money supply will shift FF to the right.

Goods market equilibrium
In Fig. 10.1(b) the goods market equilibrium is characterized by combinations of P and e for which the price level is not changing, i.e. $\dot{P} = 0$. The $\dot{P} = 0$ schedule is downward-sloping, because, as e falls, relative prices will fall (competitiveness will increase), raising the demand for domestic output and thereby leading to a higher price level. Points below the $\dot{P} = 0$ schedule represent situations where there is excess demand in the goods market. At any given price level, if the nominal exchange rate depreciates, the real exchange rate will also depreciate, and this will increase demand for domestic output and hence prices $(\dot{P} > 0)$. In contrast, points above the $\dot{P} = 0$ schedule represent positions of excess supply with prices falling $(\dot{P} < 0)$. Only along the $\dot{P} = 0$ schedule is there neither excess demand nor excess supply in the goods market.

Effects of an unanticipated monetary expansion
In Fig. 10.2 (p. 174), we combine the goods and asset market equilibrium schedules in $P - e$ space. Initially, suppose the economy is in equilibrium at point A, with the domestic price level at P_0 and the nominal exchange rate at e_0.

An unanticipated increase in the money supply will initially raise the real money supply since the price level P does not respond immediately to higher demand. The increase in the real money supply will initially lower interest rates. In Fig. 10.2, the asset market equilibrium schedule will move from FF_0 to FF_1. The lower interest rate will lead to capital outflows and an immediate jump depreciation of the exchange rate. The economy will jump to the new FF_1 schedule. Since the price level is sticky, the new equilibrium is point B, where all the movement has been in the exchange rate which falls to e_1. But this is not the final equilibrium, since although the asset market is in equilibrium, the goods market is not.

Consider what is happening in the asset market. If initially nominal domestic and foreign interest rates are equal, the expected rate of change in the exchange rate must be zero, since, from the Fisher equation, expected inflation rates must also be equal. The impact effect of a

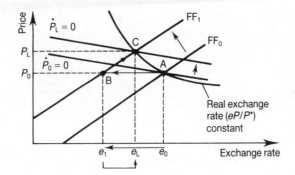

Figure 10.2   Exchange rate overshooting: the effects of an unanticipated increase in the money supply

monetary expansion, however, is to lower the domestic interest rate, while leaving foreign interest rates unchanged. Why then would investors hold domestic financial assets, if they are offering a lower return?

The answer must be because they expect the domestic currency to appreciate. But are such expectations justified? In other words, under what circumstances will the currency appreciate as expected? Point B in Fig. 10.2 represents a situation of excess demand in the goods market, especially export demand. The money supply has risen, the exchange rate has depreciated and the domestic price level is still P_0. Higher demand will raise prices and thereby reduce the real money supply, causing the interest rate to rise again. The anticipation of a higher domestic interest rate is what leads investors to expect the currency to appreciate in the long run.

As the nominal exchange rate appreciates, the real exchange rate will also appreciate, reducing the competitiveness of domestic output. This process will continue until excess demand in the goods market has been eliminated. Excess demand will be zero when the real exchange rate is restored to its original level (i.e. anywhere on the hyperbola). Point C in Fig. 10.2 represents the long-run equilibrium in both markets. Prices have risen sufficiently to bring the domestic interest rate back into line with world interest rates, and the exchange rate will again be stable.

Examining the path of the exchange rate reveals the impact effect of the monetary expansion to be greater than the long-run effect (Fig. 10.3). This is what is meant by *overshooting* of the exchange rate in response to a monetary expansion. At time t_0, the exchange rate falls from e_0 to e_1. From then on it appreciates gradually towards e_L. Note that the monetary expansion is a one-off change in the level of the money supply. Another way to understand the overshooting

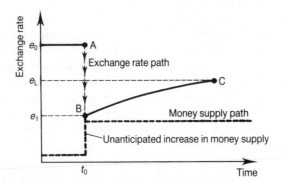

Figure 10.3   Nominal exchange rate path: the effects of an unanticipated increase in the money supply

phenomenon is to distinguish between the long run and the short run. If the supply of sterling is higher, each pound must be worth less in the long run. But from the moment after the monetary expansion takes place, and because interest rates will be rising, the currency will be appreciating. Therefore, for both of these features to exist, it must be the case that initially the exchange rate falls to a point that is lower than its long-run level. Note that, since prices are fixed in the short run, the real exchange rate will also depreciate as a result of the initial depreciation in the nominal exchange rate.

Exchange rate overshooting stories did appear reasonably convincing in the early 1980s as an explanation of sharp reductions in competitiveness associated with tight monetary policies, i.e. the opposite shock to the money supply from that analysed in Fig. 10.3. However, it could be argued that these particular restrictive monetary policies were not entirely unanticipated. After all, the Thatcher government was elected with the specific intention of controlling inflation. If investors have some advance warning of future tight policies, then the appreciation in exchange rates would have occurred when the policies were announced, not when they were actually implemented. The extent of the appreciation will also be somewhat lower in this case since the interest rate effect will be spread across a longer period. (Note that because the money supply growth rate was cut sharply by the Thatcher government, the exchange rate immediately appreciated to a level that was well above the long-run equilibrium level.)

10.2.3   Exchange rate volatility

Exchange rate volatility, the pattern of repeated and largely unpredictable movements up and down of the exchange rate, can to some extent be explained by the same mechanisms that generate overshooting. As a simple example, suppose the government believes in restrictive monetary policies (because it wants to control inflation) and has announced that monetary growth in the future will be lower. Investors therefore expect higher interest rates in the future and this will cause the exchange rate to appreciate. However, if we also assume that the government lacks complete *policy credibility*, then investors will attach a positive probability to the government reneging on its *policy commitment* and actually pursuing expansionary policies in an attempt to gain popularity (since tight monetary policies usually lead to higher unemployment at least in the short term, and this is damaging to a government's re-election prospects). Alternatively, one could envisage the uncertainty about the government's commitment arising from the possibility that the government might not actually be in office when the promised policies are to be implemented. Investors would then attach a positive probability to another political party being in office and having different objectives. If either of these two conditions holds, the appreciation of the exchange rate could be followed by an equally rapid depreciation.

Given this uncertainty, if the government announces and promises a policy of 0 per cent monetary growth and an alternative outcome is 10 per cent monetary growth (the growth rate pursued by the opposition political party if it gained power), the expected future growth rate would be a weighted average of 0 per cent and 10 per cent (depending on the likely success of the opposition party at the next general election). For example, if the electorate believes that there is a 60 per cent chance of the opposition winning the next election, then the expected monetary growth rate is 6 per cent (i.e. 0.4×0 per cent $+ 0.6 \times 10$ per cent). The exchange rate today will depreciate to the level consistent with monetary growth of 6 per cent per annum. At the actual time of the implementation of the policy, we will have either 0 per cent monetary growth if the government survives, or 10 per cent if it does not. Either way, the exchange rate will jump again. This example, although extremely simple, does bring out the role of *expectations* about the future in determining the exchange rate today.

One of the main problems with the overshooting hypothesis is that, although it can explain sharp movements in exchange rates, the adjustment path should be one where the exchange rate gradually reverts to its long-run equilibrium value along a predictable path. In practice, there are often sustained periods when currencies are overvalued or undervalued. More importantly, there is evidence that the actual volatility in exchange rates is greater than is consistent with the variations in the underlying economic variables that cause overshooting. Therefore this model, while useful, has not fully resolved the problem of exchange rate volatility.

10.3   The portfolio balance model

There are three main criticisms of the monetary model. First, the monetary model requires PPP to hold continuously, but the empirical evidence for PPP is very weak. The *portfolio balance model* does not require PPP to hold continuously. Indeed, with this approach, there can be fairly long periods when it does not hold. A second criticism of the monetary model is its assumption of perfect substitutability between domestic and foreign financial assets, something which is difficult to justify given that there are still constraints and barriers present in international capital markets, and also differences in preferences for domestic and foreign assets held by domestic residents. The portfolio balance model allows for *imperfect substitutability* between assets. This implies that investors have desired ratios between (or desired proportions of their wealth devoted to) different types of assets in their portfolios (hence the term 'portfolio balance'). They are not indifferent to the proportions of different assets that they have in their portfolios, as is the case when assets are perfect substitutes for each other. Third, throughout the analysis of the monetary model there was little mention of the current account as a factor determining exchange rates. In the portfolio balance model, the exchange rate is determined by the markets in both assets and goods. A current account deficit or surplus leads respectively to a net reduction or accumulation of foreign financial assets held by domestic residents. The current account, although not directly important in determining changes in short-term exchange rates, is important in affecting the relative supplies of domestic and foreign assets, and will therefore influence the exchange rate over the long term.

In the portfolio balance model, *the equilibrium exchange rate is such as to equate the demand by domestic investors for foreign assets with the supply of foreign assets, conditional on the relative returns and relative supplies of all assets held in the portfolios of domestic investors.* For simplicity, we will assume that the only assets held are money and domestic and foreign government bonds (i.e. we assume that there are no corporate bonds or shareholdings etc.). We therefore define the net wealth of domestic investors as consisting of the domestic *monetary base* (H), the stock of *domestic government bonds* (B) and the stock of *foreign government bonds* (F). The monetary base (also known as *high powered money* or M0) is the stock of notes and coin in circulation together with the deposits held by banks at the central bank. Bank deposits are not included in the definition of net wealth since, for the private sector, these are cancelled out by equivalent liabilities (bank loans). F/e is the domestic value of foreign bonds held domestically (where F is the value of domestic holdings of foreign bonds in dollars and e is the exchange rate measured in $ per £). Therefore total wealth measured in the domestic currency is $A = H + B + F/e$. We also assume that, for given interest rates, investors have a desired *asset mix or portfolio balance* (e.g. 10 per cent of wealth in money, 50 per cent in domestic bonds and 40 per cent in foreign bonds) and that investors will adjust their portfolios to maintain these desired proportions as their wealth changes. A change in relative interest rates will cause the desired asset mix to change in favour of the asset, the return of which has relatively increased.

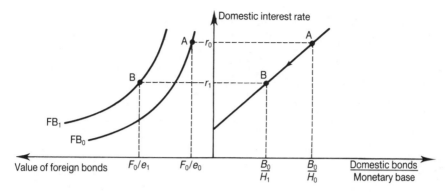

Figure 10.4 Monetary expansion in the portfolio balance model

10.3.1   Monetary policy

In Fig. 10.4, the right-hand side of the diagram shows how the domestic interest rate is determined as a function of the ratio of domestic bonds to base money. A rise in this ratio raises domestic interest rates. (As more bonds are supplied to the market, bond prices fall and yields will rise.) On the left-hand side, the FB schedule shows the value of domestically held foreign bonds at each different level of the domestic interest rate. The FB schedule is downward-sloping, indicating that as domestic interest rates rise, investors switch out of foreign bonds into domestic bonds. Suppose the existing equilibrium is at point A, with the value of foreign bonds equal to F_0/e_0 and the domestic interest rate at r_0. In other words, given the stocks of all assets (H_0, B_0 and F_0) and given domestic interest rates (r_0), the equilibrium exchange rate e_0 is determined to equate the domestic demand for foreign bonds (valued in domestic currency) with the supply of foreign banks available on the domestic market.

If the central bank increases the money supply, the ratio of domestic bonds to base money will fall, reducing the domestic interest rate from r_0 to r_1 and, as a consequence, the exchange rate from e_0 to e_1. The increase in the monetary base also leads to an increase in wealth holdings (i.e. A). The increase in wealth will shift the FB schedule to the left (from FB_0 to FB_1). Higher wealth increases the demand for all assets, including foreign bonds. However, the stock of foreign bonds held has not changed. The value of foreign bonds will rise as a result of both the increase in demand for foreign bonds and the fall in the exchange rate from e_0 to e_1. The new equilibrium is at point B. Portfolio adjustment has taken place via an exchange rate depreciation. How much will the exchange rate depreciate? That depends on the magnitude of the wealth effect that caused the FB schedule to shift to the left. The greater the wealth effect, the greater the required fall in the exchange rate since F_0 has not changed.

10.3.2   Fiscal policy

Suppose the government increases its expenditure and decides to finance this by issuing bonds, the stock of which increases from B_0 to B_1 (Fig. 10.5, p. 178). Before the increase in expenditure, the domestic interest rate was r_0 at point A, with the value of foreign bonds at F_0/e_0. Following the fiscal expansion, the ratio of bonds to money rises, and as a result, the domestic interest rate rises to r_1. Since the total stock of bonds has increased, total wealth will have risen. The FB schedule will move to the left, indicating a higher demand for foreign bonds. In Fig. 10.5, if the wealth effect shifts the FB_0 schedule to FB_2, then the value of domestically held foreign bonds will rise. Since the stock of foreign bonds has not changed, the only way that the domestic value

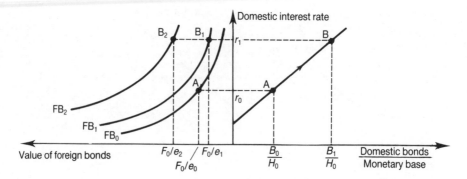

Figure 10.5   Fiscal expansion in the portfolio balance model

of these bonds can rise is for the exchange rate to *depreciate* from e_0 to e_2. However, if the FB_0 schedule only moves to FB_1, then the value of domestically held foreign bonds will fall, since, in this case, the exchange rate *appreciates* from e_0 to e_1. There are two effects operating. The *wealth effect* causes a shift to the left of the FB schedule; this increases the demand for all assets including foreign bonds. But there is also a *substitution effect*, which causes a move away from foreign bonds towards domestic bonds, since domestic interest rates are now higher than foreign interest rates. The substitution effect is represented by a move down a given FB schedule.

The analysis shows why it is often difficult to determine the precise effects of higher budget deficits on exchange rates. The actual outcome will depend on the relative magnitudes of the substitution and wealth effects. The greater the degree of substitution between domestic and foreign bonds, the more likely it is that the exchange rate will appreciate. In the case of FB_0 shifting to FB_1, the substitution effect dominates the wealth effect, the demand for foreign bonds falls and the exchange rate appreciates. In the case of FB_0 shifting to FB_2, the wealth effect dominates the substitution effect, the demand for foreign bonds rises and the exchange rate falls.

10.4   Summary

1 There are three main models explaining the exchange rate: the purchasing power parity model, the monetary model and the portfolio balance model. At best these models can identify some of the major economic influences (known as economic fundamentals) on exchange rate movements. This is because exchange rates are very difficult to predict, partly because the future is full of uncertainties and partly because the foreign exchange market is generally regarded as efficient, at least in the long term. In the short term, however, the foreign exchange market is frequently dominated by the activities of chartists, who attempt to predict future exchange rate movements by identifying patterns in past exchange rate movements that will continue into the future. The ability of chartists to make profits is evidence that the foreign exchange market is not efficient in the short term.

2 The absolute version of the purchasing power parity model states that the nominal exchange rate adjusts to equalize price levels in all countries, so that the same bundle of goods costs the same in all countries when measured in a common currency. In other words, the nominal exchange rate moves in a way that keeps the real exchange rate constant. The relative version of the model states that the rate of depreciation in the exchange rate is equal to the difference between foreign and domestic inflation rates. The PPP model does not provide a good predictor of exchange rates in the short term, since short-term capital flows are

many times larger than the trade flows designed to exploit international trade arbitrage possibilities. However, the model may well provide a good model for the long-term determination of the exchange rate.

3 The absolute version of the monetary model states that the nominal exchange rate is equal to the ratio of the foreign money supply to the domestic money supply. The relative version of the model states that the rate of depreciation of the exchange rate is equal to the difference between the growth rates of the foreign and domestic money supplies. The model predicts that a rise in the UK money supply will immediately lead to a depreciation of sterling against other currencies. The monetary model is consistent with the PPP model if the velocities of circulation of money in all countries are stable.

4 The simplest versions of the PPP and monetary models assume that prices in goods markets are flexible. In this case, the exchange rate immediately moves to its new equilibrium level following a change in the money supply or price level in one country. If the goods market is characterized by sluggish price adjustment, then the exchange rate might, in the short term, jump past its new long-term equilibrium value following a change in the money supply, according to the Dornbusch model. This property is called exchange rate overshooting and can be used to explain the substantial volatility in exchange rates observed in the markets. The main assumptions of the Dornbusch model are that: prices in financial markets adjust instantaneously, while prices in goods markets are sluggish; interest parity holds, so that the interest rate differential between countries equals the expected rate of depreciation of the exchange rate; and the international Fisher effect holds, so that real interest rates are equalized across all countries.

5 Given these assumptions, the effect of an unanticipated monetary expansion is initially to raise the real money supply since the price level is sluggish. This reduces interest rates and leads to a capital outflow and an immediate jump depreciation of the exchange rate. However, the lower exchange rate will lead to an increase in export demand and hence an excess demand for domestically produced goods. This will put upward pressure on the price level, which will reduce the real money supply and cause interest rates to rise again. The rise in interest rates leads to an increase in the exchange rate, which reduces competitiveness and export demand. Long-run equilibrium is established when the real exchange rate is restored to its original level. The reason that the exchange rate overshoots is that both interest rate parity holds and real interest rates are equalized across countries. This means that domestic interest rates and the exchange rate must both rise and fall together. This will only happen if the initial jump in the exchange rate overshoots its long-run level.

6 The portfolio balance model states that the equilibrium exchange rate equates the demand by domestic investors for foreign assets (denominated in the domestic currency) with the supply of foreign assets, conditional on the relative returns and relative supplies of all assets. This model does not require purchasing power parity to hold continuously. Nor does it require assets to be perfect substitutes internationally. Indeed, it assumes that assets are imperfect substitutes, which implies that investors have desired ratios between different assets in their portfolios. This means that changes in the relative supplies of assets will lead to changes in interest rates and exchange rates in order to restore desired ratios of assets in portfolios. For example, a current account deficit or surplus leads to a net reduction or accumulation of foreign financial assets. Similarly, monetary policy or bond-financed fiscal policy leads to an increase in the supply of domestic financial assets. In the case of a monetary expansion, the domestic money supply will increase. There is both a wealth effect (more money means investors are richer), which increases the demand for all assets, and a substitution effect, which reduces interest rates and the exchange rate. In the case of a bond-financed fiscal expansion, the supply of domestic bonds will increase. There is both a wealth effect, which increases the

demand for all assets, including foreign bonds, and a substitution effect, which causes a move away from foreign bonds towards domestic bonds, since interest rates are now higher. If the substitution effect is larger than the wealth effect, the demand for foreign bonds falls and the exchange rate appreciates. If the wealth effect is larger, the demand for foreign bonds rises and the exchange rate rises.

Exercises

1 Compare and contrast the following approaches to exchange rate determination: (a) the purchasing power parity model, (b) the monetary model and (c) the portfolio balance model.

2 'If the foreign exchange market is efficient, then chartism has no role to play in exchange rate determination.' Discuss.

3 Describe the PPP model (a) in its absolute version and (b) in its relative version. Which version, if any, is more likely to hold in practice?

4 What are the main weaknesses of the PPP model?

5 Is the following statement true or false? 'An increase in a country's money supply, holding the money supplies of other countries constant, will cause that country's exchange rate to appreciate.'

6 Briefly describe what happens in the Dornbusch model of exchange rate overshooting when there is an unanticipated increase in the money supply.

7 Under what assumptions will long-run real interest rates be equalized across countries? Rank these assumptions in order of increasing realism.

8 'Exchange rate volatility is inversely related to the degree of credibility that investors and commentators attach to a government's announced monetary policy.' Discuss.

9 Examine the effects of (a) a monetary contraction and (b) a fiscal contraction in the portfolio balance model of exchange rate determination.

10 Using the portfolio balance model, explain how exchange rate movements can depend on the degree of substitutability between domestic and foreign assets.

11 How is it possible for an expansionary fiscal policy to have an ambiguous effect on the exchange rate?

12 'Actual exchange rate volatility is much greater than that predicted by any theory of exchange rate determination. Macroeconomists have therefore not yet found the true model explaining the exchange rate.' Discuss.

Business application: Exchange rates and company performance

Although there are many measures of company performance, four tend to be given prominence in annual reports. These are sales, growth of sales, absolute profits and growth of absolute profits. For companies extensively involved in exporting, these performance indicators are directly affected by one crucial factor which is outside their control—the *exchange rate*.

The impact of movements in the exchange rate on a company's foreign sales, and hence profits, is known as its *foreign currency transactions exposure*. A UK firm exporting to America will be paid in dollars (dollar receivables) which then have to be converted into pounds sterling. The higher the £/$ spot rate, the lower the £ value of a given quantity of dollars, while the lower the £/$ spot rate, the higher the £ value of a given quantity of dollars. Thus exporters prefer a lower value for sterling on the foreign exchange market, since this boosts their revenues and profits. The problem for governments, however, is that a low, or falling, exchange rate creates upward pressure on import prices, and so is inflationary. The opposite applies to a high exchange rate, which is preferred by governments but disliked by exporters.

In 1991, ICI reported sales of £3,843m to the Americas, around 30 per cent of its total turnover. Assume, for simplicity, that all the sales took place in the USA. What we are interested in is the $ value of these sales, so that the effect of different exchange rates may be calculated. No dollar figure is given in the company report, so we will convert the £3,843m at the *average* end of month rate for 1991 which was $1.7612. This gives dollar sales of $6,768m (rounded).

To illustrate the impact of the exchange rate on ICI's turnover, these dollar sales will be converted into sterling using the highest and lowest exchange rates quoted for the last working day of each month during 1991.

1 Lowest end of month rate: £1 = $1.6215
$$\$6,768m = £4,174m$$
2 Highest end of month rate: £1 = $1.9590
$$\$6,768m = £3,455m$$

Thus if ICI had used the lowest exchange rate, sales would have been 8.7 per cent higher (£331m) than those generated, in this example, by using the average rate.

The dollar value of sales is also affected by the exchange rate, so if ICI had wanted to show how its American operations were performing in terms of the American currency, its sterling sales of £3,843m represent

1 $7,528m at the £1.9590 rate.
2 $6,768m at the £1.7612 rate.
3 $6,231m at the £1.6215 rate.

Thus the highest rate gives an 11 per cent increase in dollar sales compared with the average rate.

The impact of the exchange rate on ICI's profits is equally dramatic. Its American operations generated £391m profit in 1991. At the average exchange rate this converts to $689m.

However:

1 Lowest end of month rate: £1 = $1.6215
$$\$689m = £425m$$
2 Highest end of month rate: £1 = $1.9590
$$\$689m = £352m$$

Profits would be 8.7 per cent higher (£34m) if the lowest, rather than the average, rate had been used.

The exchange rate will also affect a company's growth. For 1990–91, ICI's growth of sales and growth of profit were calculated again using the average, highest month end and lowest month end rates.

1 Growth of sales with:
   (a) average exchange rate = 5.25 per cent
   (b) highest exchange rate = 2.67 per cent
   (c) lowest exchange rate = 4.32 per cent
2 Growth of profits with:
   (a) average exchange rate = 2.35 per cent
   (b) highest exchange rate = 0 per cent
   (c) lowest exchange rate = 1.43 per cent

These examples show that the performance of major exporters such as ICI can be significantly affected by movements in the exchange rate. A low exchange rate boosts the sterling value of dollar sales and profits, whereas a high exchange rate reduces them.

11 The money supply process in the United Kingdom

In recent years, monetary policy has come to occupy a central role in the overall framework of macroeconomic policy. Since the late 1970s, the widespread acceptance among politicians and a significant number of academic economists of the doctrine of *monetarism* is the primary reason for this. Monetarism is based on the belief that monetary growth is the primary cause of inflation. From this it followed that the only prerequisite to control inflation was to control the growth of the money supply. The main issue for designing a non-inflationary monetary policy was to select the appropriate *definition of money* and then to establish and adhere to monetary growth targets against that particular definition of the money supply. In practice in the UK, the policy of setting *monetary targets* has not been very successful. Most of the targets were never achieved, yet the policy objective of lowering the rate of inflation was achieved. Attention shifted toward other techniques of control, and also towards other indicators, especially interest rates and exchange rates. Between 1987 and 1992, the UK conducted monetary policy through *exchange rate targets* against the Deutschmark.

In this chapter, we begin by examining the process of *deposit creation*, which centres around the banking system, and then go on to outline the two main models of money supply determination, the *money multiplier model* and the *flow of funds model*. The latter is the one used by the UK monetary authorities, and we shall therefore discuss the conduct of monetary policy within this framework. Finally, we review some of the problems faced by the authorities in controlling the supply of money, and therefore in controlling inflation.

11.1   Deposit creation in a fractional reserve banking system

In order to examine how the money supply is determined, we first define *money* as *all assets that can be used as a medium of exchange* (i.e. for buying goods and services). This covers cash and bank (and building society) current account (i.e. chequeing) deposits that are used for making payments.

When banks accept deposits from members of the public (which then become the banks' *liabilities*), they know from past experience that not all deposits will be withdrawn at once. In practice, the public will withdraw only a fraction of these deposits and demand cash during any given time period. The remainder of the deposits can be used by the banks to make loans to borrowers; the loans become the banks' *assets* and earn interest for the banks. The interest from the loans is used to pay a (lower) interest rate to depositors and to give profits to the banks' shareholders. Suppose the deposits of the banking system increase as a result of higher government expenditure. (The recipients of the higher government expenditure, such as teachers or pensioners, will deposit the extra money in their bank accounts.) The banks will retain only a small fraction of these additional deposits as reserves to meet withdrawals. They will lend out the remaining fraction (i.e. make loans). If these loans are in turn used by the borrowers to make payments by writing cheques, the deposits of the banking system will rise again when these cheques are deposited. Banks will then be able to expand loans even further. This suggests

TABLE 11.1   Deposit creation by the banking system

Round no.	Liabilities (£)		Assets (£)		Reserve ratio (%)
Initial equilibrium	Deposits	100	Cash	10	
			Loans	90	10
		100		100	
1	Deposits	110	Cash	20	
			Loans	90	18.2
		110		110	
2	Deposits	110	Cash	11	
			Loans	99	10
		110		110	
3	Deposits	119	Cash	20	
			Loans	99	16.8
⋮		119		119	
Final equilibrium:	Deposits	200	Cash	20	
			Loans	180	10
		200		200	

that a given initial increase in deposits will lead to a much greater increase in total deposits. There are two reasons for this. First, banks do not retain 100 per cent of the deposits in the form of *reserves* from which the banks can finance deposit withdrawals (this is known as a *fractional reserve banking system*). Second, when the public receive loans from banks, they do not hold the entire loan in the form of cash; instead, they re-deposit at least part of the loan back with the banking system at least on a temporary basis. If the public decided to hold more of their financial assets in the form of cash, the banks would have fewer deposits and would be able to lend less.

Table 11.1 illustrates the above process by considering the hypothetical balance sheet of the entire banking system. Initially bank deposit liabilities of £100 are equal to bank assets of £90 in the form of loans and £10 in cash (the cash represents the reserves of the banking system). Suppose the banking system is initially in equilibrium, maintaining a desired 10 per cent *reserve ratio* (i.e. cash to total liabilities). In Table 11.1 this is shown as the initial equilibrium. Now suppose the public deposit an extra £10 with the banks. Deposits rise to £110 and, on the asset side, cash reserves rise to £20 (Round 1). The banks are now holding 18.2 per cent of their total liabilities in reserves, which is in excess of their desired reserve ratio of 10 per cent. The banks can therefore increase their loans by up to £9 (Round 2). The reserve ratio is again 10 per cent, and the process would stop here if the public held this extra £9 in loans in the form of cash, but this extra £9 is deposited back with the banks by the recipients of the expenditure financed by the loans, deposits rise to £119 and cash reserves to £20 (Round 3). The banks are again holding too much cash (since they have a 16.8 per cent reserve ratio). This process will continue until we reach the final equilibrium, where deposits are £200, and the 10 per cent desired reserve ratio is re-established.

In the above example, we assumed that the public were satisfied with their initial cash holdings and did not want to hold any more cash as their deposits rose. If the public do want to maintain a constant cash to total deposits ratio, there will be an additional leakage in the *deposit creation process.* In the above example, an initial increase in deposits of £10 led to total deposits rising by £100. The deposit multiplier is 10 (equal to 1/reserve ratio). A higher reserve ratio implies a lower *deposit multiplier*, since at each stage banks will be able to increase loans by a smaller amount. The value of this reserve ratio is often determined by legal requirements. In the UK there have been no reserve requirements since 1981, apart from a prudential requirement to maintain 0.45 per cent of total liabilities in cash (this is called the *cash ratio*).

11.2   The money multiplier model

In the *money multiplier model* of money supply determination, there are two important relationships that must be taken into account. First, the relationship between reserves and total deposits, and second, the relationship between reserves and the total money stock.

In Figure 11.1, the *total money stock* is defined as *notes and coin in circulation (cash) plus bank deposits.* Also *high-powered money* or *base-money* (H) consists of *cash in circulation and reserves held by the banking system.* High-powered money is any asset that banks can use as reserves in order to create deposits. In practice, reserves are held in the form of bankers' balances at the central bank. (All banks have accounts at the central bank which are used partly to hold reserves,

Definitions

$$\text{Money } (M) = \text{Cash } (C) + \text{Deposits } (D)$$
$$\text{High-powered money } (H) = \text{Cash } (C) + \text{Reserves } (R)$$

Behavioural relationships

$$C = qD$$
$$R = kD$$
$$\therefore M = qD + D = D(q + 1)$$

and

$$H = qD + kD = D(q + k)$$
$$\therefore D = \frac{M}{(q + 1)}$$

and

$$D = \frac{H}{(q + k)}$$

Implication

$$\therefore M = \frac{(q + 1)}{(q + k)} H$$

$$= \left(\frac{C/D + 1}{C/D + R/D} \right) H$$

$q = C/D$: Non-bank private sector cash/deposit ratio
$k = R/D$: Banking sector reserve/deposit ratio
$\quad H$:   Government high-powered money

Figure 11.1   The money multiplier

but also for interbank transfers: for example, at the end of each business day, as part of the cheque-clearing or *money transmission process*, banks with net debits will transfer funds to banks with net credits using their accounts at the central bank.) The total quantity of H in circulation is in principle under the control of the central bank, since it is the sole legal supplier of cash to the financial system.

Suppose that the public's desired holdings of cash is some fraction q of their total deposits (i.e. their desired cash to deposits ratio is q), and also that the banks' desired reserves are some fraction k of their total deposits, D. Substituting these relationships for cash (C) and reserves (R) into the definitions of money (M) and high-powered money (H), and rearranging terms as in Fig. 11.1 yields the *money multiplier*, which relates the total money stock to the quantity of high powered money in the economy:

$$M = \left(\frac{q+1}{q+k}\right)H$$

$$= \left(\frac{C/D+1}{C/D+R/D}\right)H \tag{11.1}$$

The money multiplier is the term inside the parentheses. Thus for any given change in H, the money multiplier will determine the change in the money stock. Changes in H will change the ability of the banking system to create money (M), since high-powered money is what the banks use as reserves. An increase in H will therefore increase M as well, assuming the public's holdings of cash (which form a major component of H) do not change significantly. But the banking system has a significant role to play in creating deposits and hence in creating money. A reduction in reserves held by banks will increase the money stock, as will a reduction in cash holdings by the public.

There are different definitions of M depending on the degree of aggregation used. Definitions of the monetary aggregates commonly used in the UK are shown in Table 11.4 (Section 11.4). In the UK, H is known as M0 or the *wide monetary base*. M2 is a *narrow money aggregate* and M4 is a *broad money aggregate*. In order to derive the relationship between H (or M0) and M2, we would include only those deposits (i.e. chequeing deposits) that are contained in M2 in the definition of the reserves to deposits ratio (R/D). For M4, the definition of deposits would also include interest-bearing time deposits. This has the effect of lowering the R/D ratio and increasing the money multiplier, so that the M4 multiplier is much larger than the M2 multiplier.

The money multiplier model provides a framework in which the determination of the money supply can be analysed in terms of the actions of the three main groups operating in the monetary sector. These are the central bank (and the government) (which controls H), the banking sector (which determines R/D), and the so-called *non-bank private sector* (or general public) (which determines C/D). The money multiplier model is popular among advocates of *monetary base control*. Under monetary base control, the central bank would control H in order to achieve a given target for the money stock, M. The main problem with monetary base control is that it requires the existence of a stable multiplier, which implies that the public's demand for cash and the banks' holdings of reserves need to be stable. In the UK, the monetary authorities have never controlled the monetary base directly, mainly due to the belief that under strict base control, the banks would find difficulty in obtaining cash on demand, and would have an incentive to encourage the public to hold less cash. A further worry is the possible increase in the volatility of interest rates that would result from strict control of the monetary base; we consider this in more detail later in this chapter.

11.3   The flow of funds model

The *flow of funds model* looks at the flows between the government sector, the monetary authority, the banking sector and the non-bank private sector. One important aspect of the government sector is its fiscal policy stance, especially in respect of the size of the budget deficit that it runs and the extent of monetary finance required to finance the deficit. The flow of funds model analyses money supply determination in terms of the three main areas of economic policy that affect monetary growth: fiscal policy, the government's debt management policy (i.e. sales and repurchases of gilts) and exchange rate policy. The advantage of this model is that it identifies the sources of monetary growth directly and enables the authorities to determine what offsetting actions need to be undertaken to counteract particular components of the growth. Furthermore, when the authorities adhered to monetary targets during the early 1980s, the model was useful in emphasizing the fiscal targets that were implied by these monetary targets.

11.3.1   Determination of broad money

To outline the flow of funds approach, we need to examine the consolidated balance sheet of the banking system (which includes the commercial banks and building societies). The sources of monetary growth lie on the asset side of the balance sheet. We first consider the changes in *broad money* from the banking system's balance sheet (Table 11.2), and then go on to relate this to action taken by the authorities (Table 11.3).

Broad money is defined as *notes and coin in circulation (NC) plus all sterling bank (and building society) deposits of the UK private sector (DP)*. These include both interest-bearing and non-interest-bearing deposits. This is the M4 definition of broad money. The banking system's liabilities include both sterling and foreign currency deposits (FC), sterling deposits being further divided into holdings by residents (DP) and non-residents (DF). On the asset side, we include all sterling lending to the UK private sector (LP), to the public sector (LG) and to non-residents (LF). Looking at the balance sheet, it is clear that not all increases in sterling lending will increase the money supply. Some of the increase in sterling lending could be financed by increases in sterling deposits by non-residents (DF) or by increases in non-deposit liabilities (i.e. increases in bank (and building society) capital (BK)). All of these items would enable banks to increase sterling lending without having to increase sterling liabilities to UK residents. From Table 11.2 we can see that the increase in broad money is derived as follows:

Increase in broad money (ΔM) = Increase in notes and coin (ΔNC)

+ Increase in all sterling lending $(\Delta LP + \Delta LF + \Delta LG)$

− Increase in sterling deposits by non-residents $(-\Delta DF)$

− Borrowing from abroad $(-\Delta FC)$

− Increase in non-deposit liabilities of banks and building societies $(-\Delta BK)$

$$= \Delta NC + \Delta LP + \Delta LF + \Delta LG - \Delta DF - \Delta FC - \Delta BK \quad (11.2)$$

Equation (11.2) expresses changes in broad money from the asset side (supply side). Relating this to the actions of the authorities in terms of the three areas of economic policy mentioned earlier, we consider the different ways of financing the government's budget deficit or PSBR.

TABLE 11.2   Determination of broad money

Broad money $= NC + DP$

Consolidated balance sheet of banking system:

Liabilities	*Assets*
DP	LP
DF	LF
FC	LG
BK	

NC = Notes and coin held by the public
DP = Sterling deposits of UK private sector
DF = Sterling deposits of non-residents
FC = Net foreign currency liabilities of banking system
BK = Non-deposit liabilities (e.g. bank capital)
LP = Sterling lending to UK private sector
LF = Sterling lending to non-residents
LG = Sterling lending to public sector

TABLE 11.3   The public sector borrowing requirement and broad money

Financing PSBR: four options

1 ΔNC Issuing notes and coin to the public.
2 ΔBP Borrowing from the non-bank private sector, i.e. sales of government bonds.
3 ΔBF External finance (includes bond sales to non-residents and foreign currency borrowing).
4 ΔLG Borrowing from the banking system.

$$\therefore PSBR = \Delta NC + \Delta BP + \Delta BF + \Delta LG$$

$$\Rightarrow \Delta LG = PSBR - \Delta NC - \Delta BP - \Delta BF$$

Substituting into Eq. (11.2):

Increase in broad money $= PSBR - \Delta BP + \Delta LP + \Delta LF - \Delta BF - \Delta DF - \Delta FC - \Delta BK$

i.e. $\Delta M = PSBR$

   $-$ Bond sales $(-\Delta BP)$

   $+$ Increase in bank lending $(\Delta LP + \Delta LF)$

   $-$ Net external finance $(-\Delta BF - \Delta DF - \Delta FC)$

   $-$ Increase in non-deposit liabilities $(-\Delta BK)$

11.3.2   The public sector borrowing requirement and broad money

The PSBR can be financed in four ways: issuing notes and coins to the public (this is known as monetizing the National Debt), borrowing from the non-bank private sector (i.e. selling government bonds or gilts to the private sector), external finance, which includes both foreign currency borrowing and sales of government bonds to non-residents, and finally borrowing from the domestic banking system. This last item allows us to relate PSBR financing to the banking system's balance sheet. As shown in Table 11.3, by substituting Eq. (11.2) into the PSBR financing equation and rearranging, we can express the change in broad money in terms of the supply side, i.e. those items or *counterparts* that create money:

Increase in broad money $(\Delta M) = PSBR$

$\qquad$ $-$ Bond sales to the non-bank private sector $(-\Delta BP)$

$\qquad$ $+$ Increase in bank and building society lending $(\Delta LP + \Delta LF)$

$\qquad$ $-$ Net external finance $(-\Delta BF - \Delta DF - \Delta FC)$

$\qquad$ $-$ Increase in non-deposit liabilities of banks and building societies $(-\Delta BK)$

$$= PSBR - \Delta BP + \Delta LP + \Delta LF - \Delta BF - \Delta DF - \Delta FC - \Delta BK$$

$$(11.3)$$

The first three items, PSBR, bond sales and bank lending, together define *domestic credit expansion*. They form the domestic sources of monetary growth. Taking each item in turn we see that the public sector borrowing requirement will add to monetary growth unless it is financed by borrowing either from the public or from overseas. The extent to which both these forms of borrowing exceed the total PSBR is known as the degree of *overfunding*. Overfunding implies that the government is selling more debt than its current shortfall between receipts and expenditure.

This simple framework, based on the balance sheet identities of the banking system and government financing, forms the basis of monetary control in the UK. Since the PSBR, bond sales and external flows can be identified with fiscal policy, debt management policy and exchange rate policy respectively, this framework shows the interrelationships between the various areas of economic policy.

11.4   Monetary aggregates in the UK

In this section, we examine the main monetary aggregates operating in the UK. The definitions of the main monetary aggregates are shown in Table 11.4.

M0 is the *wide monetary base* and includes banks' till money and bankers' balances at the Bank of England in addition to notes and coin in circulation. Narrower measures of the monetary base would include only bankers' balances at the Bank of England. Defined in this way it includes most of the liabilities of the central bank, and therefore is often cited as the only aggregate over which the authorities have any direct control.

The other monetary aggregates reported in Table 11.4 are M2 and M4, although definitions of the money supply ranging from M1 up to M5 exist. *M2 is a measure of narrow money*, that is, money that can readily be used for transactions purposes. In the past, the Bank of England's preferred measure of narrow money was called *non-interest bearing M1* which comprised notes and coin and non-interest bearing retail deposits with banks, i.e. personal sector chequeing accounts. These were the only deposits that in the past could be used directly for paying for transactions. However, in recent years building societies have also started to offer chequeing

TABLE 11.4   **Monetary aggregates in the UK**

Monetary aggregate	Definition
M0	Notes and coin (NC) + bankers' balances at Bank of England
M2	NC + retail deposits of banks and building societies
M4	M2 + building societies' share accounts + wholesale deposits of banks and building societies (including certificates of deposit)

**TABLE 11.5   UK monetary aggregates 1991
(amounts outstanding, £ millions)**

1	Notes and coin = 15,730
2	Bankers' balances = 205
3	M0(1 + 2) = 15,935
4	Retail deposits of banks = 144,737
5	Retail deposits of building societies = 117,819
6	M2(1 + 4 + 5) = 278,286
7	Building societies' share accounts = 58,494
8	Wholesale deposits of banks = 148,840
9	Wholesale deposits of building societies = 16,234
10	M4(6 + 7 + 8 + 9) = 501,854

accounts, and both banks and building societies have begun to offer deposit accounts that pay interest but can also be used for making transactions (e.g. high interest chequeing accounts). As a result of these financial innovations, the Bank of England has switched to using M2, which comprises notes and coin and the retail deposits of banks and building societies, i.e. all personal sector deposit accounts held within the banking system, whether interest-bearing or not. M2 therefore includes assets which are not held solely for transactions purposes, although they can easily be used for making transactions.

M4 is a measure of *broad money*. It comprises M2 plus building societies' share accounts (which have a different legal status from that of building society deposit accounts) plus the wholesale deposits of banks and building societies (including certificates of deposit). M4 therefore includes all the deposit accounts (both interest-bearing and non-interest-bearing) of the private sector (both personal sector and corporate sector). Before 1989, the Bank of England's preferred measure of broad money was *M3* (sometimes called *sterling M3* or *£M3*) which comprised notes and coin and all private sector deposit accounts with banks. But in 1989, one of the large building societies, the Abbey National, converted to a bank and at the time of the conversion M3 rose sharply, whereas M4 was not affected since building societies' deposits are already included in it. Since 1989, M4 has been the government's preferred broad money aggregate. *M5* comprises M4 plus private sector holdings of money market securities such as certificates of tax deposit and National Savings instruments that can be readily converted into cash. Table 11.5 shows the sizes of the UK monetary aggregates at the end of 1991.

11.5   The conduct of monetary policy

11.5.1   Monetary control

In Fig. 11.2, we illustrate the demand and supply schedules for money. The money market equilibrium condition is the rate of interest at which money demand equals money supply. Suppose the central bank target for the money supply is M_0^S, and the demand for money is known to be represented by M_0^D. In order to achieve a particular level of the money supply M_0^S, the central bank can either fix the interest rate at r_0 or it can directly control the quantity of money by supplying only M_0^S. It cannot fix both the interest rate and the quantity of money. However, with a known and stable money demand function, either method will yield exactly the same outcome in terms of interest rates and the level of the money supply.

The money supply measure here is typically a broad monetary aggregate such as M4, calculated from the product of the M4 money multiplier and the stock of high-powered money H. Supporters of monetary base control believe that the important thing is to control H and

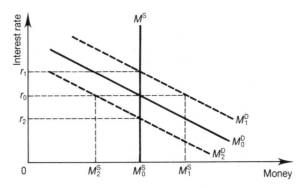

Figure 11.2 Monetary control

let the interest rate be market-determined. On the assumption that the money multiplier is stable, it is sufficient to control the growth of high-powered money in order to control the money stock. (We could quite easily extend this framework to include targets on growth rates for the money supply rather than targets for levels of the money supply.)

In practice, the demand for money relationship is not known with certainty and instead has to be estimated (using *econometric modelling techniques*). The authorities therefore will not know with certainty what the demand for money is at any given interest rate. In terms of Fig. 11.2, we do not know exactly where M_0^D is. If this is the case, then fixing interest rates or directly controlling the quantity of money does not amount to the same thing. Suppose the central bank set interest rates at r_0 and the actual demand for money turned out to be represented by the demand curve M_1^D. The Bank would have to supply whatever money is demanded at the set interest rate of r_0, with the result that the money supply would have to be set at M_1^S to keep interest rates at r_0. Conversely, if the central bank controls the quantity of money directly, changes in the demand for money will lead to fluctuations in interest rates (between r_1 and r_2 in the case where the money demand curve fluctuates between M_1^D and M_2^D). In other words, strict control of the quantity of money can often lead to substantial *interest rate volatility* if the demand for money function is not stable.

Controlling the quantity of money directly implies controlling the size of the central bank's own liabilities, i.e. the wide monetary base. In terms of the resulting broad money supply (either in levels or growth rates), the critical thing is the stability of the money multiplier. If the authorities did pursue a policy of monetary base control, changes in demand could, as we have just seen, lead to volatile interest rates. The alternative is to adjust interest rates to affect the demand for money. Thus, when the demand for money is M_1^D, interest rates would be raised to r_1; when the demand for money fell to M_2^D, interest rates would be lowered to r_2.

In the UK the monetary authorities do not operate a policy of monetary base control. The growth in the monetary base is monitored as one of a number of economic indicators, but direct control has not been exercised. In the late 1980s and early 1990s there were implicit targets for the monetary base (i.e. M0), but these were not given the same prominence that broad money growth targets (especially for M3) were given for the first half of the 1980s. Instead, the interest rate is used as the main instrument to influence monetary growth.

The UK authorities use interest rates in order to act on the supply side (i.e. on the sources of monetary growth), although when interest rates change, the demand for money will also be affected. In terms of the broad money counterparts identity (Eq. 11.3), monetary policy is conducted by first forecasting the growth of each of the components. The main ones are the PSBR (which for a few years in the late 1980s became the PSDR, which stands for *public sector debt repayment*), bank lending and external flows. Once these have been forecast, the authorities are able to determine the level of gilt sales required (or gilt repurchases in the case of a negative PSBR or positive PSDR) to achieve a particular target for broad money growth. Higher interest rates are needed to offset the growth in PSBR or bank lending, and to attract investors to gilts. But raising interest rates and selling more gilts is none other than one of the mechanisms required to reduce the demand for money. As members of the private sector purchase gilts, they run down their bank deposits, and this has a contractionary effect on money growth. In the late 1980s, gilts were being repurchased (redeemed) by the authorities, since there was a budget surplus. Yet the money stock was still growing very rapidly. The major source of monetary growth in the late 1980s and early 1990s was bank and building society lending to the private sector (i.e. the Lawson credit boom).

The main policy instrument to curtail bank lending is therefore the level of interest rates. In the UK, almost all quantity controls such as reserve ratios, special deposits etc. have either been abolished or are not used for monetary control. Bank lending, however, has proved extremely unresponsive (or at least very slow in responding) to interest rate increases (especially credit demanded by the household sector), and therefore the authorities have from time to time experimented with overfunding in order to take liquidity out of the financial system. More recently, they have recognized that higher interest rates in the short run may do little to change long-term interest rates. When the authorities have overfunded the deficit in the past, this has been mainly achieved by issuing short-dated gilts, with the result that short-term (i.e. under 5 year) interest rates have risen disproportionately relative to long-term (i.e. over 15 year) interest rates. Companies often then have incentives to switch their borrowings to long-term loans, with the effect that their demand (and therefore spending) is not curtailed by high short-term interest rates. As a result, the authorities have attempted to sell more long-dated gilts, thereby pushing up yields at the long end.

11.5.2   Monetary targets

For most of the 1980s, UK monetary policy was conducted on the basis of explicit monetary targets. This was known as the *medium term financial strategy*. The monetary aggregate that was targeted was £M3 (sterling M3). The practice of monetary targeting was abandoned in the late 1980s and monetary policy since then has been based on a variety of economic indicators. We conclude this chapter with a brief summary of the reasons behind this switch in emphasis away from quantity variables and more towards price variables, mainly interest rates and exchange rates.

The rationale for *monetary targets* was provided by the supposed stability of the velocity of circulation (equivalently, the stability of the demand for money function). Under these conditions, as we saw earlier, monetary growth was the main cause of inflation. If the *final objectives* or *goals* of the policy makers were low inflation and stable output growth, then monetary control was essential. The monetary aggregates themselves were the *intermediate variables* by which the stance of policy could be judged. As long as the monetary aggregates had a consistent and stable relationship with the objective (or goal) variables, then monitoring and controlling the money supply was considered to be sufficient for achieving these objectives. Indeed, it was argued that this was all that policy could hope to achieve. A second rationale was that if targets for money growth were set for a number of years ahead, they would provide a stable environment for private sector economic activity, and, more importantly, could help influence private sector *inflation expectations*, especially insofar as this affected wage bargaining (since the higher the inflation expectations, the higher the wage increases demanded by workers and the greater the possibility of a *wage–price spiral* developing). Adherence to targets was seen as committing policy makers to *policy rules* that would enhance their *credibility*.

The aggregate chosen for targeting was £M3 and the target range was reduced by 1 per cent each year, beginning in 1980/81 when the target range was 7–11 per cent. The choice of £M3 was determined by its apparent close relation to retail price inflation. The policy was formally abandoned in 1986/87, although as early as 1985 the authorities began to give less and less attention to monetary aggregates. If the policy had to be judged in terms of its objective, then there was considerable success, as inflation did fall significantly in the mid-1980s. However, the targets themselves were never met. In each year actual growth was considerably above the target range. For example, the target range for £M3 in 1986/87 was 4–8 per cent, but the actual growth in £M3 was 20 per cent.

A number of reasons have been offered to explain this. First, within the financial sector, the pace of financial innovation, especially that resulting from the competition between the banks and building societies to provide retail financial services, resulted in a variety of new interest-bearing chequeing accounts. Broad money aggregates were increasingly influenced by assets which contained mainly savings balances. This meant that broad money aggregates such as £M3 could actually have the perverse outcome of increasing as the authorities raised interest rates to reduce inflation, since individuals would increase their holdings of the interest-bearing components of £M3. Second, there was a fall in inflation during the mid-1980s, which increased the private sector's willingness to hold financial assets. This is because financial assets maintain their real values better, the lower the inflation rate. For both these reasons, money growth exceeded the growth in national income, leading to a substantial fall in the velocity of circulation of money. So the prerequisite of a stable velocity necessary to ensure the effectiveness of monetary targeting was not present during this period.

11.5.3 Exchange rate targets

Between 1987 and 1992, policy switched to stabilizing the exchange rate, which by definition implies that the authorities cannot pursue a monetary target at the same time. There are in principle two main reasons for switching to *exchange rate targets*. First, the relationship between interest rates (the instrument of policy) and exchange rates was thought to be far more stable (via such relationships as the interest parity equations) than the relationship between money and inflation. Unlike changes in monetary aggregates, changes in interest rates do not take a long time to influence exchange rates. Second, given the degree of openness of the UK economy, the exchange rate is one of the main determinants of domestic price inflation: a high exchange rate forces exporters to keep their prices and costs under control, otherwise they will lose their overseas markets. The objective therefore was to use the sterling interest rate to maintain a constant exchange rate between sterling and a low-inflation economy, such as Germany. This has the effect of tying the UK inflation rate to that of Germany. Fixed exchange rates (or more strictly a fixed exchange rate band or zone) replaced floating exchange rates and the UK money supply became endogenous.

Nevertheless many economists regretted the passing of monetary targets in favour of interest rate or exchange rate targets. Their argument is that, with monetary targets, it is possible to announce a precise set of monetary targets for each year of the policy (e.g. monetary growth will be no more than 6 per cent in the first year, no more than 5 per cent in the second year etc.). No such time path can be announced for the interest rate, for example. With an interest rate target, all that a central bank can do is say that interest rates will remain 'high' until inflation has been cured. The authorities also come under great pressure to ease interest rates, since at the same time that inflation is being cured, the high interest rates are generally leading the economy into recession as businesses cut back on investment and engage in destocking. This was the case in the late 1980s and early 1990s, and the government's only answer was to say, as John Major did when he was Chancellor of the Exchequer, 'if it's not hurting, it's not working'. It has been argued that precise numerical targets give a policy greater credibility than one with qualitative targets.

The UK's monetary policy after 1992 is discussed in the next chapter.

11.6   Summary

1 Money is defined as all assets that are used as a medium of exchange. This includes cash and bank (and building society) current account deposits that can be used for making payments. The two main participants in the money supply process are the government (via the issuance of notes and coin) and banks and building societies (via the deposit creation process) in a fractional reserve banking system.

2 In a fractional reserve banking system, banks (or building societies) receive deposits from the public, but they do not retain 100 per cent of the deposits in the form of reserves. Instead, they use the deposits for making loans to the public. In turn, the recipients of the loans typically re-deposit part of the loan back with the banking system, thereby allowing the banks (or building societies) to make further loans and receive further deposits. This is known as the deposit creation process.

3 The money multiplier model demonstrates that there is a multiplier relationship between high-powered or base money and the money stock. Base money consists of notes and coin in circulation and banks' reserves at the central bank. The money stock consists of notes and coin in circulation plus bank (and building society) deposits. The size of the multiplier depends on the cash ratio (or reserves to deposits ratio) required by the government, and on the desired cash to deposits ratio of the public. The higher these ratios, the lower the money multiplier, and hence the lower the money supply for a given money base.

4 There are various definitions of the money stock depending on the degree of aggregation used. In the UK, high-powered money is known as M0 or the wide money base. M2 is a narrow money aggregate and includes only bank and building society retail deposits in its definition of deposits. In contrast, M4 is a broad money aggregate and includes bank and building society retail and wholesale deposits in its definition of deposits. As a result M4 is about twice as large as M2.

5 The money multiplier model shows how the money supply depends on the actions of the government (which controls the money base), the banking sector (which determines the reserves to deposits ratio), and the non-bank private sector (which determines the cash to deposits ratio). The model is popular with supporters of monetary base control who wish to control inflation by controlling the money supply.

6 The flow of funds model analyses money supply determination in terms of the three main areas of economic policy that affect monetary growth: fiscal policy, the government's debt management policy and exchange rate policy. The model identifies the sources of monetary growth directly and allows the authorities to take offsetting actions if particular sources begin to exhibit excessive growth. The increase in a broad money aggregate such as M4 is equal to domestic credit expansion (which equals the component of the public sector borrowing requirement not financed by bond sales to the non-bank private sector, plus the increase in bank lending) plus net external finance less any increase in non-deposit liabilities of banks (and building societies). The model forms the basis of monetary control in the UK, where the PSBR, bond sales and external flows are identified respectively with fiscal policy, debt

management policy and exchange rate policy. The PSBR will add to monetary growth unless it is financed by borrowing from the public or from overseas. Bank lending (including bank lending to the government) will also add to monetary growth unless it is financed from an increase in the capital base of the banks.

7 The government can engage in monetary control either by controlling the stock of money directly, or by fixing the interest rate. It cannot do both. If the money demand function is stable, it does not matter which strategy is used. However, if the demand for money function is not stable, then there will be substantial interest rate volatility. In practice, the UK government does not operate a policy of monetary base control. Instead, the interest rate is used as the main instrument to influence monetary growth. The government forecasts each component of monetary growth (the PSBR, bank lending and external flows) and then decides on the level of gilt sales needed to achieve a particular target for broad money growth. Since interest rates will rise to encourage investors to buy the gilts, this will have the effect of reducing bank lending and money demand. If more gilts are sold than is necessary to finance the PSBR, this is known as overfunding.

8 For most of the 1980s, UK monetary policy was conducted on the basis of explicit annual monetary targets, particularly sterling M3. The rationale was the supposed stability of the demand for money function, in which case monetary growth is the main cause of inflation. Adherence to targets was seen as committing policy makers to policy rules that would enhance their credibility, especially insofar as this helped to reduce inflation expectations. The targets were never actually met, but inflation was reduced. However, the money demand function turned out to be very unstable during this period, largely because financial innovations, such as the introduction of interest-bearing chequeing accounts, reduced the velocity of circulation of money.

9 Between 1987 and 1992, monetary targets were replaced by exchange rate targets. This is because the relationship between interest rates and exchange rates is thought to be more stable than the relationship between money and inflation. The objective was to keep the exchange rate tied to that of a low inflation country such as Germany, thereby tying the UK inflation rate to that of Germany.

Exercises

1 What role does the banking system play in determining the money supply?
2 What is a fractional reserve banking system?
3 Why does a bank (or a building society) need to keep reserves?
4 What is the money multiplier?
5 You are given the following information:

    Public's cash holdings = 20
    Public's bank deposits = 100
    Bank's reserves   = 10

    Calculate:
    (a) The money multiplier.
    (b) The money supply.
6 What is monetary base control?
7 Compare and contrast the money multiplier and flow of funds models of money supply determination.

8 Using the flow of funds model, explain what determines changes to the stock of broad money.

9 You are given the following information:

Notes and coin	12
Bankers' balances at the Bank of England	2
Retail deposits of banks	140
Retail deposits of building societies	120
Building societies' share accounts	30
Wholesale deposits of banks	150
Wholesale deposits of building societies	18

Calculate:
(a) M0.
(b) M2.
(c) M4.

10 (a) What is overfunding?
   (b) What role does overfunding play in monetary control?

11 Why can't the central bank control both the interest rate and the money supply?

12 What are the main causes of interest rate volatility?

13 Suppose that you are advising the central bank. Would your preferred policy for monetary control seek to control the demand for money or the supply of money? Justify your preference.

14 What justifies the use of monetary targets?

15 What justifies the use of interest rate or exchange rate targets?

16 Why do some economists argue that a policy of monetary targets has greater credibility than a policy of interest rate or exchange rate targets?

12 The European Monetary System

12.1 Features of the EMS

The *European Monetary System* (EMS) was established in March 1979 to provide a zone of monetary stability in Europe by stabilizing exchange rates and maintaining control over inflation. There had been substantial volatility in world exchange rates following the breakdown of the Bretton Woods system in 1972. In this section, we discuss the main features of the EMS.

First, it devised a new monetary unit based on a basket of the currencies of the member states: the *European Currency Unit* (ECU). The ECU would be used as a unit of account for certain transactions between the governments of the member states. Table 12.1 shows the components and weights of the different member currencies in this currency bundle the last time the ECU was re-balanced in September 1989. When the ECU was introduced it was intended mainly for transactions between governments. In recent years, however, the ECU has been used fairly extensively in private financial markets, especially for transactions between large companies within Europe. There are now loans that are denominated in ECUs and, in 1988, the UK government introduced ECU-denominated treasury bills. The main reason for the success of the ECU was the existence of capital controls in many of the member states before July 1990. To the extent that a currency which is subject to exchange controls is partially represented in the ECU, private investors are able to replicate some of the characteristics of investing in that currency without being subject to controls.

The second feature of the EMS is that member governments each deposit 20 per cent of their foreign exchange reserves with the *European Monetary Cooperation Fund* (EMCF) and receive ECUs in exchange. Funds can also be borrowed under the third feature of the EMS, namely the *Very Short-Term Financing Facility*. These funds would then be used by the central banks for intervention in the foreign exchange markets when currencies within the EMS were moving away from their agreed ranges. The EMCF also acts to dissuade speculators and thereby reduce the currency risks to the member states.

TABLE 12.1   European currency unit (September 1989)

Number of units	Currency	Weighting (%)
0.6242	Deutschmark	30.4
0.2198	Dutch guilder	9.5
3.301	Belgian franc	7.8
0.13	Luxembourg franc	0.3
0.1976	Danish krone	2.5
1.332	French franc	19.3
0.008552	Irish punt	1.1
151.8	Italian lira	9.9
0.08784	Pound sterling	12.6
1.44	Greek drachma	0.7
6.885	Spanish peseta	5.2
1.393	Portuguese escudo	0.8

The most important feature of the EMS is its arrangement for fixing exchange rates. This is a *parity grid system* known as the *Exchange Rate Mechanism* (ERM). Each country which belongs to the ERM fixes its nominal exchange rate against each of the other members of the ERM. All currencies within the ERM are therefore on a fixed exchange rate with respect to each other, but float freely against non-ERM currencies (drachma, dollar, yen etc.). The UK first joined the ERM on 8 October 1990 at an exchange rate of 2.95 Deutschmarks per £. Each currency within the ERM is allowed to fluctuate within a target zone of ± 2.25 per cent of the agreed parities. The UK, Portugal and Spain were the exceptions. They were allowed a wider range of ± 6 per cent, due to their higher inflation rates or more volatile currencies. The UK's membership of the ERM was suspended on 16 September 1992.

When any member state's currency hits the upper or lower band, other member states within the ERM intervene to bring it back into line. The EMS therefore implies fixed but adjustable exchange rates. Realignments of exchange rates are allowed. If a member state is having difficulty reducing inflation relative to other countries, its currency will require persistent defending in the foreign exchange market. Under these circumstances it can try to seek agreement from the other member states to devalue its currency relative to that of other member currencies.

Realignments are not automatic and member states are obliged to ensure that they are attempting to keep their currencies within the agreed ranges. In order to encourage this, members of the ERM agree to a common yardstick indicating when corrective policy action is required. This is known as the *divergence indicator*. When a currency has moved 75 per cent of the amount it is permitted to move against the ECU currency bundle, the member state is obliged to adjust domestic macroeconomic policies to prevent any further movement.

In the early years of the EMS (between 1979 and 1983), realignments were quite frequent. When the system was first formed there were large differentials in inflation rates between members, and as a result, the agreed parities required frequent changes. The high inflation countries, e.g. Italy and France, were allowed to devalue their currencies in the face of considerable difficulty in controlling inflation. In the early years, therefore, the supposed benefits of belonging to the ERM, particularly that of financial discipline forced onto the member currencies by the stable German currency, did not really exist. Whenever financial discipline was required to keep nominal exchange rates within the agreed parities (i.e. by raising domestic interest rates), the devaluation route was often chosen as the less painful alternative. Realignments were not always sufficient to compensate for inflation differentials, and therefore to the extent that exchange rate realignments did not completely maintain purchasing power parity exchange rates, some financial discipline was enforced on the high inflation countries. Between January 1987 and September 1992, there were no realignments, and inflation differentials were also reduced considerably. With respect to exchange rates and the level of competitiveness (i.e. real exchange rates), the ERM countries did not experience the kind of volatility that non-ERM currencies suffered during this period.

The relative success of the EMS for nearly five years during the late 1980s and early 1990s can be attributed partly to the counter-inflationary policies of the member states converging to a common path (typically dictated by Germany), but also more importantly to capital controls. Many of the ERM countries had exchange controls which restricted the movement of capital. (Exchange controls were removed within Europe in July 1990.) If we re-examine the interest parity condition, it is clear why, if a country will not allow investors to convert their assets into foreign currency without any restrictions, it may be able to maintain a higher inflation rate relative to other ERM countries. The interest parity condition states that domestic and foreign interest rates are equalized after adjusting for the expected exchange rate change. In addition, from relative PPP theory, we know that the exchange rate depreciates at the same rate as the differential between domestic and foreign inflation rates. Suppose that a country has higher inflation than Germany. Its currency will be depreciating against the Deutschmark. If the country imposed a restriction on the actions of investors in its currency, such that they could only convert limited amounts of capital into foreign currency, this would have the same effect as a tax on domestic assets (but it would be an implicit tax rather than an explicit tax). Expectations of changes in the exchange rate are not the only thing that investors have to take into account; they also have to take into account this implicit tax. Thus part of the success of the EMS really came from barriers to capital movements. Exchange controls are only one type of barrier: others include restrictions on particular investors (e.g. financial institutions) on the amount of foreign assets they can hold. All of these restrictions imply that some member states could sustain higher inflation rates without experiencing exchange rate depreciations than they could in the absence of any restrictions.

12.1.1 EMS: costs and benefits

What are the main costs and benefits of the EMS?

There are a number of benefits of the EMS in its current form. First the EMS, by fixing exchange rates between member currencies, leads to a *reduction in exchange rate volatility*. This is regarded as an important benefit to the real sector of the economy where volatility of exchange rates can affect competitiveness. Those who have argued forcefully for exchange rate stability (e.g. the Confederation of British Industry) essentially want competitiveness to remain stable, since large and unanticipated variations in demand are difficult for companies to deal with. Those who favour flexible exchange rates argue that there is little evidence that the volatility of exchange rates affects the level of trade. So even though business men and women frequently complain about this volatility, there is very little evidence that it actually affects their businesses. However, it can be argued that the volatility of exchange rates damages activities such as investment programmes, which have longer planning horizons.

If exchange rates are fixed, it is possible that the volatility could appear somewhere else in the system (this is known as *volatility transfer*). Many economists argue that the cost of exchange rate stability is more volatile interest rates. The underlying reason is that economies are always subject to shocks. These shocks have to be transmitted through all the markets of the economy before equilibrium is restored. It may be the case that if exchange rates are not permitted to respond to changes in the supply of or demand for goods, then some markets may remain in disequilibrium, with excess demands or excess supplies persisting. However, the connection between exchange rate stability and interest rate volatility is not clear at all. Some economists have examined whether EMS member countries have suffered an increase in interest rate volatility and have failed to find any evidence. Interest rates may actually be lower.

A second important argument in favour of the EMS is that it acts as a *disciplining device for high inflation countries*. Countries such as France and Italy have benefited from membership because the EMS provided an externally-imposed constraint on their behaviour that they were unable to impose themselves. Thus although there is a disadvantage in sacrificing monetary independence, the alternative may be no worse. A country within the EMS cannot pursue an independent monetary policy, since if its monetary growth is significantly greater than that of other members (especially Germany), its exchange rate would have to depreciate, and this is not permitted. If countries are having difficulty in controlling inflation, perhaps because on their own they find it difficult to pursue a sufficiently restrictive monetary policy, then EMS membership would help. Furthermore, if one believes that monetary policy cannot help raise output and employment, except temporarily, then monetary independence may not be worth much. This is what economists call a *second best outcome*: if you are unable to do something to help yourself, let someone else help you, even if it also restricts your freedom of action elsewhere.

Related to the above argument is the issue of the *credibility* of an anti-inflation policy. Some governments that have had a long history of high inflation may find it difficult to convince the private sector (i.e. workers and firms) about their determination to reduce inflation. The consequence of this is that even if governments pursue restrictive monetary and fiscal policies, private sector inflationary expectations will not adjust downwards sufficiently rapidly, with the result that disinflation policies generate substantial recessions before they reduce inflation. For example, workers might continue to demand high nominal wage increases even though aggregate demand has been severely cut back; if these wage demands were conceded, firms would be faced with rising costs and falling demand, leading to massive redundancies and bankruptcies, the classic and painful features of a recession. In such circumstances, the external commitment of a fixed exchange rate helps, especially if it is fixed with respect to a currency such as the Deutschmark, which has proven credibility with respect to inflation control.

In the case of UK membership, there was concern over the consequences for the real sector if firms were unable to hold down production costs, especially wage costs. Those who advocated membership thought that a fixed exchange rate would force the private sector to *reduce factor input costs to maintain competitiveness*. Previous UK experience (when the degree of competitiveness was low), however, does not lend support to this view. When currencies are overvalued, the result is often *output losses* and *unemployment* rather than efforts to increase competitiveness. The experience of the UK in 1991–92 (when real UK interest rates were kept at unprecedentedly high levels to maintain an overvalued parity against the Deutschmark at a time when German interest rates had to be high to finance German reunification) appears to indicate that the earlier outcome still holds in the UK, namely recession rather than lowering of input costs.

12.2 European Monetary Union

Within the European Community, there is now a move, led principally by Germany and France, towards European Monetary Union (EMU); i.e. rather than have fixed exchange rates between the members of the ERM, these countries plan to adopt a single currency to replace all existing national currencies. Associated with this will be the creation of a *European Central Bank* which will have the responsibility for implementing *European monetary policy*, i.e. controlling the European money supply and setting European interest rates. The proposals for EMU were contained in the Delors Report of 1989 (see Table 12.2) and subsequently formalized in the Maastricht Treaty of 1991 (see Table 12.3). Stage 1 of EMU began on 1 July 1990 and Stage 2 is due to begin on 1 January 1994, with Stage 3 and a single European currency introduced between 1 January 1997 and 1 January 1999 at the latest. Table 12.4 shows the convergence criteria that have to be satisfied by each member state for it to be eligible to use the single European currency. Even if the five financial criteria had been satisfied, a member state could not participate in the single European currency unless its central bank was politically independent and that legislation had been passed to ensure this.

In this section we consider first the reason behind the proposals for full monetary union (i.e. a single European currency) and second examine the economic arguments for and against monetary union, paying particular attention to some of the implications of monetary union. There are essentially two factors that have furthered the case for full European Monetary Union.

The first is the likelihood that the EMS will not be sustainable in the long run as a result of the liberalization of capital controls within the European Community after July 1990. Member states of the EC created a *European Financial Area* (EFA) in January 1993. Exchange controls were abolished, implying free capital mobility between EMS countries. With complete freedom of capital movements (i.e. perfect capital mobility), it is not possible for countries to

TABLE 12.2   The Delors Report

Stage 1   (1 July 1990–31 December 1993)

- Removal of barriers to single market.
- Strengthening competition policy.
- Reduction of state subsidies to industry.
- Increase structural funds offering regional aid.
- Closer coordination of economic and monetary policies.
- Deregulation of financial markets.
- All currencies joining ERM.

Stage 2   (1 January 1994–31 December 1996)

- European System of Central Banks conducts common monetary policy independent of political control (now replaced by European Monetary Institute).
- Central banks pool reserves.

Stage 3   (1 January 1997–1 January 1999)

- Single EC currency (preceded by irrevocable fixing of exchange rates).
- Binding constraints on national budgets.
- Single central bank conducts monetary policy, manages all official reserves and exchange rate transactions.
- Single international policy.

TABLE 12.3   The Maastricht Treaty

The Maastricht Treaty leads to:

- Single currency by 1999 for EC member states meeting a set of convergence criteria (see Table 12.4).
- Independent European Central Bank to manage the single currency.
- Gradual convergence of EC economies, especially in respect of interest and exchange rates, government expenditure and national debt in the run up to the single currency.
- Cohesion Fund established by the richer countries to help the poorer ones (Spain, Portugal, Greece and Ireland) improve their economies.
- More social legislation governing the work-place (the UK opted out of this).
- Greater inter-governmental cooperation in foreign policy and defence, but individual member states will retain power of veto in foreign affairs except in narrow fields of non-military action; common defence policy and joint army as ultimate objective.
- Greater inter-governmental cooperation in justice, crime and immigration affairs.
- European citizenship, with full voting rights in country of residence.
- Emphasis on 'subsidiarity', with decision-making at national level except in areas where EC-wide decisions can be justified.
- New Community powers in environmental and consumer protection and setting up cross-border transport, energy and telecommunications networks in culture, education and training, and research.
- European Parliament given greater powers to confirm the appointment of the President of the Commission, to amend or veto legislation, audit EC expenditure and investigate maladministration.

maintain interest rate differentials in order to support their currencies; exchange rate realignments are not readily permitted in the ERM. Until July 1990, countries that maintained capital controls were able to support their currencies by restricting capital outflows. With no controls, countries that have higher inflation rates than other ERM countries will find it difficult to devalue (since ERM rules do not allow this), and therefore will lose competitiveness. They will

TABLE 12.4 Convergence criteria for membership of the single European currency by 1 January 1999

Each member state must satisfy the following conditions:

- Average inflation rate less than 1.5 per cent above the average of the lowest three member states during the preceding year.
- Exchange rate within the narrow band of the ERM (± 2.25 per cent) for two years.
- Average long-term interest rate less than 2 per cent above the average of the lowest three member states during the preceding year.
- Budget deficit (PSBR) less than 3 per cent of GDP.
- National debt less than 60 per cent of GDP.
- Have passed legislation guaranteeing the political independence of the central bank.

tend to experience persistent trade deficits compared with other ERM members. These trade imbalances may put considerable pressure on countries to revert back to the early pattern of the EMS, when realignments within the ERM were fairly frequent.

The argument therefore is that, since capital controls have been removed, the EMS will come under increasing strain if inflation differentials persist. Given that most countries do not want to drop out of the ERM, since this might damage the credibility of their counter-inflationary policies, further monetary integration may be the only option. Full monetary integration, where all countries agree to have a single currency, by definition implies irrevocably fixed exchange rates, so by design there can be no realignments. In other words, monetary union would have the same effect as that in a single country with different regions which all use the same currency (such as the USA). Monetary union of this form also implies a single monetary policy for all countries conducted by a single central bank.

The proposed new European Central Bank, which would, under the Maastricht Treaty, become fully operational in 1998, will have four main characteristics:

1 Its principal objective will be the maintenance of price stability; but from Table 12.4, this has been defined not as zero inflation, but as an inflation rate in any member state no higher than 1.5 per cent above the average of the lowest three member states (the central bank is also able to support the general economic policies and objectives of the EC, but without prejudice to the objective of price stability).
2 It will be independent of political interference.
3 It will have full responsibility for monetary policy across Europe.
4 It will have powers to ensure that governments do not finance their budget deficits by printing money (i.e. that budget deficits are not monetized, since this tends to be inflationary).

The precise operating procedures of the central bank in terms of the provision of banking services to the governments of member states (the original purpose of central banks), money market operations for monetary policy, the clearing and settlement of money market transactions, reserve ratios and prudential regulations have to be established by the *European Monetary Institute*.

The second impetus for monetary union came out of the European Community's plan for a single market in goods and service between member states. In the UK, the enabling legislation for this was contained in the 1986 Single European Act. At the end of 1992, the European Community removed all remaining trade barriers between member states. Workers can also move freely between member states. Associated with these trends towards freedom of movement for factors of production (mainly labour and capital), it is considered by many member states that the existence of national currencies imposes unnecessary costs on transactions in

Europe. It would be much cheaper to conduct transactions in a common medium of exchange. The adoption of a single currency is therefore part of the wider movement towards trade and capital market liberalization within the European Community.

A related development was the establishment of the *European Economic Area* (EEA) in January 1993. The EEA was formed by the twelve-nation European Community and the seven-nation *European Free Trade Association* (EFTA). The intention was to create a free trade area of nearly 400m consumers. It is regarded as a half-way house to full membership of the EC by EFTA members who are not also EC members (i.e. Austria, Finland, Norway, Sweden, Iceland, Liechtenstein and Switzerland, although Switzerland rejected this proposal in a referendum in December 1992). It also parallels the development of the *North American Free Trade Association* (NAFTA) between the US, Canada and Mexico.

12.2.1   The benefits of European Monetary Union

Lower transactions costs
If all transactions were conducted in a single currency there would undoubtedly be a reduction in transactions costs. The direct costs of converting currencies would be reduced, and there would be a reduction in opportunity costs as well. Opportunity costs are the costs in interest forgone in holding cash balances for transactions purposes. The simplest illustration of this is that tourists typically hold higher cash balances on holidays abroad than they do in their own country. However, the benefits from lower transactions costs are unfortunately not easy to quantify. Economies of scale in international transactions imply that these costs are not a simple multiple of the volume of trade or the volume of capital flows. Nevertheless, it has been calculated that the costs of transacting in multiple currencies amount to 4 per cent of Europe's GDP per year.

Reduction in exchange rate uncertainty
The private sector devotes considerable resources to both forecasting and managing foreign exchange needs and exposures. These would be entirely eliminated within Europe after EMU, as is the case within countries. The question often posed by those who favour flexible exchange rates is whether exchange rate uncertainty (and more specifically, exchange rate volatility) reduces international trade. The available evidence on this suggests that it does not, but when looking at investment, the evidence indicates that periods of fixed exchange rates have typically been associated with more stable patterns of investment expenditure.

Economic convergence
Monetary union would help considerably the process of economic convergence, and thereby facilitate the evolution of a single market in Europe. A good example of this is the Federal Reserve System in the USA which operates a single currency. To the extent that some members favour greater European political unification, monetary union may also assist this. However, it should be noted that greater monetary dependence does not necessarily entail a pooling of political sovereignty.

12.2.2   The costs of European Monetary Union

Loss of the nominal exchange rate as a policy instrument
This is by far the most serious concern of those who oppose monetary union. Their argument is essentially that if two economies are subject to different external shocks (for example, a rise in oil prices affects oil-producing countries differently from non-oil producing countries), then in a world where goods prices tend to be sluggish (recall the earlier Dornbusch overshooting

model), a nominal exchange rate devaluation may be required to restore competitiveness in the economy. In a monetary union that option no longer exists. Therefore, it is imperative for countries that are contemplating the formation of a monetary union to be similar in their characteristics; in particular they should not be subject to different types of external shock nor be affected differently by the same shock. In the economics literature, it is well established that an *optimum currency area* (i.e. a geographical area which benefits more from operating with a single currency than with a range of currencies) is one in which there is sufficient factor mobility. This means that labour and capital are able to move to regions where they could be re-employed more productively. One danger is that a particular region might become entirely depopulated if it loses its competitiveness. The single market in Europe after 1992 is therefore almost a prerequisite for monetary union. Proponents of monetary union recognize the risk of regional depopulation, but argue that most of the main European economies are sufficiently similar that the risk is fairly small. Opponents of monetary union argue that the European economies are not sufficiently similar.

Loss of monetary independence

In a monetary union, each individual member state will no longer be able to conduct an independent monetary policy. That is, monetary policy will be determined by the European Central Bank. Interest rates will be the same in all countries, as they are, for example, in different states of the USA. How serious this loss of independence is depends on the alternatives. In a world of increased capital mobility and globalization of financial markets, most countries are not able to follow independent policies anyway. In effect, independence reduces to being able to choose one's own inflation rate, and even this is not available for members of the ERM. Therefore this is not at present viewed as a large cost by most member states.

Loss of political independence

As a direct consequence of irrevocably fixed exchange rates, proponents of monetary union recognize that there will need to be something else to iron out regional disparities. That is, if countries find themselves losing competitiveness and performing worse than other members of the union, the European Community will need to institute a system of *regional transfers* operated by the *Cohesion Fund* whereby underperforming regions have resources transferred to them. This then avoids all the social problems associated with regional depopulation and the mass migration of populations. Clearly, in an idealized union, once factor mobility is sufficiently high, such transfers will be automatic via the market mechanism (e.g. regional wages will fall to re-establish regional labour competitiveness). However, at present it is doubtful whether factor mobility is sufficiently high. The disadvantage of regional transfers is that they will have to be decided on by (unelected) European administrators, and there are inevitable fears that allocation of resources by bureaucrats may not yield efficient outcomes. In other words, there are fears about the loss of political independence by national governments in deciding their own social policies. Transnational transfers also appear to increase the dangers of corruption. For example, one of the biggest beneficiaries of EC regional transfers to Southern Italy is the Mafia.

Monetary union implies fiscal policy coordination

Once there exists a single currency, control over which is the responsibility of the European Central Bank, it remains to be decided what freedom of action national governments will retain over fiscal policy. Two factors are relevant.

First, with effectively perfect capital mobility, interest rates will be equal across Europe. Therefore, if action by one government in terms of fiscal policy affects that country's interest rates, it will affect interest rates in all member states, since there will now be only one single

Europe-wide interest rate. This will impose constraints on the type of fiscal policy that governments can pursue. (Note, however, that if the securities of different governments are not perfect substitutes then interest rates do not have to be equal all over Europe. To the extent that government securities are imperfect substitutes for each other, say because one government is regarded as more risky or profligate than another government, then the more profligate government will have to pay a higher interest rate (higher *risk premium*) on its borrowings. The same is already true for more risky companies in the same country.)

Second, with respect to the setting of tax rates and social security benefit levels, governments will have to pay attention to the degree of capital and labour mobility. For example, income taxes, capital gains taxes, value added taxes etc. will to some extent have to be harmonized if there are to be no tax incentives to move from one member state to another or to buy from one member state rather than another.

With respect to government budget deficits, there is a debate at present as to whether the European Commission should have a system of *budgetary rules* that will limit the size of deficits that each government is allowed to run, or whether, as is the case under federal governmental systems (e.g. the USA and Canada), it should be left to the market to decide. The argument for the market-based approach is that if markets are efficient, they will price risk appropriately; imprudent governments will have to pay more (i.e. pay a higher risk premium) for their borrowings than those that are more prudent. Those who favour a budgetary rules-based approach have cited past experience, whereby markets, instead of imposing a gradual rising risk premium, have a tendency to curtail credit suddenly, so that an imprudent borrower cannot raise funds at any price. This is known as a *credit crunch*. The proposals currently being considered are a system of budgetary rules, preventing excessive spending by national governments. The European Commission would have to monitor whether each member state is complying with the budgetary rules and, if not, to recommend changes in the member state's policies.

12.3 The events of September 1992

For nearly five years from January 1987 to September 1992 there were no realignments of exchange rates within the ERM. Many commentators regarded this period as evidence that, after a somewhat turbulent beginning, the EMS was able finally to offer its members a stable regime of fixed exchange rates. It was this experience that provided the spur to closer European Monetary Union discussed in the last section.

12.3.1 Crisis in the ERM

However, in September 1992 there was a crisis in the ERM involving speculative attacks on sterling, the Italian lira, the Spanish peseta, the Portuguese escudo, the Irish punt and the French franc. The crisis resulted in

1. Sterling's and the lira's membership of the ERM being suspended;
2. The peseta being devalued within the ERM;
3. Spain, Portugal and Ireland reintroducing exchange controls;
4. The attack on the franc being defeated only as a consequence of massive support from the German central bank (the Bundesbank);
5. And moves towards a two-speed approach to European Monetary Union with Germany, France, Holland, Belgium, Luxembourg and Denmark in the fast lane, and the UK, Ireland, Spain, Portugal, Italy and Greece in the slow lane.

The diary of the crisis is given in Table 12.5. In this section, we examine the causes and consequences of the crisis insofar as they affected the UK.

TABLE 12.5   Diary of a Crisis

Tuesday 2 June   The Danish people reject the Maastricht Treaty in a referendum. This raises doubts about the future of the Treaty and the commitment of the European people to move towards monetary union. Sterling at 2.93 DM per £.

June, July and August   Sterling begins to slide against the Deutschmark from the end of June and continues to slide throughout July and August. This is denoted a period of 'benign neglect' for sterling, as the financial markets begin to question whether the UK is determined to maintain its parity in the ERM. The Italian lira also begins to slide during this period as the markets become concerned that Italy, with a government budget deficit of 11 per cent of GDP and a national debt larger than its GDP, will be unable to meet the Maastricht convergence criteria.

Tuesday 25 August   Prime Minister John Major and Chancellor of the Exchequer Norman Lamont have a crisis meeting as sterling begins to approach its lowest permissible limit in the ERM of 2.7780 DM per £. Sterling closes at 2.7875 DM per £.

Wednesday 26 August   Lamont insists sterling will not devalue but the financial markets are unimpressed. The Bank of England intervenes massively in the markets to support sterling which closes at 2.7950 DM per £.

Friday 28 August   EC finance ministers insist there will be no realignment of currencies in the ERM. Sterling falls back to 2.7875 DM per £.

Thursday 3 September   Lamont announces plan to borrow £7.25bn in Deutschmarks to defend sterling's value. The pound closes at 2.80 DM per £.

Friday 4 September   Italy raises interest rates to defend the lira, but the lira continues to slide.

Saturday 5 September   EC finance ministers again insist that there will be no realignment of currencies.

Thursday 10 September   Major says realignment would be a 'betrayal' for ERM. Sterling continues to slide. Privately, the Italians indicate that they have reserves to defend the lira for only the next four days.

Sunday 13 September   The lira is devalued within the ERM by 7 per cent. It is the first realignment within the ERM since January 1987.
   The Germans announce that they will cut their interest rate later in the week (the first cut for five years), thereby allowing interest rates to fall in the rest of Europe and so help to ease the Europe-wide recession. Sterling rises to 2.82 DM per £ in anticipation of the cut in German interest rates.

Monday 14 September   The Bundesbank announces a cut in interest rates of only a quarter of one per cent to 9.5 per cent. This is not regarded in London as sufficient to ease pressure on sterling which, with the realignment of the lira, has become the weakest currency in the ERM. Sterling closes at 2.8144 DM per £.

Tuesday 15 September   Sterling plunges following massive selling of the currency in the markets. Rumours of 2 per cent interest rate rise or devaluation. Sterling closes at its lowest permissible level of 2.7780 DM per £.

Wednesday 16 September ('Black Wednesday')   The events of this day are as follows:

7am	Markets open with sterling at its ERM floor.
9am	An intervention of £1bn by the Bank of England fails to lift sterling against a wave of speculative selling.
9.30am	Bundesbank and the Bank of France spend £2bn to support sterling.
11am	Lamont tells Major intervention is not working.
11.01am	Interest rates raised from 10 per cent to 12 per cent.
Midday	The Bank of England spends a further £3bn to support sterling.
1pm	Sterling falls below its ERM floor.
2.15pm	Interest rates raised to 15 per cent. The Treasury announces: 'Our policy remains to take whatever measures necessary to maintain sterling's parity within the ERM'.

3pm   The Bank of England spends another £3bn to support sterling. During the day, the Bank spends a third of its foreign exchange reserves to buy sterling.

4.45pm   The Governor of the Bank of England, Robin Leigh-Pemberton, informs Major that the situation is completely out of control.

5pm   The London market closes with sterling at 2.75 DM per £.

7.30pm   Lamont announces that sterling is suspended from membership of the ERM and that interest rates are reduced back to 12 per cent. Sterling is allowed to float freely without Central bank intervention and falls to 2.69 DM per £. The lira is also suspended from the ERM.

Thursday 17 September   Spanish peseta is devalued within the ERM by 5 per cent.

Friday 18 September   Sterling continues to fall, closing at 2.6160 DM per £. The French franc falls toward its floor in the ERM as doubts begin to grow about how the French will vote in their referendum on the Maastricht Treaty on Sunday. The Irish punt, the Danish krone and the Portuguese escudo also come under pressure.

Sunday 20 September   The French say 'yes' to the Maastricht Treaty, but with a wafer-thin majority of 51 per cent 'for' and 49 per cent 'against'.

Sterling continues its slide to 2.58 DM per £ as the markets become concerned at the policy vacuum created by the UK leaving the counter-inflationary discipline provided by the ERM. Lamont announces that the UK has no plans to return quickly to the ERM, but in the meantime, the government's economic policy would be to achieve 'sustained non-inflationary growth'. The markets take this as a change in the emphasis of government policy away from one of purely controlling inflation to one of using the lifting of the constraint imposed by the ERM as an opportunity to revive the economy. The government would also return to using the growth in the broad money supply rather than the exchange rate as the chief indicator of its counter-inflationary stance.

Monday 21 September   In the light of Lamont's Sunday announcement, the markets expect a cut in interest rates. When this does not come, sterling falls to 2.5456 DM per £.

Tuesday 22 September   Lamont cuts interest rates to 9 per cent, putting UK interest rates below those of Germany for the first time in 10 years. Sterling is steady at 2.5449 DM per £.

Lamont underlined his continued commitment to fighting inflation by warning that interest rates would be raised again if the objective of low inflation was subsequently put at risk.

Reinforcing the Chancellor's commitment, the Governor of the Bank of England announced in Washington, D.C., that the government's economic policy was based on five principles: price stability, fiscal responsibility (i.e. holding back on government expenditure), sustainable exchange rates, strengthening market forces, and working to liberalize world trade.

The Bank of France intervenes heavily to defend the French franc as the French finance minister announces that the franc–Deutschmark exchange rate is 'absolutely inviolable'.

Wednesday 23 September   The Bundesbank is successful in helping the Bank of France defend the franc by making massive purchases of francs. The Germans announce their determination that the ERM will not collapse as a result of the actions of speculators. They reveal that they have spent £23.4bn during the last week to support the ERM. The franc stabilizes.

Thursday 24 September   Spain and Ireland reintroduce foreign exchange controls, and Holland and Belgium reduce interest rates to ease speculative pressures.

There are rumours that Germany, France, Holland, Belgium, Luxembourg and Denmark plan to take the 'fast lane' to monetary union leaving the other member states in the 'slow lane'. These rumours are denied.

Major announces that the UK will not rejoin the ERM until its 'fault lines' have been ironed out. The Conservative Party is split over the benefits of further European union. The Bill to ratify the Maastricht Treaty is withdrawn until the problems with both the ERM and the Danish rejection of the Treaty have been dealt with.

Friday 25 September   The French franc makes a strong rally as the markets concede victory to the Bundesbank and the Bank of France. Germany, France, Holland, Belgium and Luxembourg reject Major's call for reform of the ERM. They state that the ERM should be 'maintained and that its rules must be correctly applied'. The UK had caused its own problems by putting sterling into the ERM in October 1990 at too high a rate.

The rumours that sterling will end up in the slow lane result in it falling to 2.5329 DM per £.

Monday 28 September Ireland raises its interest rates by 3 per cent to stabilize the punt. In the UK, expectations of a further cut in interest rates lead to a fall in sterling to 2.5103 DM per £.

There are further rumours about Germany and France preparing for a two-speed Europe, contingent on the UK being in the slow lane or even failing to ratify the Maastricht Treaty. Again the rumours are denied.

Wednesday 30 September Sterling stabilizes at about 2.50 DM per £ which comes to be regarded as the government's unofficial floor for sterling. This is 15 per cent below sterling's entry rate in the ERM of 2.95 DM per £. (Sterling did subsequently fall to an historic low of 2.3696 DM per £ on Monday 5 October 1992, but thereafter recovered to 2.50 DM per £ by mid-October.)

The UK had for nearly four years been in the deepest recession since the 1930s. Despite this, the Conservative government, in power since 1979, won an historic fourth consecutive victory in a General Election in April 1992. However, the group most affected by the recession was its own electoral supporters. These were the businesses and home-owners who were being hurt by high borrowing costs necessitated by the UK having to match the high real interest rates that Germany required to attract the funds needed to finance the costs of German reunification. The government had used up most of its goodwill in persuading the electorate that a Conservative victory at the election would reinforce the credibility of the government's counter-inflation policy and, as a result, the financial markets would reward the UK with lower nominal and hence real interest rates.

However, the lowering of interest rates did not arrive in the aftermath of the Conservative election victory. There was only further gloomy news indicating more bankruptcies, more home repossessions, more redundancies, and a bigger current account deficit. All this pointed to a deepening of the recession rather than to recovery. Every sign indicated that if the government could not cut interest rates at home to encourage investment and hence boost domestic demand, then it would have desperately liked to reduce the exchange rate to boost export demand. This was despite protestations to the contrary. However, membership of the ERM prevented sterling from falling below 2.7780 DM per £—the 6 per cent limit below the central parity of 2.95 DM per £.

It was well established that the UK had entered the ERM in October 1990 at too high an exchange rate against the Deutschmark. During the spring and autumn of 1990, John Major, then Chancellor of the Exchequer, had talked up the value of sterling from 2.70 DM to 2.95 DM per £ with promises of ERM membership, while keeping interest rates at 15 per cent. When sterling joined at a central rate of 2.95 DM per £ on 8 October 1990, interest rates were cut to 14 per cent, with expectations of further falls as the counter-inflationary disciplines of the ERM came into effect.

But the other members of the ERM had not been consulted either about the UK's intention to join or about the entry rate. The Germans certainly thought that the central rate was too high, making UK exports uncompetitive. They had also just embarked on the process of German reunification, following the collapse of the Soviet empire in Eastern Europe. This was going to keep German interest rates high and was correspondingly going to keep UK interest rates high, whatever the need for lower interest rates in the UK.

In the event, sterling traded above the central rate for only five weeks of its 23-month membership of the ERM (see Fig. 12.1). The government was boxed in with very little room for manoeuvre. With sterling almost always trading below its central parity, nominal interest rates could not be cut as frequently as the government wished. Nominal interest rates were however reduced from 14 per cent to 10 per cent between October 1990 and June 1992. But the UK inflation rate had fallen at a faster rate during this period, so the real

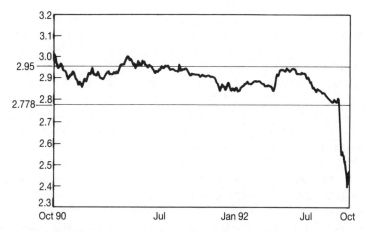

Figure 12.1 Sterling–Deutschmark exchange rate, October 1990–October 1992

interest rate was actually rising during this period and there was no sign that the recession was ending.

The catalyst to the September crisis was the Danish rejection of the Maastricht Treaty in a referendum on 2 June 1992. The train leading to European monetary and political union was derailed, if only temporarily, by what was regarded as an inner-core member of the ERM. The train was gradually put back on the tracks over the summer as the Maastricht Treaty was ratified by other member states, but its speed was not as great as before.

It was becoming clear over the summer that the Italian government budget deficit was out of control and that, as a result, Italy would find it increasingly difficult to maintain its exchange rate parity within the ERM. Also over the summer, the financial markets came to the view that the UK recession was so bad that the government would not raise interest rates whatever happened to the value of sterling.

As sterling began to slide, the Prime Minister, the Chancellor, the Governor of the Bank of England, as well as the EC finance ministers, all attempted to talk back up the value of sterling. But the markets began to sense that there was no clout behind the rhetoric, especially when sterling fell below the 75 per cent divergence indicator and the Bank did not intervene. The Bank believed that investors would not sell sterling as it approached its ERM floor because they know that it was 'impossible' for sterling to fall below the floor.

But the markets became convinced that the government would not take the only measure that was necessary to lift sterling off the floor, namely raise interest rates. Even a £7.25bn loan announced on 3 September was designed to defend sterling without having to trigger a rise in interest rates.

The speculators also knew that they had up to £600bn of 'hot money' to sell short against sterling and the Chancellor had only £7.25bn to defend it. In addition, the government did not begin the defence of the pound until, in the words of a City commentator, 'it was on the goal-line'.

The attack came on 16 September 1992 (a date which has gone down in UK financial history as 'Black Wednesday'), three days after Italy had devalued within the ERM, and so three days after the markets had realized that the move to 'irrevocable fixed exchange rate' had been put slightly in question! Currency dealers, acting on behalf of their clients, began selling massive quantities of sterling and the Bank of England was forced to buy it. They sold short; they sold forward; they did everything to drive down the price of sterling below the ERM floor, knowing that if they succeeded in doing this they could close their positions and make huge profits.

As the Bank's reserves ran out, the Chancellor was forced to raise interest rates. They were raised an unprecedented two times during the day from 10 per cent to 12 per cent, and then to 15 per cent. But is was too little and it was too late. Sterling eventually fell by 3.2 per cent against the Deutschmark during the day.

In order to fully protect investors in sterling assets from a fall of this size during a single day, overnight interest rates would have had to have risen to about 1200 per cent (i.e. 3.2 per cent × 365 days per year). The actual rise in interest rates, as with the £7.25bn loan, was wholly inadequate to protect sterling within the ERM. At 7.30pm on 'Black Wednesday', sterling was forced to make a humiliating withdrawal from the ERM. The Prime Minister was said to be 'devastated'. The total profits made by speculators on this single day were estimated to be £1bn.

The government immediately began to blame the Bundesbank and, in particular, its president, Professor Helmut Schlesinger, for helping to undermine sterling's position in the ERM. The government listed five occasions on which senior officials of the Bundesbank had used language that had undermined sterling and the ERM: on August 25 and 28, and September 10, 15 and 16. For example, on 15 September, news agencies reported sources in the Bundesbank as suggesting that a sterling devaluation could not be ruled out, and on 'Black Wednesday' itself, Schlesinger was quoted as saying that Europe's financial problems were unresolved in spite of Italy's devaluation within the ERM the previous Sunday. Following the Bundesbank's successful intervention on 23 September to save the franc, the government also blamed the Bundesbank for not doing enough to save sterling.

The Bundesbank rejected all these criticisms. Specifically, it denied that it had favoured the franc over sterling, by revealing that it had spent DM 44bn (£17.3bn) defending the pound and the lira, most of it on sterling. The Bundesbank also said that it could not be blamed for anonymous statements and rumours in the markets or for inaccurate reproduction of its statements by news agencies.

With the collapse of the main plank of its economic policy, the government found itself in a policy vacuum. Both the Prime Minister and the Chancellor reiterated their determination to control inflation—their principal policy objective—but, with possible inflationary pressures caused by a falling exchange rate, the markets had little confidence in the government's ability to achieve this objective.

The Chancellor formalized his new policy on Thursday 9 October. The main points of the policy were:

1 For the first time, an explicit target for annual inflation of between 1 and 4 per cent for the remainder of the Parliament.
2 A long-term inflation target of no more than 2 per cent.
3 No target range for sterling.
4 A growth rate target for narrow money M0 of 0.4 per cent.
5 No formal target growth rate for broad money M4.
6 House prices to be monitored as a guide to inflation.
7 Firm downward pressure on the growth in public sector pay and spending.

The objective of the policy was to control inflation by controlling the growth of narrow money and through fiscal restraint. But the new policy failed to impress the City. One City commentator argued that the policy framework was weak, since it would allow the Chancellor to use any indicator he wanted. While the inflation target was useful as a policy guide, it would be the case that responding to this target would mean responding too late to curb inflationary pressures.

An important underlying cause of the crisis was the excessive haste to economic and monetary union implied by the timetable specified in the Delors Report and the Maastricht Treaty.

Everything had to be done by the year 1999. The ERM, which had been conceived as a system of fixed but adjustable exchange rates and which the UK joined to give credibility to its counter-inflation policy, suddenly became the first stage of EMU and, therefore, became a test of commitment to EMU with its requirement of irrevocably fixed exchange rates followed by a single currency. The flexibility of the ERM was immediately taken away. The UK was expected to move rapidly to the narrow ± 2.25 per cent bands of the mechanism as a prelude to the irrevocable fixing of exchange rates.

Any thought of realignment of the ERM was ruled out of order, and any country that did realign would have lost its credibility in the financial markets, however much its domestic economy needed a realignment. Supporters of EMU argued that if a country did devalue, the markets would not believe any assurances it gave that it would not devalue again and hence would demand higher interest rates to protect investors from further devaluations.

The inevitable lesson that is drawn from this episode is that attempts to fix exchange rates between countries whose economies do not behave in similar ways are likely to be unsuccessful in the long run. Attempts to overcome the problem through the use of a single currency are likely to lead to permanent recessions in the less competitive countries within the single currency area. We are left with the famous observation of Lady Margaret Thatcher made at the time of the ERM crisis: 'You can't buck the markets. If you try to do so, you will end up getting bucked'.

12.4 Summary

1 The European Monetary System (EMS) was established to provide a zone of monetary stability in Europe by stabilizing exchange rates and inflation rates within Europe.
2 The main components of the EMS are:
  (a) The European Currency Unit (ECU): a common monetary unit of account across Europe.
  (b) The European Monetary Cooperation Fund (EMCF), into which member states deposit 20 per cent of their foreign exchange reserves to be used to stabilize exchange rates.
  (c) The Very Short-Term Financing Facility, which allows member states to borrow funds to support their exchange rate if it starts moving away from its agreed parity rate.
  (d) The Exchange Rate Mechanism (ERM), whereby member currencies are allowed to fluctuate within a parity grid system of ± 2.25 per cent of agreed parities for most currencies and ± 6 per cent for Portugal and Spain (and the UK while it was a member).
3 The main benefits of the EMS are:
  (a) A reduction in exchange rate volatility within Europe, which has the effect of stabilizing competitiveness between member states; but this might have been at the cost of more volatile interest rates.
  (b) A disciplining device for high inflation countries, together with greater credibility to counter-inflation policies; but this might be at the cost of output losses and unemployment rather than efforts to increase competitiveness.
4 European Monetary Union (EMU) is the plan to adopt, before the end of the century, a single European currency to replace all existing national currencies, together with the creation of a European central bank with responsibility for implementing a single European monetary policy. The rationale for this plan is the possibility that the parity grid system of the EMS will not be sustainable following the liberalization of capital controls within Europe after July 1990 and the creation of the European Financial Area (EFA) after January 1993. With complete freedom of capital movements, it will not be possible for any country to maintain interest rate differentials in order to support its currency in the face of inflation differentials, since exchange rate realignments are not permitted.

5 In order for each country to be eligible to use the single European currency, it must satisfy a set of convergence criteria:
  (a) Average inflation less than 1.5 per cent above the average of the lowest three member states during the preceding year.
  (b) Exchange rate movements within the ± 2.25 per cent target zone for two years.
  (c) Average long-term interest rate less than 2 per cent above the average of the lowest three member states during the preceding year.
  (d) Budget deficit less than 3 per cent of GDP.
  (e) National debt less than 60 per cent of GDP.
  (f) Have passed legislation guaranteeing the political independence of its central bank.
6 The European Central Bank will have four main objectives:
  (a) The principal objective will be the maintenance of price stability.
  (b) It will be independent of political interference.
  (c) It will have full responsibility for monetary policy across Europe.
  (d) It will not permit governments to monetize their deficits.
7 The intended benefits of EMU are:
  (a) Lower transactions costs.
  (b) Reduced exchange rate uncertainty.
  (c) Helping the process of economic convergence and facilitating the evolution to a single market in Europe.
8 The potential costs of EMU are:
  (a) Loss of the nominal exchange rate as a policy instrument; for example, in restoring competitiveness between two economies that are subject to different external shocks.
  (b) Loss of monetary independence.
  (c) Loss of political independence.
  (d) Loss of fiscal independence.
9 In September 1992 there was a crisis in the ERM involving speculative attacks on sterling, the lira, the peseta, the punt and the French franc. The crisis led to sterling and the lira's membership of the ERM being suspended; the peseta being devalued within the ERM; Spain and Ireland reintroducing exchange controls; and the attack on the franc being defeated only through massive intervention from the Bundesbank. The crisis was caused primarily as a result of the financial markets coming to the view that the exchange rates between sterling and the Deutschmark and between the lira and the Deutschmark were too high and could not be sustained. In the case of Italy, the government deficit was too high. In the case of the UK, interest rates had been lowered too much compared with German interest rates in order to help the UK out of the deepest recession since the 1930s. When the speculators began their attacks first on the lira and then sterling, the Italian and UK governments did not have the will to raise interest rates sufficiently and the ERM did not have the resources to drive off the speculators. Italy and the UK were forced to make a humiliating withdrawal from the ERM. Following this there was a move towards a two-speed approach to EMU with Germany, France, Holland, Belgium, Luxembourg and Denmark in the fast lane and the UK, Ireland, Spain, Portugal, Italy and Greece in the slow lane.

Exercises

1 What is the European Monetary System and what are its main features?
2 What are the main costs and benefits of the EMS?
3 How does the Exchange Rate Mechanism of the EMS operate?

4 When the UK joined the ERM on 8 October 1990, was the time right for it to do so?

5 What were the main reasons for the UK leaving the ERM on 16 September 1992?

6 What are the main features of European Monetary Union as proposed in the Maastricht Treaty?

7 What are the main characteristics of the proposed European Central Bank?

8 'The UK has not been successful in simultaneously achieving low inflation, low unemployment, high growth and balance of payments equilibrium by its own policy actions. It should therefore embrace EMU and allow others to achieve these objectives for it.' Discuss.

9 What fiscal arrangements, if any, might be needed to make EMU a success?

10. 'After monetary union, one country will not be able to change its competitiveness against other countries in the union; it is therefore a recipe for disaster.' Discuss.

Business application: The ERM and the control of inflation

One of the advantages claimed for the ERM is that it helps to reduce inflationary pressures. However, membership is not an economic policy instrument within the traditional sense of, for example, monetary policy or fiscal policy. Instead, the ERM provides a clear framework within which an anti-inflationary commitment is made more explicit. So by joining it, the government was attempting to add credibility to its fight against inflation.

If a country is experiencing high inflation and is near the top of its range in the ERM, the exchange rate cannot exert downward pressure on inflation by being allowed to rise. However, it is more likely that a country with high inflation will be at the bottom end of the range, since it is likely to be suffering a current account deficit. One reason for this could be expansionary government policies such as income tax cuts (e.g. the 1988 Budget) or reductions in interest rates, such as 1988–89. These would boost disposable income, which in turn would suck in imports. Alternatively, high wage settlements without accompanying productivity increases would harm the current account by making UK goods uncompetitive at home and abroad.

In these circumstances, the exchange rate must be protected, and this means raising interest rates. This will push up the exchange rate and hence export prices. UK firms will find it harder to pass on cost increases and so, to improve competitiveness, pay settlements would have to be moderated. The increase in interest rates may also push the economy into recession by squeezing demand out of the system. This should further reduce inflationary pressures. Workers, therefore, know that high wage deals will lead to inflation, balance of payments problems, exchange rate difficulties, higher interest rates and probably higher unemployment. The ERM therefore acts on inflationary expectations by providing the framework within which inflation cannot flourish.

Table 12.6 shows the impact of ERM membership on the inflation rates and pay settlements of members of the EC for 1985–90. In terms of inflation, the non-ERM members plus Italy were higher than the EC average. However, Italy's poorer performance may be explained by the fact that it operated within a ± 6 per cent currency band over the period, and so its anti-inflationary conditions were not as strict as those of the other founding members. The lowest inflation was experienced by countries in the ± 2.25 per cent band, implying some success for the ERM. However, there were a number of realignments within the ERM during its early years, particularly the devaluations of the French franc, the lira, and the krone and the revaluations of the Deutschmark. These were primarily aimed at solving balance of payments rather than inflationary problems. Overall, the realignments helped improve competitiveness and may have been partially responsible for subsequent low inflation rates.

The ERM is also supposed to create greater stability and so should reduce fluctuations in inflation rates. Thus convergence of the EC inflation rates should be facilitated. Column 2 gives an indication of the volatility, or otherwise, of members' inflation rates. Again, non-ERM countries, including the UK, experienced the greatest volatility in inflation rates. ERM members, particularly Denmark, France, Germany and the Netherlands, have much more stable inflation rates.

The impact of the ERM on inflationary expectations may be gauged by Column 3. If ERM members have lower rates of wage increases, then the exchange rate constraint may be seen to

TABLE 12.6 Inflation performance and the ERM 1985–90

Country	Average inflation (%)	Difference between highest and lowest inflation rates (% points)	Average nominal wage rises (%)	Difference between highest and lowest wage rises (% points)
1 *Non-ERM members*				
UK	5.9	4.1	7.8	4.6
Greece	16.8	6.3	17.2	13.9
Portugal	15.2	11.5	17.5	9.5
Spain	7.6	5.2	7.6	3.7
2 *ERM members*				
Belgium	3.6	4.0	3.9	4.4
Denmark	4.4	2.1	4.9	5.1
Ireland	3.9	4.1	4.9	5.6
France	4.0	2.8	2.8	3.1
Germany	2.5	1.0	3.4	1.0
Italy	7.0	2.9	9.0	2.7
Luxembourg	2.5	2.9	4.3	3.1
Netherlands	1.4	2.8	1.8	3.3
3 EC Average	5.2	1.9	6.3	2.0

Note:
Spain joined the ERM in 1989, the UK in 1990 and Portugal in 1992. The UK and Italy left the ERM in 1992. During 1979–90, Italy's currency moved within ± 6 per cent of parity. Between 1990 and 1992, the lira was in the narrower ± 2.25 per cent band.

be helping to curb wage inflation. If non-ERM members have higher pay settlements, the exchange rate constraint would be missing. The table shows that, apart from Italy, ERM members have lower average money wage rises than non-ERM members. Inflationary expectations would therefore seem to be lower within the ERM. Pay settlements also fluctuate less dramatically in ERM member countries, and so their economic environment again appears to be more stable.

Whether membership of the ERM did much to improve the UK's performance is open to debate. Even with membership of the EC, as opposed to the ERM, the UK has not been performing as well as the other industrialized members. It appears to be in the second division, alongside agrarian, tourist-based economies. Between 1966 and 1992, manufacturing employment halved to 4.4 million workers. Leaving aside any underlying long-term issues, there are many reasons for the UK's poor inflation performance during the 1980s. These include poor investment and productivity, shortages of skilled labour, large management salary increases, rising profits and hence rising pay, adherence to the 'going rate' and government policy such as increased VAT and the collapse of the Medium Term Financial Strategy. The UK's membership of the ERM between 1990 and 1992 coincided with the biggest recession in the UK since the 1930s. It was the recession more than anything else that was responsible for bringing inflation down from 10 per cent to 4 per cent during this period. The exchange rate constraint of the ERM was seen mainly as an issue in delaying the end of the recession, rather than in terms of defeating inflation.

Index